Winning
with the
News Media

A Self-Defense Manual
When You're the Story

by
Clarence Jones

T0274136

9th Edition

Winning with the News Media

A Self-Defense Manual When You're the Story

9th Edition

Copyright © 2014, 2005, 2001, 1999, 1996, 1993, 1991, 1988 & 1983 by Clarence Jones

Published by:
Winning News Media
610 Emerald Lane
Holmes Beach, FL 34217
Voice: 941.779.0242
e-mail: cjones@winning-newsmedia.com
ISBN-13: 978-1495376177
ISBN-10: 1495376176

Registered trademarks carry the ® symbol on first use in this book. On subsequent use, the trademark symbol is assumed.

Winning with the News Media **was the book's title for Editions 5 through 8. Earlier editions were titled:**

How to Speak TV, Print & Radio - (3rd & 4th Editions)
How to Speak TV - (1st & 2nd Editions)

Printed in the United States of America

Other Books by Clarence Jones:

Winning with the News Media – A Self-Defense Manual When You're the Story (e-book edition)

They're Gonna Murder You – War Stories From My Life at the News Front (Print and e-book editions)

Sailboat Projects – Clever Ideas and How to Make Them. For a Pittance (print and e-book editions)

More Sailboat Projects (a sequel, in both print and e-book editions)

Webcam Savvy – For the Job or the News (print and e-book editions)

Table of Contents

SECTION ONE - STRATEGY

About the Author – Clarence Jones, Reporter
Author, Media Consultant

He was one of America's most honored journalists. The only reporter for a local station to ever win TV's equivalent of the Pulitzer Price three times. Then he wrote this book and left reporting to be a news media consultant and on-camera coach.   *367*

Preface

The first, printed edition of this book came off the press in late 1983. The original manuscript was created with an ancient device called an electric typewriter. Remember those? Personal computers had just been marketed. I did not buy one until two years later.

I began my career with 16 years of reporting for newspapers, Then I spent 14 years as an investigative reporter in TV. I left reporting to become a news media consultant/on-camera coach when this book was first published.

A Conflict of Interest

There would have been a conflict of interest between my work as an investigative reporter and my new career, where I taught people like you to deal with sons-of-bitches like me. So I could not do both.

The printed book continued to grow through those eight previous editions. Some reviewers call it the "bible" of media relations. It is the textbook for my news media seminars, and has sold nearly 50,000 copies.

There is also an e-book version now, which can be quickly revised and updated. I had thought the 8th Edition would be the last in print. But some people still want their books to be on paper. So I decided to humor them.

So Much Easier Now

And because the technology has changed. It is *so much easier* to produce this book now. The first edition was formatted by a professional typesetter.

For the editions after that, I would compose the pages on my computer and print what they called "camera-ready" copy.

Those pages were shipped to the printer for the complicated process of photographing them, creating printing plates, running sheets of paper as wide as a wall through a press, then cutting the paper to book size, and finally, binding the pages.

The Inventory Problem

When I sent the camera-ready pages to the printer, it took about six weeks for them to print and ship the books. I ordered 5,000 books at a time. They came in a freight truck, which I had to unload. Each carton of books weighed about 35 pounds.

Storing that mountain of book cartons was a major task. Sometimes I used a rented storage locker, sometimes my garage. I was always concerned about what a fire or rising water during a hurricane could do to the books.

For those books stored in rented lockers, I had to lug several cartons home on a regular basis. Then package and ship books almost daily, driving them to the Post Office to send them to customers and clients.

Print-on-Demand

With print-on-demand now, this book is not printed until you order it from the bookseller, so there are no inventory or storage issues.

When I finished formatting this manuscript, I uploaded the file to amazon.com. It was instantly converted by their servers, and appeared for sale on their website by the next morning. If you buy it in the morning, it will be printed and shipped the same day. Revisions are quick and easy.

Compared to this process, books printed the old way are out of date by the time they come off the press. The Internet is current, and has much more depth. Space on the web is virtually unlimited. And safe from fire or flood.

And so I predict that after another generation or two, books printed on paper may become as curious to future humans as typewriters, or the linotype machines that once clattered and jingled to create the hot lead slugs that would carry my words to the newspaper's printing presses.

The Death of Newspapers

In the first edition of this book, I predicted that by 2020, the newspaper as we have known it would be extinct. My timing for the death of printed newspapers was an educated guess, but it was not far off. I had some librarians in a seminar several years ago. One of them asked, "Are you saying there will be no libraries in the future?"

"No," I said. "There will still be libraries. But they won't have many books in them. They'll have lots of computers. For people who don't own their own, or people who don't know how to use them. Mostly older folks.

"It will be your job to help those people to use the computers and find what they're looking for. Maybe read it there, or make printed copies to take home."

Changes for This Edition

This 9th, printed edition has updated and expanded the content from previous editions. Some of the earlier content is not here, because it is out of date. Some of the content in this book (like the chapter on **Webcam Interviews**) is completely new.

TV news has discovered webcams as a new, money-saving technique. If you really want to develop your new interview skills, you need to learn how to do it by webcam.

Most people who are interviewed in the future, I predict, will never meet the reporter, except by telephone or webcam.

Below is the Preface from the 8th Edition of the printed version.

I include it now because it tells about my unusual experience the morning that changed America's history and trajectory, and because it is still pertinent for those who want to learn how to deal with the news media.

A Morning to Remember

I had begun a seminar at 8 a.m. that morning at a federal training center in the West Virginia foothills of the Appalachians about 75 miles from Washington, DC.

The topic was "Crisis Management." In the audience were about 60 public affairs staffers for the U.S. Fish and Wildlife Service. They had come from all over the country.

We took the first break about an hour later. Someone from the training center's administrative team came in and told me a disaster was in the making in New York City.

They could pipe CNN into the classroom, if I chose to do so. We projected the live CNN broadcast onto a large screen.

We were watching when the second plane hit the World Trade Center building. I would learn later that some of the people in the room thought, at first, that I had fabricated the videotape as part of a class exercise.

The students voted to continue the class, alternating every 20 minutes between lecture and watching live CNN coverage.

You Must Leave Now

Shortly before noon, Rick Lemon, the director of the training center, came in and interrupted.

"This is one of the places where they run the national government during times of great crisis," he said. "The team is on the way here now. All of you must go to your rooms, pack your bags, and leave immediately."

Luckily, I had a rental car. So a few minutes later, I began the thousand-mile drive home.

Some of the class members from the West Coast, Hawaii and Alaska were stranded for weeks.

The material I had planned to deliver that September 11th became a part of the **Crisis Management** chapter of this book. It has been expanded considerably, and includes a lengthy checklist to help you design your own crisis management plan.

Planning for crisis is something we avoid. It is like buying life insurance or long-term disability insurance. We would rather not think about it.

Most organizations have written plans for fires, storms, floods. They practice those plans frequently. Should a fire or storm or flood occur, everyone will know – without thinking – what needs to be done and how to do it.

Rehearsals are Rare

Very few organizations have media crisis plans. In my experience, those that do have plans rarely rehearse them.

Most of you reading this will have a media crisis long before you have a fire or tornado or flood. Media crises in a media-driven society can be much more damaging, much more demoralizing than those hazards of nature. For organizations and careers, they are often fatal.

In my career as a news media consultant. I have said many times that I teach corporate and government executives survival skills.

Survival often depends on your reflexes. In that first moment of stark terror, there is no time to think. How you react, what you do reflexively, will often determine whether you live or die.

Life Changes After 9/11

I hope Sept. 11, 2001 has made us more willing to plan for disaster. For me personally, it also triggered a compulsion to find people who have been important in my life. So I could tell them, thank them, before it is too late.

Nine-eleven was a powerful reminder that life is short and unpredictable.

So I did that with a college professor, and a newspaper editor, and a woman I had loved intensely in 1983. I had ended the relationship, and we had no contact for 20 years. I found her and told her I had regretted ending our relationship for all those years.

Where I Sail and Write

I now live on an island in the mouth of Tampa Bay, where I write and sail. I had always planned to write the Great American Novel, but became so busy writing news stories, and then books, that the novel never started. After I got into television, I thought it would be far more satisfying to write a movie script. I wrote one that an agent could not sell.

So the same story is now underway as a novel. I write about things I know well. This one is about a TV reporter's coverage of a kidnap-murder in Miami in the years when America was waging a secret war against Cuba and Fidel Castro.

I sail a 28-foot Catalina, and can be in Tampa Bay in 10 minutes, the Gulf of Mexico in 20. I frequently publish magazine articles showing how to make things I invent for the boat. My five books now in print are listed on the **Copyright Page** of this book.

As with all the previous editions, it is my hope that this book will help you win future encounters with reporters and editors. I hope you will write your own crisis plan, and rehearse it.

If You Are Caught in the Storm

If you happen to be at the center of one of those events that becomes a major national/international story, you will be surrounded — overwhelmed — by hundreds of reporters, producers and photographers in about three hours. They may stay for weeks. It will probably be the most difficult time of your life.

I've tried to give you a lot of tips for dealing with major stories and interviews, where reporters and photographers can be a royal pain. But please don't become too defensive for the other stories you may be involved with.

For maybe 90 per cent of the stories you will be dealing with, the reporters are not out to get you. They simply need you to help them do their job. When they leave, I hope they'll thank you for helping them do that.

The truly big story, however, is quite another experience. Because the competition is so fierce, they send their most aggressive staffers to cover those. You may wind up hating some of them.

Good luck. Should you become a major player in one of those mega-media events, you're going to need all the skill and luck you can muster.

STRATEGY

Accuracy

If That's the Story, I Must Have Been Somewhere Else

It is my impression that the media are much less accurate these days. Why has accuracy deteriorated?

I believe the major cause is the intense pressure to increase corporate profits. Most daily news outlets in America are now owned by large, distant corporations. The final decision-makers are corporate executives a thousand miles away.

Managers From Far, Far Away

They closely watch ratings and circulation figures. Higher ratings and circulation mean you can charge more for advertising. That will increase the company's revenue, profits and stock price. Wall Street likes that.

But they have drastically cut staff and resources in recent years as part of that same profit motivation. News gathering and distribution is only as good as the people who do the work.

Quality suffers if there are too few reporters, editors and photographers. Or lots of young people who will work cheap and have replaced older, more experienced, higher-paid journalists.

As these cost-cutting measures take place, there is no sense that the news media are dedicated to serving the public good. The quality of writing, editing and photography decreases. The audience begins to believe they no longer need the news media, and drifts away. This is happening now with all the "legacy" media. Why don't the corporate bean counters understand that?

The Business/Newsroom Wall

In the middle part of the 20th Century, news reporters and editorial writers were completely divorced from the business side of journalism at newspapers and broadcast stations run by ethical owners.

Accuracy and fairness were the highest single goals for conscientious reporters and editors. As a young newspaper reporter, I thought it unethical to even think about circulation, or advertising, or company profit.

When I moved to TV, I was bothered by the newsroom's awareness and concern with ratings. Then I realized we had tough competition, and ratings were the scoreboard. My newspaper had not had a serious competitor. Many TV stations had a rule – no advertising people in the newsroom. The managers did not want anybody to even suspect that profit could influence news.

Profit Oozes Into the Newsroom

As the ownership of the American media changed, the drive to be profitable oozed into virtually every newsroom. Today, there is enormous pressure on reporters and editors to get the sensational story.

Too often, in my opinion, they publish or broadcast first, then check the facts later. (See **Ethics**) Unfortunately, this same competitive force makes the media echo each other's stories. They do not want to be left out of the major, breaking story which draws readers/viewers/listeners.

It is pack journalism at its worst.

And so the story generated by an unconfirmed rumor, a shaky or fictitious source, is quickly relayed from one news outlet to another. Whether true or not.

The Internet Adds to the Problem

The Internet, with its immediacy, its capacity to circle the globe within seconds, and its attraction for wackos who are wannabe publishers, has added a new dimension to the problem.

The news business has always been competitive. But there was a different motive in previous generations. Journalists took enormous pride in beating their competition. It proved they were better at their craft. They wanted the scoop, but also feared the risk of spreading a false or flawed story that could disgrace them.

Examples of Inaccuracy

Today, there are many high-profile stories that are published or broadcast too quickly; repeated by virtually every other media outlet; then found to be untrue or substantially different than first reported. In some cases, the pressure to write more colorfully has led to outright fiction in news stories that were published as truth.

Here's a sampling of stories that were inaccurate or outright fiction in recent years:

- **August, 1996** – Richard Jewell was fingered by the Atlanta Constitution in August, 1996, as the Atlanta Olympics bomber. The story was quickly echoed by virtually all media. After the stories forever altered his life, he was found to be completely innocent.

- **June, 1998** – The *New Republic* admitted that more than two dozen stories it published – all written by 25-year old Associate Editor Stephen Glass – were at least partially fabricated. Six of his *NR* articles were pure fiction. Glass had also written stories for several other national magazines.

- **June, 1998** – *Boston Globe* columnist Patricia Smith resigned after confessing she had invented both people and quotes to enhance her columns. Earlier that year, she had been a Pulitzer Prize nominee.

- **July, 1998** – CNN and *Time* retracted their June stories about "Operation Tailwind," a U. S. military foray into Laos during the Vietnam War. They had reported the raiding force used nerve gas to kill American defectors there.

- **June, 2001**– *Slate* apologized for a story about "monkey fishing" in the Florida Keys which said some people there caught monkeys with fruit-baited fish hooks. The monkey fishing technique was apparently invented by the author.

- **February, 2002** – A freelance writer admitted he had concocted an article for the *New York Times Magazine* about an adolescent slave in Ivory Coast who did not actually exist. The story was a collection of anecdotes the writer had been told by human rights workers in the African country.

- **May, 2003** – *New York Times* reporter Jayson Blair resigned after an internal investigation found accuracy problems in more than half of Blair's stories since the previous October.

  Blair quoted people he had never met, in places he had never been; and invented details which were complete fabrications. In the fallout from the scandal, *Times* Executive Editor Howell Raines and Managing Editor Gerald Boyd also resigned.

- **January, 2004** – *USA Today* correspondent Jack Kelley resigned after the newspaper said he admitted inventing a witness to corroborate a story he reported in Yugoslavia in 1998. The newspaper then created an independent committee to investigate the accuracy of Kelley's stories. He had worked at *USA Today* since it was founded in 1982, and had been a Pulitzer Prize nominee five times. In March, 2004, the committee said "Kelley's journalistic sins were sweeping and substantial ... a sad and shameful betrayal of public trust." Many of his colorful stories were completely fictitious. A month later, *USA Today* Editor Karen Jurgensen, 55, retired.

- **August, 2005** – News coverage of Hurricane Katrina in New Orleans in August, 2005, included accounts of rape and murder among storm refugees at the city's convention center. Some stories detailed how 40 bodies had been piled up inside the walk-in freezer at a restaurant there. The city's mayor and police chief seemed to confirm the news stories. But they turned out to be urban legends.

- **January, 2011** – Many news outlets reported U.S. Rep. Gabrielle Giffords had been killed in the Tucson, AZ shooting that killed six people. Giffords was among the 13 who were wounded.

- **June, 2012** – In their rush to be first, many news outlets reported that the U.S. Supreme Court had overturned "Obamacare." When their staffers inside the court building were given the printed decision, they scanned it quickly, came to the wrong conclusion, and phoned their newsrooms. The court decision in its opening pages rejected the law on one set of arguments. But then it approved the law on other grounds. In their hurry, reporters came to the wrong conclusion because they hadn't read far enough.

- **December, 2012** – Most news stories at first said the brother of the real shooter was responsible for the Sandy Hook Elementary School massacre in Connecticut. Other stories reported the shooter's mother worked at the school and was one of the victims shot there; that his father was dead, and that his girlfriend was missing. All those stories were wrong.

- **April, 2013** – The day after the Boston Marathon bombing, the New York Post website was still reporting that 12 people had been killed by the two bombs. The actual death toll was three.

A day later, CNN, Fox News, the *Boston Globe* and the Associated Press all reported there had been an arrest in the case. Reporters and photographers crowded around a federal building as news helicopters hovered overhead, waiting for the suspect to be brought there. But there had been no arrest.

The FBI took the unusual step of criticizing the false reports. Law enforcement at that point was still pleading for leads from the public. They knew that reports of an arrest would shut down some of those tips.

Good Reporters Sweat

Believe it or not, an inaccurate story is extremely painful for good reporters. They take immense professional pride in their ability to get it right. Better to miss the scoop than be wrong.

Sometimes, after a story is on the air or in the newspaper, ethical reporters suddenly realize there's one angle they didn't check. They sweat. There's a knot in the bottom of their bellies until they check that neglected angle to make sure it doesn't change anything. Good reporters also have the grace to admit it when they're wrong, and correct their mistakes.

I am concerned that the journalistic mantra "get it first, but get it right" has been overpowered by corporate executives who are not journalists, and whose primary job responsibility is to increase profits. As part of their cost-cutting, most news outlets have shut down most of their bureaus and decreased the number of editors and fact-checkers at the home office. (See **Ethics**)

Profit Overpowers Ethics

The old ethic to check and double-check will fade as more young journalists learn their craft in this atmosphere, then become editors and news directors. I remember a newscast at my Miami TV station. I was in the newsroom, and saw a script that the anchor had not yet read on the air. It contained a major historical error.

I ran to the young producer of the show and told her we needed to delay that story until we could fix the error. "Don't worry about it," she said. "It'll be over in a minute." I was stunned.

There are other factors, too, that lead journalists to be less than totally accurate.

What Do You Fear?

I often begin a media relations workshop by asking the group to talk about what they most fear when they deal with the media.

What do you dread? I ask. If you knew a reporter was coming to interview you at this moment, what would concern you most?

The results are remarkably the same. No matter where the seminar is held – no matter what they do for a living. Bank presidents, police chiefs, corporate CEOs, social workers, doctors, lawyers and accountants have the same response.

Fear of Being Misquoted

It is the fear or being misquoted or taken out of context. Why is this such a universal fear, I ask. Are inaccurate stories the result of reporter incompetence, insensitivity, or bad motives?

Sometimes one, sometimes the other. Sometimes all three. Some reporters get tunnel vision pursuing their story. They don't let the facts or what you tell them change the story. If you sense that is the case, you will need to invest a lot of energy to swing the story toward the truth.

You may need to have a meeting with the reporter's editor, or send a detailed letter to the news outlet clearly stating the facts, in contrast to what the reporter seems to believe. (See **Fighting Back**)

Preconceived Assignments

Another major factor in media inaccuracy is the preconceived story. Many story ideas are thought up by the editor, not the reporter. Remember, all of us view the world from our own, isolated cubicles. Editors are no different.

To get ahead in the news business, you do your best to please the boss. I once worked for a newspaper editor who was terrible about assigning preconceived stories. I'll call him Dave. Dave would stop at the City Desk when he arrived in the morning, voice hoarse, coughing and blowing his nose.

"We need a story on the flu epidemic," Dave would tell the city editor. "Is there an epidemic?" the city editor would ask. He knew the boss' story ideas did not always pan out.

The Flu Epidemic Story

"I've got the flu," Dave would say. "My wife and kids have the flu. Everybody in my neighborhood has the flu. Can't remember when so many people were sick at one time." And so a young reporter would be assigned to cover the flu epidemic. His first stop would be the county health department.

Lowest reports of flu in 20 years, they'd say. When the reporter's findings were put on Dave's desk, he'd shake his head. "Can't rely on those damned bureaucrats over at the health department," he'd grumble. "They could be covering it up. Put a more experienced reporter on the story."

Remember, the editor has invested the time of a reporter and photographer in this preconceived story. Most newsrooms are understaffed. They can't afford to waste resources.

Suggest a Replacement

One technique to deal with the false preconception is to suggest another, legitimate story to replace it. That way, the reporter doesn't go back empty-handed. It will be a lot easier to tell the boss the original assignment didn't pan out.

If you're the health department worker who's asked about a non-existent flu epidemic, you could say (if it's true):

"We've never had so little flu at this time of the year, but boy, the black plague is spreading like wildfire." Now *that's* a story. The editor will forget about the flu.

The Pre-Interview Interview

When a reporter approaches you on a story, your first task is to size up the reporter AND the story assignment. I call it the Pre-Interview-Interview. You need to get a handle on the reporter's story assignment, intelligence, experience, knowledge of the subject, attitude toward you and your organization. (See more on the Pre-Interview Interview in **Interview Guidelines**)

If you discover the reporter is working on a preconception that is all wrong, you need to set the facts straight IMMEDIATELY. How strongly you object to the false preconception will often determine whether the reporter changes course on the story idea.

Your first approach should be friendly and informative. "A lot of people assume that's the reason for our action, but they're wrong. Let me tell you what really happened."

Become More Aggressive

The reporter may persist with the original concept. You should become more aggressive.

Lay out your case in great detail. Suggest others who can substantiate what you're saying. Produce records that refute the preconception. Provide copies to help the reporter convince the editor the story concept is wrong.

If the reporter is not convinced, be sure your quotes make it clear you disagree, and effectively argue your point of view.

You may discover, in that Pre-Interview-Interview, that the reporter knows almost nothing about the subject matter. You will be terribly tempted to educate the reporter – to confer a Ph.D by the time the interview is over.

Don't Do That

Don't try to teach even half of what you know about the subject. You'll just confuse the reporter. If the reporter knows very little, it's impossible to prioritize the information.

"Why did they print that?" you'll say, when you read or watch the story. "They missed the whole point."

Because you gave it to them. Too much information increases the chance that the story will be off-point, inaccurate, the quotes distorted.

In a seminar for university administrators, one of my students was public relations director for a very prestigious medical school in the Northeast.

Reporters Who Know Nothing

"I've given up on TV reporters," he told the group. "They send reporters who know nothing about medicine.

"At our school, we're on the cutting edge of research. We're using extremely sophisticated, complex techniques. It takes an entire day to give the reporter a basic education.

What do we get for our trouble? Maybe 90 seconds, often inaccurate. Not worth it."

You're telling reporters too much, I said. They only need to know what time it is. You've been insisting they understand atomic clocks. The reporter's only knowledge of the subject may be a newspaper or magazine clipping.

An Opportunity for Control

Once you realize the scope of the reporter's ignorance, PROVIDE ONLY WHAT IT TAKES TO WRITE THE STORY YOU WANT. Draw the final conclusions. Get to the bottom line. Sum it all up in one or two sentences.

It gives you an opportunity to control – to a large extent – what will appear in print, or on the air.

Misquotes – Your Fault

Reporters have been conditioned to look for quotes that fit a certain formula. If you haven't learned to speak Media Language, you may discover that the reporter stitches together a phrase you spoke here, another there, as if they were spoken at one time, in one sentence. (See **Editing**)

You need to learn how to speak for quotes or sound bites in one, quick sentence. Otherwise, you might as well be speaking German or Chinese.

Don't make the reporter act as interpreter. Many quotes get lost or distorted if they have to be translated into Media-Speak. (See **Interviews** chapters – for crafting quotes that will be used and quoted accurately)

Record the Interview

If your experience with a specific reporter leads you to believe this reporter has an accuracy problem, a suggestion:

Record the interview. To make sure the taping is legal, put the recorder in plain sight. Say, "You don't mind if I record this, do you?" You can also record telephone interviews. (See more about the legality of disclosing that you're recording in **Privacy**)

The recording tells the reporter you will have a complete transcript of what you said. There will be no your-word-against-my-word dispute. (See **Defending Yourself** and **Libel** for elements of truth, news media risks & defenses)

It may be that you do everything right, and you're still misquoted. Or the facts in the story are so distorted, you wonder if you and the reporter attended the same event.

You Need to Complain

You need to complain. Set the record straight.

Not a nasty, angry complaint. A careful, straightforward telephone call or letter to the reporter and the editor, showing what was reported and what you really said. Or what really happened.

If you don't file your complaint, the flawed story goes into the newsroom library. In the future, every reporter who writes about you or the same subject matter will use the story as a resource and repeat the error. (See **Fighting Back** for details on how to file your complaint, when, and with whom; the pros and cons of corrections and retractions)

The Last Resort

As a last resort, when you have carefully documented your case, have a meeting with the newspaper's managing editor or the broadcast station's news director.

Tell them you respect their concern for truth and fairness. But — based on your experience with this one reporter — you can get neither truth nor fairness in the stories that reporter writes.

You will be happy to give interviews to ANYONE else, but you will no longer talk to that reporter. This technique may work, it may not. It will usually depend on how well you document your case against the reporter.

STRATEGY

CRISIS MANAGEMENT

Survival Often Depends On Your Reaction in the First Few Hours

In most crisis management scenarios, the outcome depends heavily on what you do and say in the first few hours. What the news media report in their first stories – and how they gauge your coping skills – will often set the tone for the entire crisis.

Chances are, the media's first impression will persist until you have overcome the problem and emerged victorious ... or you've been humiliated, fired, put out of business, arrested, sued, divorced ... the list goes on and on.

We Don't Want to Think About It

Planning for crises is something we avoid. It is like buying life insurance or long-term disability insurance. Most people don't do it because they don't want to think about the possibility of their own death or disability.

We have been forced by law and mortgage lenders to get accustomed to buying accident insurance for our cars, homeowners insurance for our houses. For most of us, medical insurance is considered a necessity.

But we still try to avoid contemplating other disasters that can lead to our death or disability; as well as the destruction of an organization that ends the careers, the productivity and the morale of the people who work there.

Perhaps the 9/11 World Trade Center and Pentagon attacks changed us, hardened us, made us more willing to face the possibility of sudden disaster that cannot be predicted.

ISIS has renewed our fears, but as terrorist attacks fade with time, we may revert and do less to prepare for crises.

The Police Shooting Model

In recommending crisis plans to my clients for 30 years now, I have told them most people do not think or function well when the crisis hits. I learned that when I was reporter, covering "officer involved shootings."

When an officer is down, or has shot someone, the call goes out on the radio. Officers rush in, sirens screaming, blue lights flashing. There is chaos at the scene. Without careful planning and training, highly excited or grief-stricken officers will do something everyone will later regret. Or fail to do something that, in hindsight, was a terrible blunder.

Things to Do

So virtually every law enforcement agency in America has an "officer involved shooting checklist." The last one I looked at had 21 things to do immediately after the shooting. Like notify the chief, wherever he/she is, whatever time of day or night.

If an officer is the shooter, isolate him/her. Offer the officer psychological and legal counseling. Relieve him/her of duty. Take custody of his/her weapon. Notify the officer's family. Do not move the corpse until it has been viewed by the medical examiner and prosecutor.

Media Crisis Plans Are Rare

Most organizations have written plans for fires, storms, floods. They practice those plans frequently. Should a fire or storm or flood occur, everyone will know – without thinking – what needs to be done and how to do it.

Very few organizations have media crisis plans. And those that do rarely rehearse them. Most of you reading this will have a media crisis long before you have a fire or tornado or flood. And media crises in a media-driven society can be much more damaging, much more demoralizing than those hazards of nature.

The checklist I've provided at the end of this chapter is a skeleton to build on. Those who use it should flesh it out, custom-tailor it to their particular needs and people. Revisit it regularly to improve it and keep it up to date.

A crisis is the imminent risk of death or serious damage. It can threaten you, people you care about, your organization, your property, your reputation, your career, your future.

If and when the media discover the crisis, your skill in influencing how they report it – or decide not to report it – are key factors that determine the outcome.

The tone of the early stories usually hinges on how well reporters and editors know you, your understanding of media strategy, your experience and reflexes in dealing with journalists.

One of the most difficult steps in crisis management is making the decision that there *is* a crisis. Wait too late, and you may not be able to save the sinking ship.

Send everybody to battle stations when hindsight shows there was no Armageddon looming, and you'll look like Chicken Little. A pathetic, paranoid manager who's out of touch with reality.

Worst-Case Scenarios

One way to determine whether you have the potential for a serious crisis is to call a meeting of top people and draw up a list of worst-case scenarios. Then ask:

- If any of these worst-case scenarios should occur, what would it do to our company/agency/career/future plans?
- How likely is it that our worst fears will come to pass?
- How and when will the media learn about it?

Call in Outside Help

If you or the organization could be destroyed or critically damaged, you've got a major crisis, and should probably call in outside public relations counsel to help you deal with it.

Inside PR staff caught up in the emotion and fear tend to not think as clearly as an outside professional. Even if they think about some of the tactics available as options, staff may not be willing to propose them.

They know how volatile and dangerous those options will seem to other, powerful insiders. Just because the options are scary doesn't mean they're not viable choices for solving the problem and ending the crisis.

Don't Put Lawyers in Charge

In far too many crises – personal, corporate and governmental – the lawyers are brought in immediately. Virtually all decision-making is turned over to them. SERIOUS MISTAKE. The attorneys need to be *a part of the crisis team* – but not run it. Why? Because their instincts for dealing with the news media will almost always be wrong. (See **Lawyers and Lawsuits**)

Winning with the News Media

Choosing Outside PR Counsel

The outside PR counsel you choose is very important. If the outside PR practitioner needs your business very badly, he/she may be no better than an insider who is afraid to speak the painful truth.

Outside PR professionals brought into the crisis MUST have extensive experience in the field.

They MUST be people of absolute integrity who will give you their best, unvarnished opinions and suggestions. They must be willing to call it as they see it, at the risk of being ridiculed and/or losing you as a client.

Sometimes their ideas will seem harsh or off-the-wall. Creativity often seems crazy. At first blush. That's one definition of creativity. Out-of-the-blue ideas nobody else has thought of.

After the boss has heard everybody's assessment of the problem and possible solutions, it's the boss's job to make the tough decisions. That's what bosses are paid to do.

Here are some basic rules for the management of news media crises:

Never Under-Estimate the Crisis

If you under-estimate, once they learn the real extent of the problem, reporters will feel like you tried to deceive them.

If you under-estimate, you can be blamed for your lack of knowledge and skill, once we know how bad it really is.

If You Over-Estimate

If you over-estimate, and solving the problem becomes a long, difficult task, the news media expected it to be, and you won't be faulted

If you over-estimate the crisis and then solve it quickly, it appears you have immense power and skill

The Media Need a "Bad Guy"

The news media need a good guy and a bad guy in every crisis. (See **Good Guys/Bad Guys**)

A crisis means the gods must be angry; and we still practice the ancient ritual of human sacrifice in this society. To appease the gods, the high priests of politics and the press must find someone to sacrifice.

If you don't understand the ritual, and how to protect yourself, you can easily become the bad guy who is thrown into the volcano.

If you did something that caused all or part of the current crisis, take responsibility, and lay out your plan to avoid repeating the error (See **Ten Commandments**).

In all your interviews, news conferences and news releases, make clear who the bad guy is.

Three Mile Island

When the radiation first leaked at Three Mile Island in March, 1979, power plant officials brushed it off as inconsequential.

When reporters found the leak was more serious than first announced, the story mushroomed into an international, five-alarm event. The earlier deception made the story bigger.

Exxon's Oil Spill at Valdez

After the oil spill at Valdez, Alaska, in March, 1989, one of Exxon's biggest mistakes was to diminish the severity of the spill and the damage to the environment. It took a long time for the president of Exxon to decide the situation was bad enough for him to take a personal look.

A company vice president was quoted putting down the media for sensationalizing the situation. No big deal, he said – after all, oil bubbles up from the bottom of the sea as a natural process.

Didn't he understand that in the next moment, TV viewers would see vivid pictures of dying seals and eagles; fishermen and their families unable to work and make a living? The unspoken media message was:

This is not important to the people who run Exxon. They don't care about the damage to the environment or the fishing villages facing financial disaster. As a global powerhouse, they only care about making money.

Deepwater Horizon Disaster

The Deepwater Horizon oil drilling platform in the Gulf of Mexico exploded April 20, 2010, killing 11 workers. British Petroleum (BP) had learned from the Exxon Valdez spill. But they did not learn enough.

The CEO's Mistakes

BP immediately began extensive efforts to take responsibility and clean up the spill. CEO Tony Hayward was at the scene quickly and became very visible. But then he said the environmental damage would be "very, very modest." Serious mistake.

He took a break to go boating with his son. He was quoted as saying "I would like my life back." Three months after the rig exploded, facing savage, worldwide criticism, he retired.

In the early days of the disaster, as oil gushed from the wellhead at the sea floor, BP had said the leak was between 1,000 and 5,000 barrels a day of crude oil. But their underwater cameras, broadcast by TV networks worldwide, showed a huge cloud of oil gushing nonstop.

The Flow Rate Technical Group (FRTG) said it was more likely about 62,000 barrels per day. BP vehemently disputed that figure. But internal e-mails discovered in 2013 showed that BP's estimate of the size of the leak in 2010 was close to the FRTG figure, while they were publicly maintaining a much lower number.

You Need to Go There

American politicians have learned to speedily go to disaster sites, fly over them in helicopters, then tell the press how much they feel the pain of those involved.

It is a political ritual, enacted for the media. But an important ritual. It must be done quickly. Ignore it at your peril. More crises:

Navy's Tailhook Scandal

The Tailhook Association is an old group of Navy pilots who flew planes launched and recovered by aircraft carriers at sea. It gets its name from the cable stretched across the carrier deck, and the hook in the tail of the planes. The hook is designed to grab the cable and stop the hurtling planes as they land.

During their convention in Las Vegas in 1991, a large group of drunk Tailhook members gathered in a Hilton Hotel hallway. As women tried to walk down the hall, they were groped, harassed and in some cases, had their clothes ripped off.

Although they were not involved in the melee, Secretary of the Navy H. Lawrence Garrett III and Chief of Naval Operations Admiral Frank Kelso had both attended the Tailhook convention. In the aftermath of the scandal, Garrett ultimately resigned. Kelso took early retirement two years later. The news media portrayed them as bad guys who were, in the final analysis, just as guilty as the drunk pilots because they had been slow to investigate the allegations.

Eventually, the careers of 14 admirals and nearly 300 Navy pilots were damaged in some way by the Tailhook scandal.

Slowness to act will often be interpreted by the media as an attempt to cover up the crime – one of this culture's very worst sins. (See **Ten Commandments** and **Good Guys/Bad Guys**)

Crash of Valujet 592

Valujet Flight 592 caught fire shortly after takeoff from Miami on May 11, 1996, and crashed into the Everglades, killing all 110 people aboard. The next day, Transportation Secretary Federico Pena held a news conference.

U.S. airlines are safe, Pena said. He was so sure the Federal Aviation Administration (FAA) was doing a good job regulating the airlines,

Pena said he would not be afraid to put his own family aboard another Valujet plane.

FAA Administrator David Hinson's media interviews echoed the same confidence.

Within a month, the media had learned about 34 safety violations in Valujet's recent history. Media stories said both Pena and Hinson knew about the violations at the time they were bragging about the safety of the airline.

They were accused of hypocrisy and deception. The FAA was cast as one of the bad guys.

FAA Conflict

Both men were caught in a conflict of interest within the Congressional mandate that created the FAA. The agency is supposed to regulate airlines and insure their safety, but it also is supposed to promote air travel.

In their management of the crisis, both Pena and Hinson had under-estimated the problem, and failed to assume responsibility for things that might have gone wrong.

Quite suddenly, Pena almost disappeared from news stories. In March, 1997, he was shifted to the Department of Energy, and a year later he resigned that post. Hinson retired at the end of 1996, seven months after the crash.

The careers of both men were badly damaged by their missteps in the early hours of the crisis.

The TWA 800 Crash

There was a sharp contrast in the way National Transportation Safety Board (NTSB) vice chairman Robert Francis handled the media in both the Valujet crash and the TWA Flight 800 crash two months later.

When the TWA 747 enroute to Paris exploded off Long Island the night of July 17, 1996, all 230 people aboard died. Francis by that time had logged a great deal of experience in crisis management.

The TWA crisis was especially difficult because there were recurring rumors the plane had been destroyed by a bomb or a missile. At every news conference, Francis was exceptionally skillful at reminding the media:

- How difficult it would be to prove what caused the crash
- That the NTSB would leave no stone unturned
- That the investigation would take a very long time
- That nobody should jump to conclusions before all the evidence was in

Despite fatigue, sunburn and days in the international spotlight, Francis was unusually patient with reporters who asked stupid, repetitive or antagonistic questions.

Virginia Tech Shooting

When 33 people were shot and killed on the Virginia Tech campus on April 15, 2007, University President Charles Steger was even more visible and helpful to reporters than Francis had been.

The university had failed to realize after the first person was shot that this was just the beginning of a major massacre. They were late in locking down the campus.

It could have easily cost Steger his job. But Steger worked incredibly hard to help the news media cover the story. He seemed to be available non-stop for media inquiries.

A Standing Round of Applause

After many days of intense stress and very little sleep, Steger held a news conference to tell reporters he was so exhausted he would have to take a break and get some rest. In a highly unusual response, the reporters gave him a standing round of applause to thank him for his efforts on their behalf.

Even though some mistakes had been made the day of the massacre, Steger's genuine effort to work with reporters made them downplay those mistakes.

He was not blamed, and there was never any major threat to end his presidency at the university.

Gary Condit's Gaffe

A very different case history: in April, 2001, Congressional intern Chandra Levy disappeared. The media quickly learned that she had been having an affair with California Congressman Gary Condit; that the affair had gone sour, and that she had planned to leave Washington shortly before she disappeared.

Media stories began to suggest that Condit might have killed her to prevent her destroying his reputation. For months, Condit refused to talk to reporters.

Finally, he was persuaded by his handlers to appear on ABC's *Prime Time Live* with Connie Chung four months after Levy's disappearance.

When Chung pounded the congressman with blunt questions about his affair with Levy, Condit began to side-step.

CHUNG: Would you like to ... tell the truth about the relationship with her?

CONDIT: I've told you and responded to uh, the relationship question. And I think the American people, and people watching out there understand. I think they understand that ... that I'm entitled to some of my privacy. My family's entitled to some of their privacy. And certainly the Levys are, as well.

Condit's evasion made him look even worse than his previous silence. In March, 2002, Condit was trounced in the Democratic primary, ending 14 years in Congress.

Two months later, Levy's body was found in a remote area of Rock Creek Park. Her skull had been crushed, but law enforcement never even hinted that Condit might have been her killer.

Nothing is Off-Limits

Moral of the story? If you decide to talk to the media after the crisis has broken, nothing is off-limits. You must be willing to talk about ANYTHING and EVERYTHING. (See **Ten Commandments** - Commandment # 9 – The Big Dump)

Priests Abusing Children

Perhaps the greatest news media crisis of the last century is the epidemic of stories about the sexual abuse of children by Catholic priests.

The *Boston Globe* won a Pulitzer Prize in 2003 for a series of daily stories that had begun in July, 2001. Virtually no media outlet in the United States has failed to run lengthy stories about the scandal since then.

Ten years after the first stories broke in the U.S., the scandal had spread world-wide. One study in 2010 estimated the Church had already paid $6 billion in damages as the result of civil lawsuits – a third of that in Ireland. And many more were pending.

The story had been there a long time. Lengthy, in-depth newspaper investigations about priests who were serial abusers of children were published as early as the mid-1980s in scattered parts of the country.

So how could an organization as rich, powerful, and connected as the Catholic Church have possibly mismanaged its crisis so badly? It now threatens the Church's financial structure, its reputation, the recruiting of young priests, and some of the Church's most sacred doctrines.

Principles of Crisis Mismanagement

Crises often become disasters because the climate within a large organization instills a complex set of reflexes in those who make critical decisions. Some general principles:

- **Success** can be a terrible handicap. If the organization is not broke, why fix it? Why change the way things have always been done? The early exposes about priests abusing children did not cause any great damage to the church. So the same tactics for handling them continued.

- **Internal authority**, with little or no advice or pressure from outsiders, can prevent those making decisions from seeing the big picture.

- **Bureaucracies reward** those who are conservative and follow old, established procedures. Those who rise in the ranks are not boat-rockers. Once at the top of the power hierarchy, they are inclined to use old techniques for dealing with new issues.

- **Allegiance to the organization** can lead to decisions that do not carefully weigh protecting the organization versus protecting individuals. The news media's value system is heavily weighted in favor of individual rights.

- **Hypocrisy** is one of the juiciest news stories. We love to see the mighty fall, especially if they violate the values they were supposed to defend. A fire chief charged with arson – a respected accounting firm which helps falsify the reports of a major client – will always get top billing in the news. Certain kinds of organizations – like religious groups – are particularly susceptible to this kind of crisis.

▪ **Power corrupts.** Those in power tend to believe they can go outside the law or conventional ethics, if necessary, to protect the organization they lead. The watershed event in the *Boston Globes'* investigation of priests' child abuse was the newspaper's successful effort to unseal old court records.

They showed Cardinal Bernard F. Law's long involvement in hiding the scandal. The court records showed that Law had testified under oath that he knew about Priest John Geoghan's sexual abuse history as early as 1984.

▪ **Covering up** has become inexcusable in the United States. Richard Nixon was driven from the White House by news stories that documented his role in trying to cover up the Watergate scandal – not because he was a conspirator in the burglary itself. Bill Clinton was impeached for his effort to evade and deceive – not because he had an extra-marital affair.

Stock Market Crises

In the stock market crises of 2002 and 2007, many of the same elements of crisis mismanagement gave the securities industry a very bad name. Highly respected financial firms, as it turned out, had been hypocritical in recommending investments when they knew the companies were about to fail. In some cases, they were actually betting against investments they were recommending to their clients.

CPA firms were also involved in covering up what was happening. Those in power at a number of corporations believed that they could lead lavish lifestyles and spend company money for personal luxuries, not having to abide by the usual standards of corporate behavior.

Keep Reminding Yourself:

If you're caught in one of those national or world-wide crises, you need to keep reminding yourself:

▪ **I have a job to do**; reporters have a job to do. If they didn't understand what I said, I'll say it over and over, without getting testy, until they do understand

▪ **If I behave badly**, the world will see reruns a thousand times

▪ **If reporters behave badly**, it will probably not be reported

▪ **I will be a more effective** spokesperson if I can remain human, humble, sensitive

- **It is OK to admit** that I don't know, but I'm working very hard to:

Find the answer

Solve the problem

Prevent it from happening again

When I know the answer, I'll tell the whole world

Bring the Media Inside Your Crisis

Bring the news media inside your crisis. Brief them frequently. Let them watch at close range how you handle the crisis. At first glance, this seems absolutely absurd. But it works. Here's why:

- Reporters are, by nature, gossips

- Being inside gives them special knowledge, power and prestige

- By watching your decision-making process, reporters can better understand the options

- They are more likely to report you were the good guy who did the right thing, and made the best of a bad situation

- The Stockholm Syndrome takes over

The Stockholm Syndrome

In August, 1973, a group of robbers armed with submachine guns tried to rob the Sveriges Kreditbank in Stockholm, Sweden. The robbery went bad when police responded to a silent alarm and surrounded the bank. The robbers holed up in the bank vault with four hostages. The hostage crisis lasted five and a half days.

Psychologists and police officers who later interviewed the hostages were amazed that they were sympathetic to the bank robbers, not the police officers who rescued them. The phrase "Stockholm Syndrome" was born. A number of hostage situation studies since then have documented the same bonding phenomenon.

Ruthless Attitude Softens

Lengthy, close contact in a hostage crisis also leads the captors to identify with their prisoners. Their original, ruthless attitude is softened as they learn more about their prisoners as human beings.

Both hostages and hostage-takers are unified by the knowledge that the rescue operation may harm or kill them all.

Bringing the media into your crisis has similar psychological effects. Those outside, surrounding and threatening you, will be perceived as the bad guys. Those inside become the good guys.

The Tylenol Disaster

Johnson and Johnson CEO James Burke saved the company after the Tylenol poisoning of five people in Chicago in September, 1982. Within an hour after news broke that someone had planted cyanide in Tylenol capsules, Burke was enroute to Chicago to supervise the company response.

He also let the media see the innermost decision-making process. Mike Wallace and a *60 Minutes* camera crew were allowed to film an executive committee meeting at the height of the crisis, with no holds barred.

Reporters were briefed regularly. Even though cyanide deaths occurred only in Chicago, Tylenol was recalled worldwide.

When you help reporters cover your crisis, you've done them a favor. They sort of owe you one. This will never be spoken or acknowledged. But reporters are human, too.

Confine the Story

The real damage occurs when a story breaks out of the local media and goes national or worldwide.

My advice is to drop everything and concentrate all your resources and skill on local coverage with disaster potential. If you're not guilty, and you succeed in minimizing or killing the local story, wider coverage can be avoided.

If your organization slipped up and made a terrible mistake, tell the local reporter that. Admit your crime, correct the problem, do what you can to prevent its ever happening again.

The Targeting Phenomenon

Once a story begins to spread nationally, a strange phenomenon occurs. For a while, anything that is even remotely associated with an element in the story gets a huge amount of media attention.

If a Boeing 737 crashes, for months afterward, any slight problem that occurs with *any* 737 will get major coverage. The little problems would not normally be news.

One reason some situations deteriorate into full-fledged crises is the fear of staff to make quick, creative decisions on their own.

To do things differently usually requires high-level approval. Perhaps by the CEO or chairman of the board. That takes time.

Risky to Wait for Approval

The Allies' Normandy invasion in World War II might have been repelled if the German officers in France had ordered a shift in German forces to the invasion site.

Instead, they waited for permission from Berlin. By the time it came, it was too late.

In the new, media-driven world where crisis news circles the globe in a matter of minutes, everything is on a much faster track. One of the serious hazards in crisis management is ignoring media reports because you know the allegations are not true.

Crisis at Coca Cola

The scare about contaminated Coca Cola in Europe in June, 1999, is a good example. Coca Cola staffers in Europe believed from the beginning that their drinks were not the cause of the illness. Their certainty kept the company from responding quickly.

It took nine days for the Coca Cola board chairman to fly to Europe to show top-level concern about reports that Coke had caused illness in hundreds of people.

Government investigations later determined that Coke was not the culprit. But media stories (and government reaction to the coverage in Europe) cost the company an estimated $100 million in recalled products that summer, and reduced sales for months.

The company's stock price, its reputation, and a number of careers were also hammered.

If Fault is Uncertain

It is not enough to proclaim your innocence, if you are the accused. If it appears that you *might* be at fault, you must quickly take bold, visual, expensive, public, media-savvy steps to make sure things are safe and under control.

The Firestone/Ford Crisis

Firestone and Ford were badly hurt in the 2000 crisis over tires on Ford Explorers throwing their treads and causing scores of deaths. The most damaging accusation was that the companies had indications of problems years earlier, but covered them up, or did nothing.

It was possible that other brands had the same propensity to disintegrate at high speeds if the owner did not keep them properly inflated. At the beginning of the crisis, both companies pointed their fingers the each other, rather than creating better defenses.

Toyota's Sudden Acceleration Crisis

Stories began to spread in 2009 that some Toyotas had suddenly accelerated to more than 100 miles an hour while the drivers stood on the brakes, unable to slow or stop the cars. Toyota's response was very reserved, and very unusual.

Most of the company's reaction as the story grew was released in written statements. Perhaps because the corporation's top executives were Japanese and did not speak fluent English, American news outlets did not hound them as they would have if the owners of Detroit-made cars had reported the acceleration problem.

There was another element in that issue. Perhaps the drivers themselves were to blame. It is not unusual for drivers to mistakenly hit the accelerator and not the brake.

And for cars speeding out of control, simply turning off the engine or putting the transmission in neutral would have quickly solved the crisis.

Planting Doubt Slows Crises

Planting the element of doubt can slow an impending crisis. For many years, the tobacco companies used that technique to win lawsuits that blamed cigarettes for causing lung cancer. Eventually, the evidence was so overwhelming, the doubt defense no longer worked.

The same tactic is now being used to fight warnings of climate change and reforms that would slow air pollution. Maybe higher temperatures are just natural swings, the opponents argue – and not the result of man-made pollution.

Expensive Recalls and Settlements

Toyota went through several very expensive recalls, conceding that some floor mats may have been snagged by accelerators when the drivers pushed the pedal to the floor.

A second recall was initiated when accelerators for some Toyotas – supplied by an American company – were shown to have collected moisture, making them slow to return to idle speed when drivers released the pedals.

Both NASA and the National Highway Traffic Safety Administration conducted extensive investigations and said they could find no evidence that the electronics in Toyotas were to blame for sudden acceleration.

Toyota quietly settled some lawsuits and paid fines for delaying their recalls and reporting of complaints. The crisis eventually eased out of sight.

A Crisis Management Checklist

Here's my checklist to help you design a crisis management plan:

1 **Begin with a list of examples to define a crisis and help executives make the decision to implement the crisis plan**

2 **A crisis can be sparked by violence or a natural disaster**

   ▪ Murder, accidental death or injury within the organization

   ▪ A major fire, earthquake or storm that threatens or has harmed employees, customers, services, facilities, assets

3 **A crisis might be caused by other events that might cause a major breakdown or threat to:**

   ▪ The public

   ▪ The environment

   ▪ Product or service quality

   ▪ Employee morale

   ▪ Customer confidence

   ▪ The organization's equipment or facilities

4 **A crisis can erupt if internal problems are discovered by the news media like:**

   ▪ A major internal theft

   ▪ Failure to conform to a contract, industrial or quality standard that could damage the reputation, income, or profits of the organization

   ▪ Major conflicts of interest on the part of insiders

   ▪ A real or suspected blunder that could cause great financial or physical harm

5 **Action by outsiders**

   ▪ Allegations published – or about to be – that say the organization is guilty of any of the problems in the previous bullet point (whether true or not)

   ▪ The arrest or criminal investigation of a staffer

   ▪ Elimination of funding, resources, utilities, etc.

   ▪ A strike, major protest movement or boycott aimed at the

organization

- A major lawsuit against the organization. Or the announcement, filing or passage of legislation or regulatory action that could dramatically affect the organization

6 **The plan should make it very clear who has the power to call the organization into crisis mode**

- The plan should set up a chain of command, in case those authorized to initiate the crisis plan are unavailable

7 **Detail who should be notified, and how**

8 **Itemize standard procedures that should be altered**

9 **Create an executive committee to deal with the crisis and decide:**

- Who should be members
- Who should head the committee
- How the committee will communicate with both insiders and outsiders, and who will speak for the committee

10 **One of the first steps for the committee is to determine: how serious IS the risk?**

11 **If it is VERY serious, the plan should direct the committee to consider hiring:**

- Outside legal counsel
- Outside public relations counsel

    (Lawyers and public relations experts on staff may not be willing to say what needs to be said. Because they work for the company, they have a personal investment that amounts to a conflict of interest)

12 **If large numbers of journalists are converging:**

- The CEO should be visibly present on the scene to demonstrate the organization's concern and its efforts to solve the problem
- The CEO should be available for media interviews
- If there have been deaths or injuries, the CEO should visit victims and/or survivors

13 **Establish a media center that is staffed 24/7 with:**

- Wi-Fi, adequate phone lines, power outlets, restrooms, tables, chairs, air conditioning, a briefing area with a multiple mike system (if possible) and your own video camera

- Issue credentials for entering the media center
- Feed reporters and photographers

14 Create a Media Committee

- Include all types – newspaper, TV, Internet, radio, periodicals
- Tell them you will help them cover this story IF they follow the rules
- Ask the committee to help you set up the rules, so that peer pressure becomes a powerful enforcement tool
- Make it clear that your unusual efforts to help ALL media cover the story will be severely curtailed if ANYBODY breaks the rules
- Meet with the Media Committee often

15 Create a private number, recorded message and/or a password-entry website for up-to-the-minute media information

16 Brief the media often

- Tell them as much as you can so they will like you, believe you, trust you
- Make and keep your own video of every briefing so you can prove what you said and what they said
- Tell them you expect COURTESY, ACCURACY, FAIRNESS
- Praise them when they live up to your expectations

17 Bring reporters inside the decision-making process whenever possible

- The Stockholm Syndrome will take over
- They will owe you one – or two – for helping them cover the crisis

18 Use techniques like pool cameras and pool reporters

19 Shoot and release your own pictures and video to give close-up coverage with less confusion and intrusion

20 Set up areas for interviews that will leave ingress and egress clear

- Establish parking areas for satellite trucks and other large media vehicles

21 Try to arrange information-sharing with reporters you

trust

22   Put caller ID on all your phones to trace threats and other nuisance calls

23   Remember that some media offer large bribes to insiders who will leak

24   Be aware that the media spotlight and celebrity status can dramatically affect the behavior and personalities of some of your staff

25   Take good care of your staff

- Order catered meals to help your people avoid the media gauntlet at mealtime
- Bring in bedding and clean clothes for staffers who may not go home for a while
- Give them frequent breaks and ability to contact their families
- Constantly monitor fatigue levels
- Sleep deprivation and stress can severely damage stamina, performance and decision-making

Crisis Plans MUST Be Rehearsed

Creating a crisis plan is only the first step. The plan must be reviewed and rehearsed regularly. Running your people through realistic drills will uncover defects in the plan, so it can be revised to solve those problems.

The CEO and anyone else who is expected to speak for the organization during a crisis should be given tough, on-camera training. Unless you can simulate the beating they will get at the hands of aggressive reporters, they will be overwhelmed when the real crisis occurs.

The CEO's Involvement

The CEO's involvement is critical. All employees get their cues and priorities from the person at the top. If the CEO telegraphs that crisis planning is important, the entire organization will become believers. Make sure the organization's lawyers also are involved, and that they understand the priorities and the process.

Bring in outsiders to get their perspective on your plan, and to monitor your crisis drills. They can often see flaws that are simply not visible to insiders.

The most valuable outsiders will be those who have been in the spotlight of a national story. Their personal war stories and what they learned can convince even the most skeptical staffers that crisis planning and action are crucial.

STRATEGY

ETHICS

Do They Make Up the Rules As They Go Along?

When I mentioned journalistic ethics in a seminar, a middle-aged police chief interrupted. "Reporters have no ethics," he grumbled. "They'll do whatever it takes to get a story. They have no conscience. They make up the rules as they go along."

Sometimes, I conceded, that's true. Since the beginning of this nation, the media's ethics have been in constant flux. Some of the ethics are written, some spoken, some taught at journalism schools. Some guidelines are simply tradition, which is understood among editors and reporters. That's what makes it seem so amorphous and strange to outsiders.

Who Regulates the Media?

The ethics for many professions are enforced through state or federal law, usually through regulatory bodies created by statute. Many people who deal with the news media believe there should be similar supervision of the news media. But the First Amendment keeps popping up:

Congress shall make no law ... abridging the freedom of speech or of the press ...

There was a period in the 1970s and 1980s when the media did a lot to clean up their act. Part of it was the aftermath of Watergate. The media had turned the spotlight on public officials in a new, no-holds-barred way.

Before Watergate, the media had often participated in a conspiracy of silence about certain kinds of things that went on behind the scenes in government; certain kinds of behavior among power people, politicians, and media people themselves. (See **Privacy**)

Stone-Throwers & Glass Houses

People who live in glass houses, the old saying goes, shouldn't throw stones. Journalists have traditionally been the stone-throwers in this society.

If we're going to hold politicians and public officials to a certain standard, the media reasoned, we'll have to live by those same standards.

And for the first time, the media were willing to report on each other without pulling their punches. Another contributing factor for that was new, increased competition.

Newspapers were especially eager to trash their new television competitors, whom they feared and despised. (See **Selling Your Story**)

Ethics Erosion in the 90s

Unfortunately (in my opinion) a much sharper increase in competition and the drive to make publicly held media corporations profitable has led to a massive erosion of media ethics and responsibility.

I blame that deterioration primarily on a shift in American media ownership. A few large, distant corporations now control television networks, many local TV stations, and the overwhelming majority of all daily American newspaper circulation.

This is a major cultural shift for the United States. Until the 1970s, most American newspapers were locally owned, and very provincial. Today, the locally owned, independent newspaper is very rare.

Few National U.S. Dailies

Unlike other industrial countries, the U.S. has very few national dailies that are sold all over the country. *The New York Times, The Wall Street Journal* and *USA Today* are about the only ones.

With weekday circulation averaging 2,378,827 copies in 2013, *The Wall Street Journal* was America's largest daily. Japan's largest daily, *Yomiuri Shimbun*, was averaging 13.5 million copies that year.

By 2013, *The New York Times* was selling off other newspapers it owned. *The Wall Street Journal* and *New York Post* were owned by Rupert Murdoch, the Australian billionaire who also owned the Fox TV Network and some of Great Britain's largest newspapers.

The Washington Post was sold that year to Jeff Bezos, the founder and CEO of amazon.com. Bezos had no experience as a journalist. But many journalists expressed their hope that his genius at making money with new technology might stop the slide of American newspapers into extinction.

The Bottom-Line Mentality

The people with final power in the corporations that own today's media rarely have experience as reporters or editors. They have no experience with journalistic ethics.

They have a bottom-line mentality. Their primary allegiance is to profit and their stockholders. They crave Wall Street's blessing. Their careers depend on their ability to maximize profits. If there is a conflict between public service and profit, public service is almost always abandoned.

The ethical slide is also accelerated by the decline of the newspaper as the dominant source of news and information.

"The Cereal Killer"

One of the early, and most publicized ethics battles between news and profit began when Mark Willes was named CEO of the Times Mirror Corp. in 1995. The *Los Angeles Times* was the company's flagship newspaper. Willes came to *Times Mirror* from his job as vice-chairman of General Mills, the cereal company.

He quickly alienated reporters and editors by going through the entire corporation, slashing jobs and killing highly-regarded publications that were not profitable enough. Journalists within the company gave him the nickname "The Cereal Killer."

Willes' next move was an attempt to move the advertising department into the newsroom. Editors were teamed with advertising "partners" so they could work together to merge the goals of both news and advertising. In June, 1999, Willes appointed as publisher Kathryn M. Downing. She had no newspaper background.

The Willes strategy was financially successful. He made a compelling argument that journalists will have nowhere to publish what they write if their publication does not make a profit.

Guerilla Warfare Behind the Lines

Throughout Willes' reign, there was constant guerilla warfare in the newsroom. Stories about what was happening at the *Los Angeles Times* became staples in the *Columbia Journalism Review* and *American Journalism Review* — the self-appointed monitors of ethics in U.S. journalism. Many of the details were leaked by disgruntled staffers on the *Times* editorial staff.

In late 1997, Shelby Coffee III, 50, the highly-regarded *Times* editor who had led it to four Pulitzer prizes, resigned. He claimed it had nothing to do with Willes. But few believed him.

The Final Battle

The final battle was a 162-page Sunday supplement published October 10, 1999, about the Staples Center – a proposed $400 million sports and entertainment arena in downtown Los Angeles.

The supplement contained $2 million worth of advertising. *New Times* – a local weekly – then disclosed a secret deal to give the proposed center half the $2 million generated by the Sunday supplement.

Otis Chandler, the retired former chairman of Times Mirror, had been largely silent about the business for 13 years. With news of the Staples supplement deal, he could stay quiet no longer.

In a four-page letter of protest, he savaged Willes' regime as "the single most devastating period in the history of this great newspaper."

Journalists' Personal Interest

One of the sacred tenets of American journalism ethics has barred reporters and editors from having an undisclosed financial interest in anything they cover.

Downing – the *Times* publisher – admitted that she had kept the Staples Center financial arrangement secret from the editorial staff. In the uproar, she published an apology for the entire incident.

In mid-2000, Times Mirror was merged with the Tribune Co. – parent company of the *Chicago Tribune*. Both Willes and Downing were dumped in the merger.

As more old, family-owned newspapers were sold to big corporations in the years that followed, *The Los Angeles Times* drama set the pattern for dozens of other fights between corporate executives and journalists.

A Constitutional Crisis

For the first time in American history, scholars are beginning to question whether the news media in America have become simply another money-making business venture. They pose a question that makes the Founding Fathers shiver in their graves:

Does the press deserve Constitutional protection if its primary goal is no longer the public enlightenment that is necessary for a democracy to thrive and survive?

Newspapers' Terminal Illness

The newspaper as we have known it cannot survive much longer. The old economic model has broken down. Because they had been dominant so long, it took a long time for newspaper executives to realize they could no longer deliver their product to customers' front door and still make a profit.

When they finally grasped what was happening in the mid-1990s, they went into survival panic mode. In the evolution of organisms and organizations, the will to survive is often much more powerful than the will to be responsible and ethical.

Corporate executives with no background in journalism seem to have a tin ear for ethical tunes. They simply do not understand what all the fuss is about.

The Founding Fathers could not have foreseen the media's evolving financial structure. When journalists break their own rules, there are things you can do about it, if you understand the traditional ethic, and the levers of power.

I'll try to explain some of those rules, and how you can wield power as a reader/viewer/listener/consumer.

The Out-Take Ethic

For outsiders, there is no ethic more baffling than editors and reporters who refuse to give up out-takes. Out-takes are pictures, audio or video that were never published or broadcast. In the editing process, they were taken out.

The out-take issue took on national significance in the summer of 1968, after the street demonstrations during the Democratic National Convention in Chicago. Prosecutors decided it was time to treat protesters more harshly.

Chicago - the 1968 Riots

They went to newspapers and television stations with subpoenas, demanding all film (videotape was not yet used by TV news) and still pictures taken during the demonstrations. From those pictures, they planned to prosecute anyone they could identify.

Many editors and news directors had never dealt with the issue before. Some quickly handed over their out-takes, without a fight. Others refused, saying they would destroy the pictures, if necessary, and risk contempt of court.

People outside the media could not understand why reporters, photographers and editors thought themselves immune to subpoenas and court orders. The police were using pictures already printed and broadcast to round up protesters. What was the difference between those and the out-takes?

First Amendment Theory

The argument against giving up out-takes uses a First Amendment theory. The news media argument goes like this:

> If we give you these pictures, and you use them to prosecute people, then our photographers become police agents. At the next demonstration, the mob will attack our photographers to prevent their gathering evidence for the police. We will not be able to do our job. Therefore, the government subpoena violates our First Amendment rights. It abridges the freedom of the press to cover future events.

After the 1968 hassle, many news organizations adopted a broad policy that says:

> We will never give up out-takes to any governmental agency. We will destroy the pictures or hide them and risk contempt of court rather than handicap ourselves in future news gathering.

Setting Up Precedents?

The hard-liners counter that if you do it once, you set up a precedent that will make it harder to refuse out-takes next time.

The Case-by-Case Approach

Other news organizations take a case-by-case approach. In some instances, they believe they can give up out-takes without jeopardizing future freedom to gather news.

It is a tough question.

Suppose, for instance, that a television reporter is shooting a standup for a story in a downtown park. The reporter flubs several times. The sun goes in and out behind the clouds. The photographer is unhappy with the light, so they do it once more. An airplane passes over and the sound is ruined, so they do it again.

They use one of the standups in a story for the six o'clock news. The flawed standups become out-takes.

The next morning, a homicide detective shows up at the newsroom. "I understand you were shooting video in Downtown Park yesterday," the officer says.

"I'd like to look at that tape. There was an armed robbery in a jewelry store across the street from the park at 2:05. A clerk in the store was killed. Your photographer may have unknowingly captured the killer entering or leaving the store. Right now, we have no other leads."

A Murderer on Tape

Is there now a reasonable argument to deny the police access to the out-takes? Some organizations will give them up in a narrow circumstance like this.

There is a loophole for the station with a rigid "no out-takes" policy. They could look at the video, and if it does show someone going in or out of the jewelry store, they could run it on the news.

"Do you recognize this man?" Great follow-up to the murder story. Once on the air, it would no longer be an out-take, and the station could honor a subpoena without violating its policy.

Too Cozy With the Police

Fifty years ago, there was little concern about reporters becoming police agents. Law enforcement and reporters often collaborated.

The police gave reporters story leads. Reporters passed information to the police. A two-way street.

Many people in the news business now question that kind of coziness. It is not the media's job to make criminal cases, they say. That is a function of the criminal justice system. To become a police informant, they say, compromises a reporter's independence.

In the old days, most newspapers assigned, one reporter to cover the police beat. For all intents and purposes, the reporter on the police beat became a closet cop.

In that old setup, if there was a critical story about the department, another reporter did it. Ethical reporters who investigate police misconduct were careful not to give or accept any favors from law enforcement.

As profits at newspapers tanked, there were mass layoffs of reporters, editors and photographers in most newsrooms. The old beat system was abandoned at most newspapers.

Reporters As Witnesses

Some news organizations have severe misgivings about their employees testifying in a criminal trial, or before a grand jury.

In the early 1970s, three reporters in separate incidents refused to even go inside grand jury rooms. They had been subpoenaed to testify about illegal activities they had witnessed and written about.

They said they arranged to watch those activities by promising they would never disclose the names of the people involved. If they went into a secret grand jury session, they argued – and their sources were later arrested – the sources would believe the reporters had betrayed them inside the grand jury room.

U.S. Supreme Court's View

The U.S. Supreme Court combined the three incidents because they were so similar. In *Branzburg v. Hayes* (408 U.S. 665 - 1972) the Court ruled reporters have no First Amendment immunity from grand jury subpoenas.

The justices said a reporter might refuse to testify about certain things once in the witness chair, and that refusal might have to be argued in court; but there are many other subjects reporters – as citizens – are obligated to talk about.

Some journalists strongly disagree, and have been willing to risk jail if they were subpoenaed.

Deception Through Staging

Television coverage of civil rights and war protest demonstrations made "staging" a major issue in the 1960s. TV was new. It was still exploring the power of the picture.

If the TV crew got there after the rocks were thrown, photographers would sometimes ask demonstrators to throw more rocks, with the camera rolling.

The FCC established severe penalties for stations who broadcast scenes that appeared to be spontaneous and unrehearsed when – in fact – the event had been staged for television. At some stations, rules were written that instructed staff:

> *If you get to the scene of a demonstration, and nothing is happening, it may become clear they were waiting for you to arrive. Leave without filming anything if you determine the demonstration was staged purely for TV.*

Photo Opportunities

This is a slippery concept.

In the 1950s, politicians and celebrities quickly learned to create "photo opportunities" for both TV and print.

A publicist announces a politician will go to the scene of a chemical spill for a personal inspection. Is that staging?

Yes. It is an event created primarily for media exposure. The argument that he needs to visit personally, as part of his campaign or government duty, is very transparent.

Enhanced Media Events

An event can be greatly enhanced for the cameras through staging. During presidential campaigns, if the candidate is in a motorcade, it is not unusual for campaign workers to recruit people to enlarge the crowd.

Large crowds are arranged in the vicinity of the TV cameras. There may be blocks without a single person to wave at the candidate. But the crowds near the cameras give the perception that multitudes were hysterically enthusiastic along the motorcade route.

It is staged. It is deceptive. Sometimes the media tell us about the staging. Sometimes, they don't.

Dramatizations

In 1989, the use of dramatizations became popular in TV news. In a dramatization, actors re-enacted an event for the camera. The agreed-upon ethic decreed that if dramatizations were used, the audience must be told very clearly this is not the real event.

One of the landmarks in this issue was an ABC News television story about an alleged espionage case. ABC videotaped a re-enactment of a State Department employee handing national security secrets to a Russian agent.

The Phony Spy Tape

In broadcasting the story, it was not made clear this was a re-enactment. The videotape had been shot amateurishly, as though it were authentic counterspy surveillance. The story caused such an uproar, many TV news organizations for a time outlawed all re-enactments and dramatizations by their news departments.

Computer animation has become today's substitute for dramatizations. The audience knows the scene they're watching is not an actual recording. That it was created from details the reporter learned, and the animation simply makes clearer what happened.

Exploding Truck Scandal

An even larger ethical debacle took place in November, 1992, when *Dateline NBC* ran a safety story about General Motors pickup trucks. The videotape showed a broadside crash which seemed to cause the truck's gas tank to explode. The fuel tanks were mounted on the underside of the chassis.

General Motors began an intense investigation to defend its design and disclosed in early 1993 that the *Dateline* crash had been rigged. A contractor-technician for NBC had attached incendiary devices to the truck to make sure it would explode.

The disclosure led to a major investigation within NBC; the resignation of three *Dateline NBC* producers; and the reassignment of the correspondent to a network-owned station.

Print Holier-Than-Thou

Newspapers are particularly holier-than-thou in their coverage of any television news controversy. But virtually every newspaper in the nation publishes staged pictures every day. If you've been at the award ceremony, you know the still photographers line people up, position them, and then tell them to hold still for "one more."

Are the standard "grip and grin" pictures in virtually every newspaper staged? Yes. But because the action is so innocuous, we don't seem to mind.

Spot News Photos Rare

Television news from the beginning invested heavily in helicopters and other equipment to reach news events and broadcast them live. That was an important element in their becoming the dominant source of news for most Americans.

Because television does this so well, many newspapers no longer tried to photograph most breaking news stories. In 2013, the *Chicago Sun-Times* fired all its photographers and said they would depend on photos their reporters and readers took.

Television has conditioned Americans to expect video of major events, as they happen. If we see it, it must be so. Not necessarily.

Doctored Photographs

The ethics of doctoring photographs has now become a major concern for all news media.

With complex software, still photographs and video can be altered, and the manipulation cannot be detected. One of the most blatant examples occurred on New Year's Eve, 1999. Dan Rather anchored the *CBS Evening News* from Times Square in New York. Over his shoulder, you could see a large billboard advertising CBS.

The billboard was not really there. It had been inserted electronically to cover the *real* billboard, which advertised NBC.

When other news media ran stories about the billboard cover-up, Rather said he did not know about it until after the newscast. But he said nothing publicly until news stories about the billboard broke almost two weeks later.

Jennings' Precaution

ABC Anchor Peter Jennings was wary that he might be accused of similar visual sleight-of-hand at the political conventions in 2000.

In each newscast, Jennings told his audience the convention floor that appeared to be behind him was not really there.

Jennings would then let the audience see a shot from the side. He was in the convention hall, but he was sitting in front of a blank wall.

The live shot of the convention auditorium that viewers saw behind him was inserted electronically. (Read how weather maps are created the same way in **Newscast**)

No Photographic Manipulation

Because the public is so wary of dishonesty in the news media, there is now a blanket policy at many outlets that forbids any manipulation of any photo or video. Even if it is done to remove a distraction and has no effect whatever on what the image portrays.

Long before computers, newspaper artists routinely used air brushes to remove distracting objects from pictures. They sometimes pasted people into photographs. But that was much easier to detect.

Junkets and Freebies

More than a century ago, P. T. Barnum learned how to get free advertising when the circus came to town.

First, he hired schoolboys to paste circus posters on the side of every barn within 20 miles. They did it for nothing if you gave them free circus tickets.

Newspaper reporters could also be recruited. For a handful of tickets, a reporter would write a glowing story about that wondrous extravaganza of excitement, that colossal collection of color and courage, that stunning display of spine-tingling skill waiting for you under the Big Top. It still works.

Reporters routinely cover the Ringling parade of animals from the circus train to the Big Top, and are offered a chance to ride an elephant for a better, personalized story.

Until the early 1970s, it was not unusual for reporters to accept all sorts of freebies. Travel writers took elaborate trips, with an airline or a resort picking up the tab.

Political writers traveled with a candidate in planes the candidate paid for. Tickets to sporting events were passed out like candy.

Press rooms were provided in public buildings for free. Theater critics received free tickets to the events they reviewed.

The Free Ticket Furor

In the late 1970s, an investigative story in a magazine showed how sportswriters at major newspapers routinely accepted large numbers of season tickets, which they could sell or pass out to their friends. Embarrassed newspapers began announcing they would no longer accept free tickets to sports or cultural events.

Many news organizations drew up — some for the first time — codes of ethics for their staffs. Most now forbid accepting anything of value from anyone a reporter might expect to cover.

Some are so strict, they won't even let their employees accept a cup of coffee. Or lunch. They pay their pro-rata share of transportation costs when they travel with candidates, and they pay rent for the use of space in public buildings.

Massive Freebies Still

But there are still freebies on a massive scale. Tourist attractions fly reporters, photographers and their families in for a VIP weekend when they open a new section or celebrate an anniversary. Many accept. Media people know a phone call is all it takes to get free tickets at some attractions.

Airlines invite the media along for first-class service when they open a new route. TV networks have huge, week-long, expense-paid parties to unveil the new season's shows. Some TV critics accept the freebies, others pay their own way.

Those policies are still evolving. Those who refuse freebies argue that if they report conflicts of interest among public officials and corporate executives, they have to keep their own skirts clean.

Others don't seem to care. Some alibi that travel, sports and entertainment coverage is not real news, and has a different ethic.

Media Moonlighting

Some media celebrities don't tell their readers/viewers about their own moonlighting. Well-known journalists accept lush payments to speak to special interest groups.

They rarely tell their readers/viewers they've accepted money, travel and other gifts from those they're writing about.

This is a clear violation of the Code of Ethics endorsed by both the Society of Professional Journalists (SPJ) and the Radio-Television News Directors Assn. (RTNDA). The full text of both codes is reproduced at the end of this chapter.

In many cases, journalists who violate the Code of Ethics are so valuable to the profits of their employers, nothing is done about it. Sort of like star athletes who misbehave, but aren't disciplined.

A Duty to Be Fair

Reporters have an obligation to be fair. To get both sides of the story. To interview you, and give you a chance to answer the allegations against you. The story should be balanced and objective, unless it is clearly labeled as an editorial, a column for the journalist's personal opinion, or commentary.

Truth and Accuracy

Media stories should be accurate and true. Reporters have an obligation to go beyond the obvious in search of the truth – particularly if the story will damage someone.

Reporters who accept information with strings attached are morally obligated to honor that contract, which is often a verbal agreement that is virtually impossible to enforce. (See **Off-the-Record**)

Breaking the Law

The U.S. Supreme Court has ruled that reporters and editors must live by the same laws that other citizens do. The Constitution does not give them special dispensation to trespass, to break and enter, to harass you, or wiretap your telephone.

In the real world, reporters break minor laws in order to expose a problem. As an investigative reporter, I bought illegal numbers (local lottery) tickets and bet on horses in illegal bookie joints to show that law enforcement was not doing its job.

Playing God

My editors and I played God. We decided the public service that would be performed by those stories outweighed the misdemeanor.

But I never wiretapped a telephone or hacked into a computer system to get information for a story.

That kind of journalistic behavior nearly brought down the government in Great Britain early in this century, and resulted in the arrests of many tabloid journalists and executives at Rupert Murdoch's newspapers.

Undercover Reporting

Undercover work to obtain a story is hotly debated within the news media. Some say reporters should never pose as anything but reporters. Instead, they should interview insiders to get the story.

As an investigative reporter, I took the opposite position. If truth and fairness were my goals,

I needed to see, hear, record and photograph for my audience exactly what was going on.

If you're doing a story on a home improvement scam, do you go to the contractor's office, introduce yourself, and say, "Hi, I'm Clark Kent of the *Daily Planet* and I want to know whether you've been bilking little old ladies."

Not if you want the truth.

The Food Lion Case

This was exactly the issue in the landmark Food Lion v. Capital Cities/ABC case. In 1992, ABC's *Prime Time Live* sent two producers to a Food Lion store in North Carolina to apply for jobs in the meat department. After they obtained the jobs, they worked for several weeks wearing hidden cameras and microphones.

On November 5, 1992, *Prime Time Live* broadcast a riveting segment in which secretly videotaped Food Lion supervisors showed the undercover producers how to dip tainted meat in bleach to kill the smell, then re-package it for sale.

Food Lion sued ABC. But not for libel (defaming its reputation). The truth of the story was not challenged at the trial. Instead, the grocery chain based its case on the producers' deception in applying for their jobs, their trespassing in the stores where they worked, and for invading the privacy of Food Lion employees. (See chapters on **Libel** and **Privacy**)

Jury Awards $5.5 Million

The jury was not even allowed to see the ABC story. The issue was not the story. It was how the reporting was done. In cross-examining the producers who had worked under cover, Food Lion attorneys questioned their ethnicities and income, picturing them as highly-paid yankees who came into the South to embarrass local folks.

In December, 1996, the jury returned a verdict against ABC with a judgment for $5.5 million in punitive damages. The damage award was later overturned by an appellate court.

After the verdict, newspaper columnists clucked their tongues and shook their fingers at ABC for doing something naughty that newspapers would *never* have done.

The print writers seemed to overlook *The Wall Street Journal's* 1995 Pulitzer Prize for Tony Horwitz' undercover series that included his working inside a chicken packaging plant. Or Jane Lil's undercover job in a garment factory in 1996 for *The New York Times* to document sweat shop conditions.

Because so many investigative reporting teams have been shut down in recent years, a lot of the undercover photography and video that shows illegal or immoral activity is now done by activist groups which then provide it to the media. Typical in this area is photographic proof of animals or employees being mistreated.

Now that everyone has a cell phone with a camera, the best video of major catastrophes is often shot by amateur photographers, not the news media pros.

The Entrapment Issue

Some journalists argue that inviting the aluminum siding salesperson into your home for the sales pitch is entrapment.

But entrapment is a part of criminal law that protects innocent people from being framed by police and prosecutors. The law says defendants cannot be persuaded to break the law, and then be prosecuted. To be scrupulously ethical, reporters working undercover must be very careful in what they do and say, so the targets of their investigations act on their own, without being coerced or encouraged to do something improper.

Where a hidden video camera is used, the audience can judge for itself whether the target was improperly influenced. In some states, however, hidden microphones cannot legally be used by reporters. (See **Privacy**)

"Sneaky" Reporters

"Sneaky" is the word often used to criticize stories and pictures obtained by reporters posing as potential victims or fellow thieves. I maintain that some stories and some criminal cases can never be accomplished any other way.

Journalists often polish their public service halos. Is the public interest served when the news media disclose an undercover police investigation to infiltrate a terrorist group? Or the government's secretly buying land for a new road, to keep the price down?

Public Service Responsibility

Journalists say they must defend the "public's right to know." The counter argument asks − if the story had been held a little longer, would not the public good have been better served?

The same debate rages over how much the public should know about a criminal case before it goes to trial. Does the public's right to know outweigh the defendant's right to a fair trial? Those issues will be debated as long as democracy exists.

Anonymous sources are another continuing ethical debate. Some recent major stories where the media got it wrong were the result of trusted sources who gave reporters false information. But other, major media disclosures would have been impossible without confidential sources. (See **Off-the-Record**)

Confidential sources are especially prevalent in stories about government and politics, where the media have virtual immunity from lawsuits. (See **Libel** and **Privacy**).

Checkbook Journalism

The public seemed unaware of checkbook journalism until the mid-1970s. Mainstream news media had always considered paying for information or an interview highly unethical.

Interestingly, *Life Magazine* in the 1960s had signed a lucrative contract with the original group of astronauts for their exclusive, personal stories. That was checkbook journalism, but there were few protests.

Despite that old ethical boundary, CBS quietly paid H. R. Haldeman $25,000 for a lengthy interview. Haldeman had been Richard Nixon's White House chief of staff. All through the Watergate scandal, Haldeman had been silent. The CBS payment leaked out, and the interview became a coup that backfired.

Other media piled onto CBS for the transgression.

But in the 1980s and 90s, the rapid proliferation of tabloid-style TV shows − and then Internet websites that pandered to sleazy topics − began to erode the old ethic. The new outlets also had to compete directly with print tabloids like the *National Enquirer*, where paying interview subjects was an old, established custom.

An Established Custom at the Enquirer

The *Enquirer* had paid for the photo that showed model Donna Rice sitting on the lap of U.S. Sen. Gary Hart. The 1987 photo ended Hart's campaign for the Presidency.

More recently, photos and information were bought by the *Enquirer* to show U.S. Sen. John Edwards' relationship to Rielle Hunter, and her child that Edwards fathered.

And the same process propelled *Enquirer* stories about Tiger Woods' extra-marital adventures. The *Enquirer* has even advertised: "Got News? We'll Pay Big Bucks."

The increased pressure for ratings and profit has now pushed "establishment" media to do the same thing. Although they all have guidelines that say they forbid paying for interviews, they have invented elaborate workarounds that disguise what's going on.

They can truthfully say they don't pay people to be interviewed. But they don't tell us that they paid a go-between. Or paid a "licensing fee" for photos and video provided by the person they interviewed.

How Interviews are Peddled

Sheelah Kolhatkar, an editor at *Bloomberg Businessweek*, produced an astounding article for the September, 2010 *Atlantic* magazine titled "The News Merchant." It broke open the topic most mainstream media had avoided.

The *Atlantic* article showed in great detail how Larry Garrison, a former Hollywood bit actor, had become a spectacularly successful broker for checkbook journalism.

He approaches people inside major news stories to become their "agent." Particularly tabloid-type stories that involve sex, big money, celebrities, grisly murders and political scandal.

Arranging Media Availability

Garrison's behind-the-scenes business surfaced when he represented Natalie Holloway's father, arranging his TV appearances and co-writing a book about the disappearance of the 18-year old blonde during a school trip to Aruba.

The *Atlantic* story showed how ABC News paid the family of Casey Anthony $200,000 for an exclusive "license" to broadcast photos and video of Anthony's murdered two-year-old daughter.

Then they got exclusive interviews with the mother. She was later charged with murder. The payment leaked out during pre-trial discovery. A criminal court jury later found her not guilty.

Valuable Cell Phone Photos

When the "underwear bomber" tried to bring down an airliner over Detroit on Christmas day, 2009, a passenger with a fuzzy cell phone picture was able to sell the photo to various news outlets for a reported $18,000.

The *Washington Post* reported that Michael Jackson's father was paid $200,000 by ABC for some rare family home movies. That same story told how Gawker Media, which runs several gossip websites, offered $10,000 for a "before" picture of singer Faith Hill without makeup.

Gawker found a seller, the *Post* said, and then resold the photo to *Redbook* magazine for a cover story about the illusion of glamour and beauty in the entertainment industry.

Media Elite Play Catch-Up

"While it's clearly troubling for a publication to fork over cash for trash," the *Washington Post's* TV critic wrote, "the condescending media elite are often forced to play catch-up."

One of the women who received "sexting" photos from U.S. Rep. Anthony Weiner reportedly sold them to the news media for between $10,000 and $15,000.

The gossip website www.mediabuffet.com claimed that competitor TMZ.com (owned by Time-Warner) paid $62,500 for police photos of singer Rihanna's battered face after she was allegedly beaten by her boyfriend.

Once you understand how checkbook journalism has become so common, and lucrative, you can better grasp why celebrities are hounded by the paparazzi.

The Credibility Issue

When the media pay for an interview, it raises the same questions that come up when a paid informer testifies at a trial.

Can you believe people who've been paid to talk? Was there an agreement to avoid certain subjects? Have they enhanced their stories to make them more valuable? Would they have told more if the price had been higher?

Is this really a form of bribery?

In my seminars on media ethics, newspaper editors often say, self-righteously, that they would *never* pay someone for an interview. That would be unethical.

But as I move the hypothetical along, they say they *would* charter a jet to help a crime victim confront the defendant; pay for the transportation to reunite a family; fly a critically ill child to a well-known medical center.

And of course, the transportation arrangements would be made with a promise of exclusive coverage for the news outlet that paid the bill.

They have a very hard time explaining why providing transportation or hotel rooms is different from cash. I suspect the code of ethics in some editors' minds is there because it has been the custom – not because it has been carefully thought out.

Previewing Stories

Interviewees often ask if they can see a story before it's published or broadcast. That's considered a no-no. If you saw it, and didn't like what the reporter wrote, or the way it was presented, you'd say so.

The reporter might be influenced, and lose independence. In effect, you would become an editor for a story about yourself. You're not very objective about something you're personally involved in.

Some reporters – particularly beginners who have been hired to replace better-paid veterans –will let you do it. They don't know any better. So it doesn't hurt to ask. If the reporter has no objections, it's to your advantage to preview the story.

Everything I Say, or Nothing

If you're doing battle with a news organization, you may not trust their editing of what you say. Many people in this situation say they'll submit to an interview only if the reporter agrees to print or broadcast everything they say, unedited. This kind of offer is difficult to sell. Editors don't like to be told what they can print or broadcast.

As a part of their FCC licensing, broadcasters are responsible for everything they air.

In effect, they would be handing that responsibility to someone else. They can be sued if you use their station to libel someone. You might be irresponsible in other ways, like using four-letter words the FCC frowns on.

There's a way around the problem. Draw up a letter of agreement in which they agree to print or broadcast everything you say – or nothing at all. That leaves them complete editorial control.

But if you expect them to use what you say under that agreement, it has to be brief, factually accurate, and to the point.

Questions in Advance

Interview subjects often ask if they can have the questions in advance. Normally, that is considered unethical. The interview – particularly on television – is supposed to be a spontaneous, unrehearsed conversation between you and the reporter.

Knowing what the questions are going to be would let you research your answers in advance. It would be like letting the lawyer for a witness at a trial whisper the answer to every question.

Most reporters consider it ethical to give you a broad idea of what the interview will cover, but not specific questions.

Questions in Writing

In some cases, however, you can insist, and win. This sometimes happens with highly-placed officials, celebrities, or people facing major criminal charges. Look, they say, I'll answer your questions, but only if you submit them to me in writing. Take it or leave it. Play it my way, or not at all.

In that situation, the media will sometimes play by your rules, but tell their readers, viewers or listeners the terms of the interview so they will not be misled.

Journalists in Politics

Most journalists consider it unethical for reporters and editors to participate in any kind of political activity. That includes giving political advice; contributions of work or money; bumper stickers on their cars; signs in their yards, attending a political meeting where they are not working as reporters or editors. Some will even register as "Independent" to avoid any suggestion of bias toward a political party. The extremists do not register at all and do not vote.

Journalists Draw Different Lines

Some purists in the media also refuse to do work for a charitable organization or serve on any board – private or public. Every journalist draws a different line.

It is common in many communities for newspaper editors and broadcast executives with news responsibility to work in local United Way fund-raising campaigns. Some reporters in those newsrooms chafe when their bosses accept those positions.

Hard-liners suspect the people who run United Way chose the boss because they believe they can get better news coverage that way. They probably can.

National Codes of Ethics

There are two nationally endorsed codes of ethics for American journalists. One by the Society of Professional Journalists (SPJ) – also known as Sigma Delta Chi – the other by the Radio-Television News Directors Assn. (RTNDA).

The codes are only models. But many news organizations endorse them. Some have much more stringent and specific guidelines for their employees.

When you complain to the media about their coverage, citing either code is a powerful tool if you believe the media have acted improperly. (See **Fighting Back**)

The original SPJ code was adopted in 1973. The current version was adopted at the SPJ's September, 1996, convention, and is badly in need of updating. The complete text. of the SPJ code begins on the next page.

Subheads are part of the code.

Full Text - SPJ Code of Ethics

Preamble

Members of the Society of Professional journalists believe that public enlightenment is the forerunner of justice and the foundation of democracy. The duty of the journalist is to further those ends by seeking truth and providing a fair and comprehensive account of events and issues. Conscientious journalists from all media and specialties strive to serve the public with thoroughness and honesty. Professional integrity is the cornerstone of a journalist's credibility. Members of the Society share a dedication to ethical behavior and standards of practice.

Seek Truth and Report It

Journalists should be honest, fair and courageous in gathering, reporting and interpreting information. **Journalists should:**

Test the accuracy of information from all sources and exercise care to avoid inadvertent error. Deliberate distortion is never permissible.

Diligently seek out subjects of news stories to give them the opportunity to respond to allegations of wrongdoing.

Identify sources whenever feasible. The public is entitled to as much information as possible on sources' reliability.

Always question sources' motives before promising anonymity. Clarify conditions attached to any promise made in exchange for information. Keep promises.

Make certain that headlines, news teases and promotional materi-

al, photos, video, audio, graphics, sound bites and quotations do not misrepresent. They should not oversimplify or highlight incidents out of context.

Never distort the content of news photos or video. Image enhancement for technical clarity is always permissible. Label montages and photo illustrations.

Avoid misleading reenactments or staged news events. If reenactment is necessary to tell a story, label it.

Avoid undercover or other surreptitious methods of gathering information except when traditional open methods will not yield information vital to the public. Use of such methods should be explained as part of the story.

Never plagiarize.

Tell the story of the diversity and magnitude of the human experience boldly even when it is unpopular to do so.

Examine their own cultural values and avoid imposing those values on others.

Avoid stereotyping by race, gender, age, religion, ethnicity, geography, sexual orientation, disability, physical appearance or social status.

Support the open exchange of views, even views they find repugnant.

Give voice to the voiceless; official and unofficial sources of information can be equally valid.

Distinguish between advocacy and news reporting. Analysis and commentary should be labeled and not misrepresent fact or context.

Distinguish news from advertising and shun hybrids that blur the lines between the two.

Recognize a special obligation to ensure that the public's business is conducted in the open and that government records are open to inspection.

Minimize Harm

Ethical journalists treat sources, subjects and colleagues as human beings deserving of respect. Journalists should:

Show compassion for those who may be affected adversely by news coverage. Use special sensitivity when dealing with children and inexperienced sources or subjects.

Be sensitive when seeking or using interviews or photographs of those affected by tragedy or grief.

Recognize that gathering and reporting information may cause harm or discomfort. Pursuit of the news is not a license for arrogance.

Recognize that private people have a greater right to control information about themselves than do public officials and others who seek power, influence or attention. Only an overriding public need can justify intrusion into anyone's privacy.

Show good taste. Avoid pandering to lurid curiosity.

Be cautious about identifying juvenile suspects or victims of sex crimes.

Be judicious about naming criminal suspects before the formal filing of charges.

Balance a criminal suspect's fair trial rights with the public's right to be informed.

Act Independently

Journalists should be free of obligation to any interest other than the public's right to know. ***Journalists should:***

Avoid conflicts of interest, real or perceived.

Remain free of associations and activities that may compromise integrity or damage credibility.

Refuse gifts, favors, fees, free travel and special treatment, and shun secondary employment, political involvement, public office and service in community organizations if they compromise journalistic integrity.

Disclose unavoidable conflicts.

Be vigilant and courageous about holding those with power accountable.

Deny favored treatment to advertisers and special interests and resist their pressure to influence news coverage.

Be wary of sources offering information for favors or money; avoid bidding for news.

Be Accountable

Journalists are accountable to their readers, listeners, viewers and each other. ***Journalists should:***

Clarify and explain news coverage and invite dialogue with the public over journalistic conduct.

Encourage the public to voice grievances against the news media.

Admit mistakes and correct them promptly.

Expose unethical practices of journalists and the news media.

Abide by the same high standards to which they hold others.

RTNDA Code of Ethics

The Radio-Television News Directors Assn. adopted the following code at its convention in September, 2000. It is a major expansion of the brief Code of Ethics that had previously been in effect. Subheads are part of the code. Here's the full text:

FULL TEXT – RTNDA CODE OF ETHICS

The Radio-Television News Directors Association, wishing to foster the highest professional standards of electronic journalism, promote public understanding of and confidence in journalism, and strengthen principles of journalistic freedom to gather and disseminate information, establishes this Code of Ethics and Professional Conduct.

Preamble

Professional electronic journalists should operate as trustees of the public, seek the truth, report it fairly and with integrity and independence, and stand accountable for their actions.

Public Trust

Professional electronic journalists should recognize that their first obligation is to the public. **Professional electronic journalists should:**

Understand that any commitment other than service to the public undermines trust and credibility.

Recognize that service in the public interest creates an obligation to reflect the diversity of the community and guard against oversimplification of issues or events.

Provide a full range of information to enable the public to make enlightened decisions.

Fight to ensure that the public's business is conducted in public.

Truth

Professional electronic journalists should pursue truth aggressively and present the news accurately, in context, and as com-

pletely as possible. **Professional electronic journalists should:**
Continuously seek the truth.

Resist distortions that obscure the importance of events.

Clearly disclose the origin of information and label all material provided by outsiders.

Professional electronic journalists should not:

Report anything known to be false.

Manipulate images or sounds in any way that is misleading.

Plagiarize.

Present images or sounds that are reenacted without informing the public.

Fairness

Professional electronic journalists should present the news fairly and impartially, placing primary value on significance and relevance. **Professional electronic journalists should:**

Treat all subjects of news coverage with respect and dignity, showing particular compassion to victims of crime or tragedy.

Exercise special care when children are involved in a story and give children greater privacy protection than adults.

Seek to understand the diversity of their community and inform the public without bias or stereotype.

Present a diversity of expressions, opinions, and ideas in context.

Present analytical reporting based on professional perspective, not personal bias.

Respect the right to a fair trial.

Integrity

Professional electronic journalists should present the news with integrity and decency, avoiding real or perceived conflicts of interest, and should respect the dignity and intelligence of the audience as well as the subjects of news. **Professional electronic journalists should:**

Identify sources whenever possible. Confidential sources should be used only when it is clearly in the public interest to gather or convey important information or when a person providing information might be harmed. Journalists should keep all commitments to protect a confidential source.

Clearly label opinion and commentary.

Guard against extended coverage of events or individuals that fails to significantly advance a story, place the event in context, or add to the public knowledge.

Refrain from contacting participants in violent situations while the situation is in progress.

Use technological tools with skill and thoughtfulness, avoiding techniques that skew facts, distort reality, or sensationalize events.

Use surreptitious newsgathering techniques, including hidden cameras or microphones, only if there is no other way to obtain stories of significant public importance and only if the technique is explained to the audience.

Use the private transmissions of others only with permission.

Professional electronic journalists should not:

Pay news sources who have a vested interest in a story.

Accept gifts, favors, or compensation from those who might seek to influence coverage.

Engage in activities that may compromise their integrity or independence.

Independence

Professional electronic journalists should defend the independence of all journalists from those seeking influence or control over news content. **Professional electronic journalists should:**

Gather and report news without fear or favor, and vigorously resist undue influence from any outside forces, including advertisers, sources, story subjects, powerful individuals, and special interest groups.

Resist those who would seek to buy or politically influence news content or who would seek to intimidate those who gather and disseminate the news.

Determine news content solely through editorial judgment and not as the result of outside influence.

Resist any self-interest or peer pressure that might erode journalistic duty and service to the public.

Recognize that sponsorship of the news will not be used in any way to determine, restrict, or manipulate content.

Refuse to allow the interests of ownership or management to influence news judgment and content inappropriately.

Defend the rights of the free press for all journalists, recognizing that any professional government licensing of journalists is a violation of that freedom.

Accountability

Professional electronic journalists should recognize that they are accountable for their actions to the public, the profession and themselves. **Professional electronic journalists should:**

Actively encourage adherence to these standards by all journalists and their employers.

Respond to public concerns. Investigate complaints and correct errors promptly and with as much prominence as the original report.

Explain journalistic processes to the public, especially when practices spark questions or controversy.

Recognize that professional electronic journalists are duty-bound to conduct themselves ethically.

Refrain from ordering or encouraging courses of action which would force employees to commit an unethical act.

Carefully listen to employees who raise ethical objections and create environments in which such objections and discussions are encouraged.

Seek support for and provide opportunities to train employees in ethical decision-making.

In meeting its responsibility to the profession of electronic journalism, RTNDA has created this code to identify important issues, to serve as a guide for its members, to facilitate self-scrutiny, and to shape future debate.

STRATEGY

FIGHTING BACK

I'm Mad as Hell & I'm Not Gonna Take It Any More

When a news story is inaccurate, libelous, unfair, slanted, absurd – or just outrageously stupid – what can you do about it? In the old days, you challenged the editor or reporter to a duel. Or thrashed him (female editors were extremely rare back then) with your cane.

Those techniques have gone out of style, unless you want to be the lead story in tomorrow's paper and perhaps make the wire services and network news. Great idea, if that's the kind of coverage you're looking for.

Most people react angrily, in ways that often create more bad stories, and worse public images for themselves. It may make you feel better – just as it would to punch the reporter – but in the end, you'll lose the fight. Here are the most common reactions:

Throw Them Out

Vow never to talk to a reporter – any reporter – again. Hire a bouncer. Issue orders to your staff that any reporter or photographer who sets foot on the premises is to be violently ejected.

This will endear you to all newspaper editors and broadcast news directors. On slow news days, it means they can count on you to liven their news.

"Hey, Gorilla," they'll yell across the newsroom, "Go over to Neanderthal's place and try to get in. Keep the camera rolling. We need something to fill the second block."

Great stuff. Will probably earn you a special award at the next Emmy or Pulitzer ceremony. Most Valuable Resource to Increase Ratings and Readership. Marvelous for your public image.

Shut Them Out

Punish the offending station, network, magazine or newspaper by shutting them out. Feed lots of stories to their competition. Hold news conferences and invite everyone else, but conveniently forget to include the offenders.

This is the most common reaction in government agencies – particularly police departments – when they're unhappy with a story. It rarely works.

Another common way for law enforcement to retaliate is to follow and give traffic tickets to staffers. Just one more way to be featured as the bad guy in more stories.

Public Records Are Public

Most of the records reporters need for daily coverage of a public agency are – by law – public. If you shut them out, they'll go to court, and win easily. The stories about the court process will get lots of coverage. In all of them, you'll be the bad guy.

The news of your fight with the reporter will prompt disgruntled people within your office to make anonymous calls, leaking more dirt and ammunition to the reporter.

You'll wind up with a big LOSER tag around your neck. It'll look like you're trying to hide something. The story of your shutting them out will be a better story than those you're feeding the competition.

Look at the Compelling C's in **Selling Your Story**. One of the most powerful elements is CONFLICT. Creating a conflict with the news outlet is another NO-WIN RESPONSE.

Stop Your Advertising

Cancel your advertising at the offending station or publication. Call your friends who advertise there and urge them to pull their commercials or ads. In a small town this may have some effect. Otherwise, you're a real candidate for Suicide Bomber School.

Your business probably needs to advertise a lot worse than the news outlet needs your money.

At a broadcast station, magazine or newspaper with ethical management, the advertising staff is completely divorced from the news operation. To prove that advertisers have no voice in news judgment, the news department may come after you with even more vigor than before.

If it is a station with low ratings, or a declining newspaper, dropping your ads can punish them.

But it'll hurt you a lot more, months from now, when you come back with your hat in your hand, asking if you can place some new advertising with them.

Not a great solution. But in narrow circumstances, better than the first two.

Complaining is Important

But it is absolutely vital that you complain when you feel strongly that a news outlet has published or broadcast an incompetent, unfair, or dishonest story.

You probably don't want a retraction or correction. That often makes matters worse. In the correction, the reporter writes, "What we published yesterday was not exactly right. It's actually much worse."

But if you don't complain, the error will be repeated in every future story. Once it is printed three times, the error becomes accepted fact. Almost impossible to correct.

The complaint should not be made in anger. Wait until you've cooled off to decide how you'll complain. If this is the first time an editor or news director has received a complaint about a reporter's story, you may get no discernible reaction.

But if yours is the second or third complaint about the same person, the editor or news director will begin to wonder whether there is a problem staffer who could get the company into much more serious trouble. Or an expensive lawsuit.

Truth, the Perfect Defense

Remember that in a libel suit, truth is the perfect defense. Editors these days are very concerned about lawsuits. Jurors who feel the media abuse their power have a way to even the score.

We're not talking about small amounts here. Libel and privacy suits usually ask damages in tens of millions of dollars. So a reporter who can't report accurately is a multi-million-dollar lawsuit, just waiting for the right assignment.

Editors and news directors need to know when they have a reporter who can't write truthfully. For whatever reason. It can be incompetence. Or the inability to leave personal prejudices out of the copy. The reporter's supervisors are vitally concerned. (See **Libel**)

Editors Need/Want to Know

In the same way, privacy suits are often lost because of the way the reporter or photographer acted at the scene of the story.

Editors and news directors need to know if they have a staffer who likes to bully people. Someone willing to break the norms of human behavior – perhaps the law – if that's what it takes to get the story. (See **Ethics** and **Privacy**) Editors and news directors have no way to know about their employees' inaccuracy, incompetence, or nasty behavior if you don't tell them.

How to Complain

Let's go through some of the ways in which you can complain with maximum results.

Suppose the story is inaccurate. Names misspelled, titles wrong, errors in numbers that are not really damaging to you or your organization. A letter is probably the best way to complain. I'd suggest writing the reporter, with a copy to the immediate boss. It should read something like this:

Dear Reporter: The story you wrote in yesterday's newspaper/newscast contained several inaccuracies. I thought you should know, so future stories will not repeat those inaccuracies.

In the first paragraph, you called my organization the Amalgamated Association of Aardvarks. The proper name is The National Association of Aardvark Advocates.

In the second paragraph, you said we spent $3 million lobbying the state legislature last year. The correct figure is $300,000.

Correction? Be Careful

You may ask for a correction or retraction. But remember that reporters and editors have big egos. To distract from the mistake, in the same story that corrects the error, they may unload new information that is even more damaging.

As an investigative reporter, I learned to hold back a trump card. If my target complained, I turned over my ace in the hole.

If You're Going to Sue

If you have any idea of filing a suit because the story damaged you in some way, consult an attorney before you complain. In some states, the form and timing of the complaint can have a major effect on your rights in that future suit. (**Libel** and **Privacy**)

If an inaccurate or unfair story has caused real problems for you or your organization, a face-to-face meeting may be the best way to make your case. Here again, I'd suggest that you call the reporter and/or the editor to set up the meeting.

You will need to document how the story distorted the truth, or how outrageously the staffer acted.

Radio & TV Station Hierarchy

It is critical that you reach the right person with your complaint. The organizational structure at most radio and television stations goes something like this:

The station's **General Manager** hires and fires the **News Director,** who is responsible for everything in the news department. The news director may have an assistant.

The **Assignment Editor** decides how the station's news staff will be used every day. How their time will be invested. Who will cover what. The assignment editor is expected to know what's happening in your area, and cover it, if it's important.

At most stations, the assignment editor is not responsible for the quality or accuracy of the stories, and will not have much input into how those stories appear in the newscast.

Combined Duties

Unless you're unhappy with the station's persistent refusal to cover stories you suggest, the assignment editor is probably not the person to see. Understand that with today's cutbacks in resources, the same person may be both news director and assignment editor.

Each newscast has a **Producer,** who's roughly the equivalent of a page editor at a newspaper. The producer decides which stories go into the newscast – how long they'll be, in which order, and in what form.

At larger stations, there will be an **Executive Producer**, who supervises the producers of each newscast, and whose duties may include reviewing scripts for accuracy and fairness. The executive producer is often a sort of assistant news director, with a variety of responsibilities.

Power to Hire & Fire

The news director does all the hiring and firing within the broadcast station's news department. Reporters and photographers work under the direction of producers and the assignment editor, but their competence and any disciplinary action will eventually be decided by the news director.

Most station managers will meet with or talk to their news directors several times a day. Newscasts can be the major local revenue and image producers for many TV stations.

Remember, if the station is a network affiliate, the station has no control or responsibility for the content of network programming it broadcasts.

News directors and station managers are human, too. When you complain, their natural reaction will be to defend their employees, and their stories.

Make Your Own Recording

Documenting a broadcast error can be difficult. In the distant past, the FCC required broadcasters to keep a copy of their scripts or a recording of their broadcasts. Not anymore. They are not required to provide you with a copy of what they said.

If you have any advance warning that a story may be slanted or antagonistic, you should at least make an audio recording of the broadcast.

A video recording of a television story is much better, because part of the inaccuracy or slant may be created visually. Your recorded audio or video will be the only way you can prove you were misquoted, or how the story was inaccurate.

Newspaper Hierarchy

At newspapers, the top editor in charge of everything to do with news is the **Managing Editor** or **Executive Editor**, who may or may not have jurisdiction over the editorial page. Many newspapers have an autonomous **Editorial Page Editor**.

The person with overall supervision is the **General Manager** or **Publisher.** But in most cases, the general manager or publisher is more concerned with the paper's mechanical and financial operations. They leave journalism to the top editor.

At most newspapers there will be a **City Editor** or **Metro Editor** who supervises all stories in the local area. A **State** Editor (if they have one) will be in charge of stories and reporters outside the local area but inside the state. There may be a **National Editor**, a **Political Editor**, an **Investigative Projects Editor.**

Here are the steps to take if you have a complaint about a story:

Complaining, Step One

Call the reporter. Discuss the story. Find out who the reporter's immediate supervisor is, or the editor who was in charge of the story you're unhappy with. If it's a simple complaint to correct numbers or names for future stories, tell the reporter you'll send a letter confirming the call. A letter is better than an e-mail because it can be copied and filed for future reference. If you're unhappy with the reporter's response, take the next step.

Complaining, Step Two

Write the reporter's editor or news director a detailed letter describing your complaint with the story or a staff member's behavior. Quote from the offensive story and write, in detail, your version of what happened; or how the story was inaccurate or unfair.

Repeat. *Don't file your complaint in anger.* Suppose you've headed a study commission that produced a final report. The story about your study is grossly inaccurate. If you're writing a newspaper editor, you may want to include a copy of the study, a copy of the story, and something like:

Dear Editor: I thought you would want to know that a story you printed Monday was very inaccurate. If you'll compare the enclosed study with what your reporter wrote about it, I think you'll come to the same conclusion.

If you are badly misquoted, your letter to the news director should say something like:

Dear News Director: I thought you'd want to know that I was quoted entirely out of context in the story you broadcast Monday night. I recorded the entire interview with your reporter. I'm enclosing (or attaching) a transcript. The way in which my interview was edited created a false and very damaging impression. Once you compare the story with the transcript, I think you'll come to the same conclusion. If you'd like to see the video (hear the audio tape), I'd be glad to meet with you.

If you're still unhappy with the results, go to Step Three.

Step Three for Radio & TV

Write the station manager the same kind of detailed, registered letter. This time make it clear you're angry. Send a copy to the president of the company that owns the station. Ask for a return receipt and proof of delivery. You can usually get the name and address by calling the station manager's secretary.

If not, go to the station and ask to see the **Public File**. This is a file required by the FCC which will include fairly complete details of station ownership and corporate officers; and what the station committed to do when it applied for its license with the FCC. If your complaint involves fairness or deception (which might lead to a lawsuit or formal FCC complaint) send another copy of this letter to the corporate vice-president for legal affairs.

Newspaper Ombudsman

If the newspaper has an ombudsman, take your complaint there. An ombudsman is assigned to hear complaints from readers, and act as a sort of hearing officer. They often write columns critical of the reporter or editor who is the target of a complaint. Or report that the complaint was unfounded.

Next Step for Newspapers

If your newspaper doesn't have an ombudsman:

Write the managing editor or executive editor a detailed letter, making it clear that you're angry about what the staff did, or what was published. The top editors will usually be included in the masthead on the editorial page.

Corporate officers are easily obtained from corporate websites or the corporation's filings on the website of the Securities and Exchange Commission (SEC) – http://www.sec.gov.

Complaining, Step Four

Now it's time to write the president or CEO of the corporation directly, if you're still unhappy. The masthead on the editorial page will usually tell you which corporation owns the paper. On the Internet you can find the names of corporate officers, and the corporate headquarters address.

The president or CEO of the corporation will normally not read all letters that come in. But a staffer who works in the boss' office will, and if your complaint is justified, it will get to the boss.

Broadcasters More Responsive

Local radio and TV stations are usually more responsive to complaints than newspapers. They're always concerned about their public image. Anything that turns off viewers lowers ratings.

What they charge for advertising time is directly related to how many people watch. It's a lot easier to change channels than to change newspapers. In most cities, you *can't* switch to another daily newspaper. There's only one.

At many stations, the telephone switchboard operators keep a daily log of calls – both complaints and praise. The managers study the logs daily. It gives them a daily survey of audience reaction to their programming.

Ascertainment Interviews

Until the mid-1980s, the Federal Communications Commission required broadcast stations to compile voluminous "ascertainment interviews" as part of the licensing process.

These were personal interviews with people from all segments of the community, asking them to list and rate the community's major problems and issues.

At license renewal time, the station was supposed to show how its programming had served the community's needs, as outlined in those interviews.

No Longer Required

As part of the deregulation of broadcasting that began in the 1980s, ascertainment interviews are no longer required. But veterans in the business still reflexively respond when you complain that the station is violating its public trust and responsibility.

If you're contemplating a lawsuit against the station, you should consider having your lawyer look at each of your letters before you send them.

Tell the Competition

Competing local media may be interested in reporting the competition's goof or breach of journalistic ethics.

Regional magazines and business publications frequently cover local media better than newspapers or broadcasters.

This idea of the media tattling on each other is fairly new. In some cities, they still refuse to report each other's indiscretions. After all, editors think, the next embarrassing story could be about me, if this thing gets out of hand. But that's changing.

Media Critics

If the newspaper has a TV critic, there might be a story there. Newspaper people hate TV and the people who work in it. They're always ready to jab TV for the slightest slip or indiscretion.

Newspaper Sunday supplements are often interested in stories that expose shoddy television reporting or policy.

A few TV stations have media critics. They're rare, but they're always looking for material. They'd love to hear from you if there's a story of sloppy, inaccurate reporting or slanted, unfair treatment. Particularly in the print media.

Westmoreland vs. CBS

In 1983, *TV Guide* published a scorching story criticizing a CBS documentary that suggested Army General William Westmoreland conspired to hide or distort reports on enemy strength and casualties in Vietnam. Mike Wallace was the correspondent on the documentary.

Hodding Carter, former press secretary for the State Department, also did an investigative special for Public Broadcasting about the same CBS documentary. Eventually, Westmoreland sued CBS for libel. After weeks of testimony and high-intensity media coverage, Westmoreland dropped the suit, claiming a moral victory. (See **Libel**)

At the time, one medium criticizing another so harshly was highly unusual. But things have changed. Like tobacco companies, the media have been a favorite target lately and are much more vulnerable to critical coverage by other media.

The Time-Warner Flap

In 1995, a major public debate erupted over the content of Time-Warner's "gangsta rap" music on CDs and video. The lyrics were sexually explicit, depicting women as sex objects who should be abused. Some encouraged the assassination of police officers.

Former U.S. Education Secretary William Bennett, as co-chair of the advocacy group Empower America, attacked Time-Warner as a corrupting influence on American life. Because Bennett was very media-savvy, his efforts were covered by virtually all news outlets.

Politicians began introducing legislation to censor obscene and violent media. Although it claimed the decision had nothing to do with the controversy, Time-Warner quickly sold the division that was producing gangsta rap.

There are several national publications that might be interested in your complaint about how the media have covered you.

Columbia Journalism Review

The *Columbia Journalism Review*, founded in 1961, is generally considered the conscience of American journalism.

In the first edition, it stated its purpose:

To assess the performance of journalism in all its forms, to call attention to its shortcomings and strengths, and to help define – or redefine – standards of honest, responsible service ... to help stimulate continuing improvement in the profession and to speak out for what is right, fair, and decent.

The *Review* is published every other month by the Graduate School of Journalism at Columbia University. In each issue, there is a section called "Darts and Laurels," in which the magazine praises or roasts networks, local stations, and the print media. The section pans or praises specific incidents, journalists, and stories. The editors are always looking for articles about the media, particularly performance or policy that violates journalistic ethics.

CJR's readers are mostly journalists, journalism professors, and public relations people. Take your complaint to:

The Columbia Journalism Review
729 Seventh Avenue, Third Floor
New York, NY 10019
Internet: http://cjr.org

American Journalism Review

Founded in 1977 as the *Washington Journalism Review*, and privately owned, the magazine was given to the University of Maryland's Journalism School in 1987. The name was changed to *American Journalism Review* in early 1993.

The Journalism School was able to maintain the commercial look and appeal the original publisher gave it.

In July, 2013, the print edition was abandoned. *AJR* became an online-only publication. That online-only format is too new, as this is written, to know whether it will continue the print-version tradition of slickly produced content, with sharp, interesting writing, often by journalists rather than academics.

Its stories historically had the flavor of "insider" intrigue during power struggles at places like *The New York Times*, the TV networks, *The Atlanta Journal-Constitution*, and *The Washington Post*.

This is what the dean of the Journalism School wrote about the shift to online-only:

The model for publishing has clearly shifted to digital formats as online readership has grown," said Merrill College Dean Lucy A. Dalglish. "It no longer made financial sense for the award-winning AJR to continue producing a print magazine because most AJR readers accessed content on the Web. In addition, philanthropy has long been an important source of funding for print magazines devoted to media criticism. That support has steadily declined over the past 10 years.

She said the magazine's website would be maintained. Most of its articles back to 1991 are available online. You can contact *AJR* at:

American Journalism Review
University of Maryland
Philip Merrill College of Journalism
College Park, MD 20742-7111
Internet: http://ajr.org

SPJ and Quill

The Society for Professional Journalists (SPJ) – also known as Sigma Delta Chi – has created the most widely-recognized code of ethics for journalists.

You'll find the complete text of the SPJ code in the **Ethics** chapter. Most major cities have a local SPJ chapter. In most of those chapters, newspaper people will be much more active than broadcasters. Call the city desk at the local newspaper to find the name of the SPJ president in your town.

The initiative and strength of the local organization vary considerably from city to city. A strong chapter, incensed over a story that was inaccurate, unfair or unethical, might pass a resolution condemning the offender.

Quill is SPJ's national magazine, published six times a year. *Quill* also publishes articles that criticize journalists' performance, but its circulation and influence have always been smaller than *CJR* and *AJR*. Its readers are primarily working journalists. Contact:

Quill
3909 N. Meridian St.
Indianapolis, IN 46208
Internet: http://spj.org/quill.asp

Local Journalism Reviews

Some cities have local journalism reviews, often written and distributed among local journalists. They are usually semi-underground publications, where local reporters write anonymously about scandals inside their own workplace.

Complaining to a Network

Effectively complaining about a network news story is much more difficult than complaining locally. The networks have regional bureaus across the country. Correspondents work out of those bureaus. They spend about four days a week on the road.

If you're interviewed by a network correspondent or producer, you'll probably never see either of them again. Their supervisor will be a bureau chief hundreds of miles away. The people with the real power are in New York, Atlanta or Los Angeles.

Know the Producer

If you're contacted for a story by a network, find out which bureau is originating the story and who is the field producer.

A network crew will usually include the correspondent, field producer, photographer and sound technician. The correspondent is the one you'll see and hear when the story is broadcast. The producer scouts the story, sets up interviews, gathers documents, manages travel arrangements, and often writes the script the correspondent voices.

As TV news shifts to online, webcam interviews, you won't have any personal contact with anyone from the network. (See **Webcam Interviews**)

Work Your Way Up

If you were interviewed in person, and try to call a network bureau to complain, the correspondent or producer will probably be running to catch a plane halfway around the world. So start working your way up the hierarchy.

Phone the bureau chief. Give your assessment of the story and its failings. During the conversation, ask who the bureau chief's immediate supervisor is. Each network is organized differently. If you're not satisfied –

Write the bureau chief's supervisor. At each stage, send a copy of your letter to the next one up the ladder. If you're still unhappy –

Write the head of network news. The title of the news division boss varies from time to time. It may be president of XYZ News, which is a division of the XYZ Network. Or the network may have several vice-presidents – one of them in charge of news. Remember to be detailed and specific with your complaint.

If You're Still Not Happy

And if you're still not happy –

Write the president of the network. If there's any thought of a lawsuit, send a copy to the vice-president for legal affairs. You can get the names and addresses of network executives on the Internet, or by calling ABC, CBS or NBC in New York. CNN is headquartered in Atlanta; Fox in Los Angeles.

Call the local affiliate to get addresses for smaller broadcast networks, the local cable company for cable TV and satellite networks.

Complaining to the FCC

The FCC processes complaints on virtually every kind of problem in broadcast or cable news – from allegations of unfair or distorted coverage to technical gripes about the quality of the picture or sound.

The FCC's Investigations and Hearing Division handles complaints involving non-technical issues such as the broadcasting of obscene and/or indecent material, hoaxes, radio and TV station contests, and the broadcasting of telephone conversations. This division also acts as trial staff in Commission hearings.

Most of the people who complain receive a form letter asking for more detailed information. Here – more so than with a complaint to a station or network – great detail is extremely important if you expect to have any impact.

You Must Give Details

You must give them the station or network that broadcast the story, the date, which newscast, the correspondent or anchorperson who read it, quotes from the story (a transcript of exactly what was said will impress them) and why the story was inaccurate, unfair or deceptive.

The FCC website is extensive, and includes the rules that govern broadcasters. You can even file your complaint there. Send your complaint to:

Federal Communications Commission
Enforcement Bureau
445 12th St. S.W.
Washington, D.C. 20554
Internet: www.fcc.gov/complaints

The revocation of a broadcast license is extremely rare. Virtually every revocation in the history of the FCC was based on some kind of deception. But the loss of its license is so threatening, any complaint that prompts an FCC inquiry will get their attention.

Schools of Communications

A school of journalism or communications in your area probably has personal contact with many people who work in local news. The editor or news director may be a graduate. While a journalism school usually has no formal way to investigate or criticize poor journalistic performance, the dean might be able to quietly shake his finger and influence the station or newspaper the next time a similar situation occurs.

Special Interest Groups

A number of national organizations are designed to fight for specific issues – particularly television's coverage of those causes. They lobby for what they believe would be good for society. Things like less violence, better children's programming, less sexuality, no smoking or drinking in dramatic shows, more programs of one kind or another.

Some of these organizations have money and staff to help you carry a complaint to court, to Congress or the FCC. Most of them, however, will be interested in your complaint only if it fits their narrow area of interest.

Accuracy in Media

One of the most vigorous of the special interest media watchdogs is Accuracy In Media, a politically conservative, non-profit group formed in 1969. AIM says it is:

A grassroots citizens watchdog of the news media that critiques botched and bungled news stories and sets the record straight on important issues that have received slanted coverage. to combat what it feels is a liberal slant in American journalism.

AIM sends members a daily, e-mailed update on current media issues, produces books, radio and TV reports, documentaries, magazine articles and syndicated newspaper columns.

AIM buys advertising in major newspapers to castigate the media, and also owns a token amount of stock in some major media corporations.

An AIM staffer who tries to get on the agenda has become a fixture at annual stockholders' meetings. The group also sponsors a speakers' bureau. You can reach AIM at:

Accuracy in Media
4350 East West Highway, Suite 555
Bethesda, MD 20814
Internet: http://aim.org

FAIR – a Different View

A more liberal perspective on media criticism is available at Fairness and Accuracy in Reporting. With about 40 per cent of its funding from foundations, FAIR describes itself this way:

We work to invigorate the First Amendment by advocating for greater diversity in the press and by scrutinizing media practices that marginalize public interest, minority and dissenting viewpoints. As an anti-censorship organization, we expose neglected news stories and defend working journalists when they are muzzled. As a progressive group, FAIR believes that structural reform is ultimately needed to break up the dominant media conglomerates, establish independent public broadcasting and promote strong non-profit sources of information.

FAIR was created in 1986. It publishes a bi-monthly magazine, a newsletter, a syndicated radio show, a syndicated newspaper column, how-to kits for activists, and operates specialized research and review sections.

If you think FAIR would be interested in your complaint, contact:

Fairness and Accuracy in Reporting
104 W. 27th Street, Suite 10B
New York, NY 10001
Internet: www.fair.org

STRATEGY

LAWYERS & LAWSUITS

In a Media Crisis, Your Lawyer Will Be Wrong

When you get to work and find the *60 Minutes* crew waiting in your reception area, you know it's going to be a bad day. The first thing many executives do is call their lawyer. Particularly if they know a lawsuit has been filed – or is about to be filed.

Some don't need to call the attorney to find out what to say to the reporter. They've been told that all lawsuits automatically mean "no comment."

WRONG.

If you take news media problems to an attorney, you'll usually get bad advice. My presentation at a symposium sponsored by the American Bar Association was titled: "In a Media Crisis, Conventional Wisdom, Your Reflexes, and Your Lawyer Will Always Be Wrong."

Lawyers Do Not Understand

You need to call your lawyer for LEGAL advice. But NOT for advice about dealing with the news media. All over America, executives in both government and industry have abdicated. In any kind of crunch, they hand over their power to their attorneys.

They ask them what to do, and then do it religiously. Even when their high-priced media consultants are telling them to do something entirely different.

In my 30 years of working with organizations who had a media crisis, their lawyers were my biggest problem.

Most lawyers do not understand the news media game. This is a different arena. A lawyer's training and experience – the instincts developed in the courtroom – will often lead to disaster in the media. By following the attorney's advice, you will probably lose the media battle, and perhaps the war.

And/or the corporation. And/or your job.

In many cases, critical media coverage will do much more damage to your organization than a jury's verdict. Even if that verdict costs you millions of dollars. Bad media stories can destroy employee morale and productivity, turn customers away, depress stock prices, and influence future jurors who will go into court already prejudiced against you.

I maintain that it is your job as an executive to listen to *both* your lawyer and your media consultant, then decide what to do. It is *your* job and *your* responsibility to make the final decision, not your lawyer's.

The Lawyer: 'Say Nothing'

I know exactly what most lawyers will tell you if a lawsuit is looming. "Say nothing. Tell them no comment. Whatever you say to a reporter can come back to haunt us in court."

But "no comment" has taken on many dark shades of meaning in today's media-driven society. (See **Ten Commandments of Media Relations**) Newspaper readers and television watchers hear something else. When they see you or your attorney running away from the cameras, perhaps holding your hand over the lens, they think:

The plaintiff in the lawsuit must be right. The defendants are guilty. Otherwise, they would talk to the reporter. They must have something to hide. Or –

The rich, powerful people who run that organization (or the rich, powerful person who is the defendant) don't even care about this poor plaintiff. They're as insensitive now as they were when the damage was done.

Many people in my seminars have said – because lawyers have said it so often – that it is illegal to comment on a case that is in litigation.

THAT IS SIMPLY NOT TRUE.

I tell lawyers that they may be guilty of malpractice and unethical conduct if they tell their clients to stonewall the media.

Why are so many good lawyers so dead-set against talking to the media – or having their clients talk to the media?

Why Do Lawyers Avoid the Media?

- **They don't understand the media**, and have few media skills or instincts. They don't want to mess around in an area where they feel incompetent and inexperienced. They don't want to show their lack of expertise.

- **They live and work in an isolated, insulated system**. The legal system has a long history of elitism, dating back to its foundation in England. American lawyers do not wear robes and wigs, as British barristers do. But once they are admitted to the Bar, they are members of a private club where commoners are not allowed. Attorneys get their strokes, recognition and prestige from fellow lawyers who judge them by what happens inside the legal system.

- **In the legal system, there are very rigid rules**. The lawyer wins who best knows the rules and how to manipulate them. The legal system is based on precedent and history. There are written, predetermined guidelines for almost everything. The media have very few rules, and those that do exist are constantly changing. The precedent that drives today's news decision is whatever the competition did yesterday.

- **Reputable attorneys are ashamed** of some of their colleagues who use the media to advertise their practice. The headline hunters are more interested in getting their names out to the public than in serving the best interest of their clients. Some very good, successful lawyers are so offended by their ambulance-chasing colleagues, they avoid doing anything that would even suggest that they are seeking publicity.

- **Some lawyers truly believe it is unethical** to talk to the news media. They cite sections of the Canons of Ethics that are designed to protect the right to a fair trial. But there is also a Canon that says ethical lawyers must represent the best interest of their clients. To act as if the news media do not exist, I maintain, is often not in the best interest of a client.

Some Cases Will Always Be News

I am not suggesting that an attorney take a case to the media to influence the judge or the jury. Some high-profile cases, because of the status of the litigants – or the human interest in the circumstances – simply cannot be kept out of the spotlight. If the attorney happens to represent that kind of client or case, I maintain the legal ethic now *demands* helping that client deal successfully with the media.

If attorneys for the other side are presenting their evidence in the media, it is suicidal to sit back and say nothing.

Lawyers like to win. That's why you hire them. But remember that their primary responsibility is winning *in court*. It is your job to find the delicate balance between winning in court and winning in the media. Often, you can win in both places.

Just remember that the attorney will always err on the side of caution to protect the legal case. If you do something that might put the court case at risk, you are jeopardizing the attorney's reputation for winning there.

Attorneys Never Admit Fault

Lawyers have been trained and conditioned to never admit their client is guilty or at fault. Yet one of the best media strategies (if your client is guilty, or at fault) is to quickly confess your error and tell the world how you will make it right. (See **Ten Commandments of Media Relations**)

A repentant sinner asking for forgiveness is hard to kick. If you have made it right, and the plaintiff is now trying to make a lot of money off your mistake, media coverage can make the plaintiff look like a bully, and level the playing field.

Hypocrites Make Great Targets

A hypocrite who appears guilty but claims innocence makes a wonderful media target. If you goofed, a quick confession and promise to mend your ways will often end the story.

The court system is different. There, even the most guilty defendants plead innocence and often beat the system. But not if they have pleaded guilty. So attorneys will almost always tell you not to admit fault.

In the media, the lie or cover-up become the story. It's much more newsworthy than whatever you're trying to hide.

The Media Love Victims

The media love victims. So do juries. Especially little people who have been damaged by big, bad corporations or government bureaucracies. Often it is not a matter of whether the jury will find the company at fault. It is just a matter of how much money the litigant with deep pockets should pay the tragic victim/plaintiff.

Journalists also consider it one of their Missions From God to make things right. To bring justice to a world full of injustice.

A civil suit often casts the plaintiff as one of those victims. These kinds of cases make great human interest stories, too. Reporters love to play folk hero, rescuing the "good guy;" wreaking vengeance on the "bad guy." (See **Good Guys/Bad Guys**)

The Overly Aggressive Lawyer

Some of the best lawyers are extremely aggressive. Human dynamos with the killer instinct. This kind of lawyer will try to prevent your carrying out the most disarming media strategy – admitting you made a mistake and making every effort to fix things. "I don't want to look like a wimp," this kind of lawyer will tell you, "We're not going to give an inch."

In the judicial process, this kind of posture often leads the other side to cave in and settle quickly, rather than become involved in a very long, expensive legal battle. But the media can make that aggressive lawyer look like a voracious money-grubber.

It Doesn't Have to Be True

If a lawsuit is filed against you, the media can report the plaintiff's claim with impunity. It doesn't have to be true. The filing of the suit makes it a public record. The allegations can be published or broadcast with no verification, so long as the news story simply repeats what is in the court record. (See **Libel**)

If you are the defendant, and you don't tell the media the other side of the story, readers and viewers will believe everything said by the plaintiff is true. *After all*, Joe Sixpack thinks, *they couldn't put that stuff on TV or in the newspaper if it wasn't true*.

WRONG.

In America, you are supposed to be innocent until proven guilty. If they were ever taught this in high school civics, most people in American seem to have forgotten. With massive media coverage of allegations against you, the reverse is true.

Guilty Until Proven Innocent

Media stories will make you look guilty unless you maintain or prove your innocence.

I believe the ethical lawyer representing you needs to be constantly telling the media there is another side to this story.

If the evidence you have can't be disclosed now for tactical reasons, you should at least be reminding the audience that there is more to this than meets the eye.

Or the camera.

Too Many Facts Get in the Way

When you're not guilty, you have been led to believe that you will be exonerated, once the public knows all the facts. All you have to do is give a detailed, well-organized, reasoned explanation to reporters. This cloud of suspicion and malevolence will lift.

WRONG AGAIN.

Many court cases have very powerful, emotional angles that appeal to a mass audience. This increases circulation and ratings.

Corporate lawyers have great success with smart, talented judges by designing well-reasoned arguments. No emotion. Lots of footnotes and legal citations. They often use that same technique when they talk to reporters. It doesn't work. Reporters don't have time for the lengthy, technical reasoning. Get to the point! How do you feel? In less than 10 seconds, tell us what this case is about.

Emotion Sells Ideas, Too

We sell products and ideas in America through emotion, not reason. Commercials for personal hygiene products are based on the fear of offending, failing, losing someone you love.

Luxury cars are sold in TV commercials by suggesting visually that the people who drive this car are wealthy, powerful, sexy, respected, smart. Candidates are sold by appealing to the most basic human emotions – fear; the desire for safety and security; love of family or country; anger at some real or imagined injustice.

Criminal attorneys with a lot of jury experience understand this. They appeal to jurors with high drama and emotion. Something like:

Let me explain to you what was going on in the mind of this defendant. If you had been there, you would have done exactly the same thing. You would have been (fill in the blank) afraid/ angry/ proud/ satisfied this was the right thing to do. My client is only guilty of being human, and should not be punished.

That doesn't mean the defendant didn't do it. It just means he/she was justified in doing it. The client is not *morally* guilty. Once the litigant on the other side invokes one of those emotions in a news story, it is very difficult to change the public's attitude.

Wait Until We Know More

Lawyers have learned in legal cases not to move too quickly. Never make a motion or take the testimony of a witness until you know everything. They want to learn as much as they can before they make their move.

Attorneys who have not dealt with the media do not instinctively understand that the news media's deadlines are absolute. The media do not grant continuances.

Lawyers have been conditioned to believe they can present their case later, when they know more. If you are to defend yourself effectively, you should be quoted in the first news stories about your case. First impressions are hard to change.

We Can Always Appeal

Another reflex serves lawyers badly when they are dealing with the news media. In court, if you lose at the trial level, you can always appeal. In the judicial system, it is very important to build a meticulous record. This is your backup. In the news media, there is no appeal process, once they decide you're guilty, and slant their coverage that way.

Incomplete Court Transcripts

Appellate judges never see the witnesses or the evidence. In the distant isolation of their chambers, they read the court transcript. It is only words. So lawyers become terribly concerned with words. Court reporters do not record the tears, the smiles, the quick glances, the smells, the murmur from the spectators.

Timing is everything, they say. Trial transcripts do not convey the timing, either. Whether the lines were delivered with a shout or a whisper. Milliseconds make all the difference for standup comedians delivering their punch-lines, and for lawyers delivering their final arguments to a jury.

When lawyers do decide to speak to the media, many do not seem to realize that style can be much more powerful than the words themselves. Trial lawyers who try jury cases understand this. Corporate and property attorneys frequently do not.

The Lawyer's Leverage

Lawyers have enormous leverage. You have invested a lot of money in their advice. To ignore it seems stupid. They sometimes tell you they will abandon you if you don't do everything they say. Just the thought of starting all over again with another lawyer is terribly frightening.

In-house public relations staffers are often former reporters. They rarely have a higher rank in the organizational pecking order than the vice president for legal affairs. If they suggest taking your case to the media, the CEO may believe they are catering to the media because of some inherent, pro-media prejudice.

The outside PR consultant, brought in for the crisis, is pitted against the in-house lawyer who better understands the corporate culture.

The CEO's Bias

The CEO carries a bias from personal experience. The CEO socializes with lawyers; plays golf with them; respects their wisdom, skill and loyalty; has invested a lot of money in them. They have walked through a lot of fires together, and emerged victorious. Perhaps built the company together.

Most CEOs have a lot more experience with lawyers than with reporters. When the media crisis surfaces, that past experience can lead the CEO to quickly accept the lawyers' advice, and dismiss the counsel of the public relations expert.

That decision may put the organization in great peril. It is a difficult balancing act. It is easy to turn everything over to the lawyers. It is hard to hear both sides, and then make the tough decisions.

But that's what bosses are paid to do.

STRATEGY

MEDIA POLICY

You Mean I Can't Tell Them to Buzz Off?

I believe most organizations should have a written media policy. The larger the organization, the more detailed the policy should be. Once the policy is written, the boss should personally tell employees why the policy is there. AND WHAT IT REALLY MEANS.

If you don't make your intentions very clear, you'll get a lot of different interpretations. Staffers should be given specific scenarios in which reporters might approach the organization, and how they should handle it.

Too Many Thou Shall Nots

Too many media policies are just lists of Thou Shall Nots. Don't talk to reporters. Don't talk about company policy. Don't let reporters or photographers enter without an escort. Don't violate client confidentiality. Don't contradict the governor's political stance.

Don't. Don't. Don't. With all those don'ts, many employees decide the safest course of action is to avoid reporters at all costs. If a reporter shows up, cover your face and hide under the desk.

Corporations and government agencies send their top executives to my seminars, to learn how to deal effectively with the media. But they are rarely reporters' first contact. The reporter's first contact is often an entry-level employee, like a receptionist, who knows nothing about media relations. They're frightened. They become very defensive.

A Bad First Impression

The reporter may interpret that employee's response as the official company line. A story that was slightly critical may suddenly head toward a full expose of scandal in the executive suite.

That's why the written policy is so critical. I suggest that written policies stress the positive aspects of media relations first. Then get around to specific things you should not talk about, and how to refer the reporter up the ladder of command.

At the end of this chapter, I've reproduced portions of model policies I've written for clients. They can be easily modified to fit your organization.

The Basic Points

I believe every media policy should contain these basics:

1. **We need to tell the public who we are and what we do.**

2. **Public knowledge of our organization is vital to our success.**

3. **Reporters and photographers need to be treated courteously and diplomatically. Their impression of you becomes their impression of the entire organization, and that is reflected in their stories.**

4. **Discuss with reporters only those facts you personally know about. Don't speculate.**

5. **If you don't have personal knowledge or policy responsibility, say that. Then help the reporter reach someone who does.**

6. **If you would give a customer or a client *public information* the reporter is asking for, give it without hesitation to the reporter.**

7. **Let a designated executive (usually the PIO) know as soon as possible after any contact with the media. We need to be aware of stories that involve us, so we can provide additional information.**

8. **Refer media questions about policy or complicated technical issues to the PIO or other designated executive.**

9. **Return all reporters' calls as soon as possible. If a message is left and the person the reporter called can't be reached, someone else should return the call. "Can I help you?" We do not want to be surprised by tonight's newscast or tomorrow morning's newspaper. A story about this organization should never say we "could not be reached for comment."**

10. **Every story about this organization should include our perspective or point of view. That can't happen if we**

don't talk to the reporter.

11. Never say, "No comment." It sounds like you're hiding something.

12. Certain kinds of issues should not be discussed with reporters because of (fill in one or more): (a) the law; (b) our ethics or rules of procedure; (c) client confidentiality; (d) business competition; (e) some major harm that might result. Make sure the reporter understands why you cannot answer the question. Refer the reporter to a designated executive.

13. The news media have a legal right to observe, to photograph and to record any event or any person in a public place.

14. Any other elements that fit your organization in Ten Commandments of Media Relations.

Only the Boss Talks

Some organizations have a policy that says only the boss can talk to reporters. If the boss can't be reached, stories will be written without the organization's point of view.

If only the boss is allowed to speak, reporters get the idea the boss doesn't trust the staff. They're either too dumb to speak for the company or have been muzzled because there's something to hide.

There may be a need to designate specific spokespeople for special kinds of situations.

In a police department, for instance, the lead investigator working a homicide may be the only proper source for the media on that case. That investigator is best qualified to know whether the release of certain information might harm the investigation.

A fairly open policy will — in the long run — best serve most organizations. The single most disarming factor for a suspicious reporter is a friendly, wide-open media attitude.

I recommend the Home Depot technique. When a customer asks an employee where something is, the Home Depot employee doesn't just tell the customer where power saws are. The employee *takes* the customer there. The customer feels: *this company cares about me and my business. I like that. This is a good place to shop.*

In the same way, your staffer should refer the reporter to the PIO (perhaps call the PIO and hand the phone to the reporter) or to someone who is better situated to answer the reporter's questions.

A Policy for Bankers

Private corporations and government agencies need to approach media policy with a slightly different tone. Here are portions of a model policy I suggest for my banking clients. It can be modified easily.

A Suggested Media Policy for Bankers

To better serve our customers and the community, we need to tell them more about who we are and what we do here at the bank.

That message is often conveyed by the news media. And so the entire staff needs to be more aware of how we can cooperate with the news media, in ways that will best accomplish that goal.

A Word About Confidentiality

Never forget that the confidentiality of our customers' financial affairs is a sacred trust. Every employee of the bank can protect that confidentiality, and still be courteous and cooperative with members of the media.

Reporters Are Part of the Public, Too

Reporters have the right to answers for any questions you would answer for any member of the public.

EXAMPLE: "What is the bank's current interest rate on new car loans?" We'd answer that question for any potential customer who's shopping for a car. We'd be unusually helpful. We want their business. You should give reporters that same kind of information and help.

Be sure your answers to reporters' questions are accurate and current. If you don't know the answer, make a special effort to find the person in the bank who CAN get the information.

Reporters Have Deadlines

Remember, reporters are working against a deadline. They usually need their questions answered quickly. A prompt, courteous reply is good public relations for the bank. It's good business.

Banking News Is Important

The public today is more involved in finance than ever before. Reporting on banking and business is at an all-time high. This is a complicated subject. Good reporters need explanations and data we can provide. In doing so, we perform a major public service.

When a reporter asks about a generic financial or banking concept, you should – within reason – use your knowledge and the bank's resources to help that reporter.

EXAMPLE: "What is the relationship between banks and the Federal Reserve?" Or, "How does the Federal Deposit Insurance Corporation work? What must a bank do to qualify as a member? What does it cost the bank?"

The answers to these questions are available elsewhere. They're not specifically tied to our bank. But by helping the reporter, we build a relationship with that reporter that's important to us. That reporter will come back to us in the future, both as a reporter and as a customer.

Notify Our Media Specialist

As a matter of policy, after you've given this kind of generic information to a reporter, notify the bank's media specialist. The media specialist's job is to work closely with reporters.

We'd like to keep track of how reporters use the information we give them. Perhaps we'll call later with follow-up suggestions after the story is printed or broadcast. If the reporter's inquiry would require extensive use of bank employee time or resources, you should also clear that with the bank's media specialist, before you commit to do the research.

Matters of Bank Policy

If the reporter's question involves a policy of the bank, or a specific incident or personnel decision, the reporter should be courteously referred to the bank's media specialist.

These questions are sometimes sensitive, in terms of our competitive position with other banks. How much information we provide the public is often a policy decision that can only be made at the administrative level of the bank.

EXAMPLE: "We have a tip that you plan to open a new branch and appoint Mary Moneycounter as president of that branch. Can you confirm that?"

OR: "To compete with other financial institutions, some banks are offering innovative Internet services to checking account customers. Is your bank considering such a service?"

We might be, but we might not want to advertise it just yet. The bank's media specialist will confer with top officers of the bank before deciding how we should answer that question.

Remember, on some questions you can give away the answer just in the way you say you can't answer. So refer the reporter to the media specialist without hinting at the answer.

Never Lie or Try to Deceive the Media

It's much better to say, "I'm sorry, I can't answer that question right now," than to give a deceptive answer. Explain why you can't answer. Avoid saying "No comment."

Reporters respect honesty more than any other character trait. So do our customers. In fact, honesty is our stock-in-trade. We must NEVER give even a suggestion that we're evasive or deceptive. If you give that impression to a reporter, it will probably be passed on to the reporter's readers, viewers or listeners.

Our Bank Is the People Who Work Here

Our bank is not a building or a corporation. It is the people who work here. We are constantly judged by the public's perception of our staff. When a customer or a reporter finds an employee helpful and friendly, then our bank builds its reputation as a helpful, friendly place.

When an employee is grumpy and uncooperative, then that customer or reporter gets the idea that everybody in the bank is that way.

What Is News?

News is the unusual. It can be good or bad news.

News is information people need in their daily lives. It can be information that makes their lives more enjoyable and profitable.

It can be information that warns them to take special precautions. Bad news always seems to leak out. Gossips thrive on stories of human frailty or failure. And once they spread their gossip, the media have a responsibility to publish or broadcast it, if they decide it will serve the public interest.

But news is also simple, human stories that remind us of life's joys and special times. Stories that renew our hope in humanity.

"Good news" often goes unreported. Because they never heard about it.

One of your responsibilities here is to make sure our media specialist knows about possible human interest stories. The media specialist will know who to call in the local media to see if they're interested. But the call will never be made unless you bring the story to the specialist's attention.

EXAMPLE: After a customer had a heart attack in the bank lobby, a group of tellers took CPR classes on their own time. If it happens again, they'll be better prepared to help until the paramedics arrive.

EXAMPLE: An elderly customer cashed a check and left $100 in cash on the ledge at the teller's window. The next customer in line – high school student – found the money and told the teller. When the elderly customer returned in panic, she and her cash were re-united. Without it, she wouldn't have been able to pay her rent.

EXAMPLE: A group of students who couldn't find summer jobs wanted to start a service to "house-sit" the homes of people on vacation. But they had no money to advertise. The bank's loan de-partment decided they were a good risk, and loaned them the money to get started. They've built a very successful business.

News Pegs

The news media are constantly looking for local stories that tie to a national story. They call these stories "news pegs." They're lo-cal stories pegged to a larger, national or international story. There are many national financial stories that could generate lo-cal news pegs. The local media may not know of the local angle unless we tell them.

Keep that in mind when you know that we're somehow involved in some banking activity that could be pegged to a national or inter-national incident. Tell the bank's media specialist so the story can be passed along.

Cameras In the Bank

Reporters and photographers have the same right to enter public areas of the bank as any other citizen. They do not have the right – in this privately owned, public place – to interfere with banking business or our customers' expectation of privacy.

When a news photographer enters the bank and begins taking pic-tures, the media specialist or a bank officer should be notified immediately. The officer should approach the photographer cour-teously and ask what the pictures are for.

Remember, rudeness – on camera – always gives a bad impres-sion of the bank. If the reporter or photographer is rude, we won't see that in the news. But if YOU are, we'll probably see just HOW rude on tonight's news. And tomorrow's news. And in future sto-ries about this bank.

As a matter of policy, we'll be glad to help the news media photo-graph banking operations. We'd like to know in advance just what they want and need, so we can arrange the photography with the least interference to our customers, bank security, and our normal business.

If the photographer is belligerent and uncooperative, politely ask him to leave. In this kind of conflict with the media, make sure you're not the one who behaves badly.

A Policy for Human Services

The following is a model policy I suggest to human service agencies. By law in most states, these agencies cannot discuss anything about a client. The law and their professional ethic make it extremely difficult to defend the agency when it is attacked unjustly, by people making false allegations. This policy can be easily modified to fit most government agencies.

A Suggested Media Policy for Human Service Agencies

This department exists to serve the public.

The people in this community are vitally concerned with human services. How we meet the needs of those who cannot provide for themselves determines, to a large extent, the character of our community – its priorities and standards – its conscience and human dignity.

The people of this community provide the financial support and encouragement that make effective human services possible. They have the right to know, through the news media, how we carry out our duties and responsibilities. We have nothing to hide. We will not have the support that we deserve as dedicated public servants unless the community is fully aware of the problems we face, and how we deal with them from day to day.

The News Media Can Help Us

The news media can often help us do our job. Many of our clients and potential clients cannot be reached in any other way. They will not know of our services if they do not hear about them through the media. News stories can rally the community to provide special needs in times of crisis. The news media are often invaluable in helping locate elderly clients who wander away from home; in identifying abandoned babies, and other similar cases.

It is Our Policy to Help the News Media

It is the policy of this department to make information available to the news media as quickly and completely as possible, except in those instances where the release of that information might violate the client's right to confidentiality or interfere with the fair administration of justice. When we cannot release information for legal or ethical reasons, those reasons should be carefully explained to the reporter. In some cases, it might be helpful to give the reporter copies of the law and the regulations governing what we can and cannot discuss publicly.

Returning Reporters' Calls

Every reporter's phone call should be returned as quickly as possible. If you cannot be reached, make sure your staff returns the call, and refers the reporter to someone who can answer the reporter's questions.

We never want it to be said that we "could not be reached for comment." We do not want to be surprised by tomorrow's headline or tonight's newscast. Stories about us should always include our response or point of view.

Client Confidentiality

We have a legal and ethical responsibility to protect the confidentiality of our clients. In some cases, the legal process removes that cloak of confidentiality. If it has not been removed, we can still talk to the media about the way we help clients without naming a specific client.

We can explain to reporters, just as we would to anyone who asked, the rules and regulations concerning our services; the way those rules are put into effect; the numbers and amounts of money involved that are a part of the public record, or will eventually become part of the public record.

Every Staffer May Speak

Every staff member is free to speak to the media about departmental matters so long as the basic policy set forth here is not violated.

The employee at the site of our services is often the best witness and can give the most accurate account of what happened.

Public Information Office

It is the role of the Public Information Office (PIO) to serve as coordinator of information with the media. A sort of tour guide.

Reporter's inquiries should be referred to the PIO unless they can quickly be handled by the staffer who is contacted.

Often, the reporter simply needs a number or an explanation of how a program works. You may be better qualified to give that explanation than the PIO. But it is a good idea to let the PIO know about the reporter's inquiry.

There may be other activity on the same subject within the department that you are unaware of. If the PIO is fully informed, they may be able to give more assistance to the reporter and improve our rapport with the media.

Have Personal Knowledge

You should speak to the media only about those matters of which you have personal knowledge. Do not speculate. This restriction is intended to prevent the relaying of inaccurate information to the news media.

Human Interest Stories

The news media are always looking for strong human interest stories. We often complain that the media cover us when we have problems and ignore us when we do things right. This is a chance for us to tell the public about our successes. It is the responsibility of the PIO to suggest these stories to reporters and editors.

But the PIO cannot know about them unless you alert them. Remember, some of these stories need substantial lead time for the media to cover them effectively. Let the PIO know as soon as possible about clients or staffers who are involved in human interest situations that offer news story possibilities. Because it is the job of the PIO to work closely with the media, they can often arrange ways to cover those stories that do not invade clients' confidentiality.

Legal Rights of Privacy

The news media have a legal right to observe, to photograph and to record any event or any person in a public place. On private property, the owner of the property has the final word on who shall be allowed inside the premises.

A court order which gives our staff the right of entry does not automatically give that same right to members of the news media. So long as the media are physically on public property — or on private property with the consent of the owner — they have the right to observe, photograph and record events that may be occurring on private property.

On-Scene Coordination

Many of the conflicts between human services staff and the media occur at the scenes of great human emotion and suffering. Under these difficult and often confusing circumstances, many members of the media will arrive about the same time we do. The ranking staff member on the scene should be responsible for coordinating release of information to the news media until a public information officer arrives.

Who Should Discuss Policy

Staff members should make every effort to be courteous and diplomatic in dealing with the news media. In matters of policy, the reporter should be referred to a staff member responsible for setting or carrying out that policy.

Not to Be Released

Staff members shall not release for publication, or in a manner which is likely to result in publication, information in the following categories:

1. The identity of a client, or confirmation that a person is a client, without the written consent of that client.

2. The names and addresses of victims of sex offenses.

3. The names and addresses of juvenile offenders.

4. Until next-of-kin have been notified, the names and addresses of people who die. The names shall be released after a reasonable time if notification of next-of-kin cannot be accomplished.

Reporters may be given the names of dead people so long as they pledge that they will not publish or broadcast them until next-of-kin have been notified, or until the department approves release of the names.

This can be done as a convenience to the media when notification of next-of-kin is expected before a reporter's deadline.

5. Information which might jeopardize an investigation.

6. Any opinion as to guilt or innocence of a client, or the merits or evidence in a case where a client's identity has become public through an arrest or other action outside this department.

7. The performance of any medical examinations or tests; their results, or the refusal of a client to submit to a medical examination or test.

8. The home address or telephone number of staff members, without the express consent of that staffer.

The purpose of this provision is to strengthen the off-duty privacy and safety of the staffer and his/her family, not to make the staffer inaccessible to the media.

Media requests for information that may be known only by an off-duty staffer can often be relayed to the staffer by the PIO or the staffer's superior without giving reporters a home phone number.

9. *(Insert other localized items)*
Records That Are Public

State and local ordinances provide that the following records shall be open to the public:

(Insert local application)

Records That Are Not Public

State and local ordinances and departmental policy provide that the following records shall not be open to the public:

(Insert local application)

Beyond these explicit guidelines, members of this department are encouraged to be open and cooperative with the news media.

Although the department has a public information office, its existence does not imply that staff members should refer all inquiries to that office.

Every member of the department is expected to know the contents of this policy, and to abide by it. The director is willing to trust your judgment about what to say to the news media, and how to say it .Every member of this department is a public information officer.

STRATEGY

PIOs

What Exactly Do Public Information Officers Do?

Most companies and government agencies of any size now have at least one public information officer (PIO). When they get that assignment, many PIOs have no training or experience with the media.

Many of them don't have the foggiest notion of what they're supposed to do. Or how to do it. Nor does the boss.

I guess you write press releases, and answer reporter's questions?

Right. But …

A Difficult Position to Fill

There's a lot more to it. The learning process can be very painful for the PIO, the boss, the organization, and reporters who have to deal with a new PIO.

If you're the boss, choosing a PIO is one of the most difficult personnel decisions you'll ever make. You'll need to consider:

- Should the job be full-time or part-time, and –
- Should it be a veteran employee who knows the company, but may not know much about the media, or –
- Should it be a journalist who can be persuaded to leave the news business and represent you

More important than any of these, I believe, is the PIO's basic personality, intelligence and motivation. Does this individual personify the organization?

How hard is this person willing to work? Can he/she handle being on call 24 hours a day? How well does this person perform under stress?

How Reporters Rank PIOs

As a reporter, these are the things I valued most in PIOs:

- **Good PIOs are bright**, and they learn quickly
- **Good PIOs have great people skills**; they're patient; they know how to communicate, negotiate and mediate
- **Good PIOs have integrity**; they will not lie; they project sincerity and credibility; reporters, photographers, trust them. AS WELL AS the people within their own organization

The most common misuse of PIOs occurs when the boss creates the position and announces the PIO will be the spokesperson for the organization. Often in this kind of structure, no matter what happens, only the boss or the PIO speaks to the news media. The boss often wants to use the PIO as a buffer, to keep the media at a safe distance. Not good.

Relays Are Too Slow

In this kind of setup, , the PIO becomes an information relay. It takes a lot of time to get the answers to a reporter's questions approved, and then get back to the reporter, who by then has thought of several other questions.

If you miss the reporter's deadline as a result of a lengthy search, your point of view will not be in the story.

Every time information passes from one hand to another, it becomes more stale and less personal. The chance for error multiplies.

How Did It Feel?

Most important – the PIO wasn't there when it happened, and can't answer the media's most pressing question – How did it feel? (See chapters on **Interviews**)

A cop is shot in the chest at close range. His only injury is a bad bruise. His bulletproof vest saved his life. Reporters want to talk to the officer, not the PIO. They want pictures of the bruise.

How did it feel to be shot and live to tell about it? What went through your mind? How much pain is there when a slug slams into a bulletproof vest? Do you wear the vest all the time? Only the officer can answer those questions.

The PIO's function *should be* to arrange the interview, NOT to speak for the officer.

Tour Guides for the Media

Good PIOs are tour guides for the media. They are walking encyclopedias. They know the organization as well as the boss – perhaps better. They can quickly lead reporters and photographers to the right place, the right people, the right information.

Good PIOs are credible. If they know the answer, but can't tell the reporter, they say so. One deception, and the credibility can never be restored. Reporters have very long memories. They have ways to get even.

Good PIOs are respected and trusted by their colleagues within the company or agency. They can be trusted not to leak. Unless the boss wants something leaked. And when that happens, They know how to leak so nobody will know who did it.

The Chain of Command

Which leads to the chain of command. Who should the PIO answer to?

In the best organizational structure, the PIO or public relations director reports directly to the chief executive officer. The PIO has constant access to the decision-makers and is included in all major discussions and decisions.

If the PIO is not included, information can be released to the media that's not true. The PIO *thought* it was true.

When reporters learn the truth, the PIO becomes – in their minds – either a liar or a flack who's out of the loop and doesn't know what's happening within the organization.

Public vs. Private

PIOs for government agencies and private companies should have different perspectives.

Similar, but different.

In the private sector, part of the job involves putting the company's best foot forward. It is part public information, part marketing and promotion for the company.

Too many public information officers in government fail to understand the perils if they adopt those same objectives. They think it is their job to make the boss, or the agency, look good. In doing that, they may stall, or try to block a story.

They may fail to disclose something. They may lie.

Switching to Attack Mode

The news media seem far less critical of deceptive games when private industry plays them than when the players are government officials or employees.

Nothing switches reporters to attack mode quicker than a lie or the belief that you're hiding something. It whets their appetites. There's got to be a Pulitzer Prize somewhere under that mountain of misinformation, they think. They dig harder.

Simplified Media Relations

In its simplest definition, good media relations tells the public:

WHO are you?

WHAT do you do?

If your organization has good people who do a good job and provide a good product or service, that's the message you need to convey.

In a society drowning in information, PIOs have to become more and more creative to get the media's attention, so they can deliver the basic message. (See **Selling Your Story**)

News Conference Role

At news conferences, the PIO's role is to:

- Choose the best place and time
- Alert the media and invite them to attend
- Act as stage manager, to make sure the physical layout will accommodate both the spokespeople and the news media
- Provide handouts before the news conference begins
- Explain any special ground rules, and introduce the people who will take reporters' questions
- Close the conference when a pre-set time limit is reached, or when questions taper off
- Help set up individual interviews if reporters ask for them after the conference (See more in News Conferences)

PIOs Are Always On Call

PIOs should generally be on call 24 hours a day. News does not operate on a schedule. Your organization needs to have its perspective in every story that mentions it. In some types of operations – fire, law enforcement, medical and emergency services, utility companies

– you may need assistant PIOs on call at night or on weekends. Otherwise, the PIO will never be able to sleep.

Spend Time With Media

PIOs need to spend time with the reporters and editors who will be covering their organization.

The PIO for a large bank should have lunch regularly with the business editor of the dominant newspaper in the area. The PIO for a hospital should do the same with medical reporters.

PIOs should ask to spend a day or half-day occasionally watching news people do their job. Ride with a television news camera crew, then watch them edit the story. Try writing an accurate newspaper headline in the limited space for headlines. Sit in on the staff conference that sets news priorities.

It gives you a much better understanding of the problems media people have getting their stories in the paper or on the air. Accurately and on time.

Enlarge Your Contact List

Watching over their shoulders not only educates you. It sends a strong message that you're interested in what media people do. That you want to do a better job, helping them.

In that visit, you'll enlarge your list of media contacts. Next time you call, trying to sell a story, they're much more likely to listen.

The single most important strategy in dealing with the media is to convince them you're willing and anxious to help them get a better story.

Becoming a Resource

Reporters need resource people. Major national associations realize that, and run advertisements in magazines that cater to the media. "If you have questions about our industry, we have people with answers," the typical ad says.

One of your goals as a PIO should be to have your name, phone numbers and e-mail address in the contact list index of every reporter and editor in your community – and perhaps at the TV network news desks, and major publications like *The New York Times, USA Today, The Wall Street Journal,* and *Bloomberg Businessweek.*

Every time you're quoted, with your company affiliation, it's free advertising. It creates prestige and name recognition for the organization. It won't hurt your career, either.

Knowing all that, the full-time vs. part-time question really depends on how many media outlets the PIO must handle. You may want to begin with a part-time assignment, keep track of how the PIO spends the time, then decide whether it should be expanded to full-time.

The Staff Must Understand

Part of managing an organization also involves educating the entire staff to function as a team with the PIO. Public information officers can't be everywhere at once. They need to be tipped by others within the organization when there is a potential favorable news story or media problem.

I believe every organization of any size should have a written media policy, so there will be no doubt about exactly what is expected of employees. Managers need to let staff know precisely what the policy means. Particularly if it has been changed.

I recommend periodic staff meetings to go over hypothetical situations to make sure employees understand the organization's stance when dealing with print and broadcast news outlets. (See **Media Policy**)

In a crisis, remember – the media's first contact will not be with a highly-trained, media-skilled executive. *Every* staff member should be aware of your organization's media attitude and policy.

STRATEGY

SELLING YOUR STORY

Wow! Have I Got A Story For You!

Many people try to get the news media to cover their story, fail repeatedly, and can't understand why.

They don't realize that their approach turns off editors. They don't know what news is. Or how to sell it.

News is the exception. The unusual.

Mayor Sober Today

If the headline says, "Mayor Sober Today," we assume he is drunk most of the time. What would your reaction be if tonight's newscast told you:

- No children were murdered today
- No airliners crashed
- No bridges collapsed
- No banks failed

News Is What's Different

News is what happens that is *different*.

It is news when a doctor walks into a hospital with an assault rifle and kills half a dozen people before turning the gun on himself.

It is not news that thousands of other physicians spent the day saving lives and relieving the misery of their patients.

Information We Need

News can also be information people need. Information that will in some way affect their lives. In a democratic society, we need to know that the school board is contemplating a tax increase so we can support, or try to stop it. We need to know that a certain brand of sardines is contaminated so we can throw them away and not get food poisoning.

To successfully sell stories on a regular basis, you must know your media market, the specific styles and audiences of each outlet in that market.

Visually Interesting for TV

Many of the stories that are staples for newspapers are not visually interesting for television, and have no appeal whatever for radio. Video of the school board's hearing on property taxes is not nearly as visually appealing as a warehouse fire.

The debate in all newsrooms is whether to give the public what they need, or what they want. The spreading ownership of media outlets by very large corporations seems to be making the latter choice. Stories that get larger audiences and profit get a higher priority than public service.

An old saying in television news: If it bleeds, it leads.

The Compelling C's

Here are eight broad categories for news story content in all media — I call them the Compelling C's:

Catastrophe	**Crime**
Crisis	**Corruption**
Conflict	**Color (human interest)**
Change	**Celebrities**

If you, your department or your company are going to be in the news, the story will usually need an angle that fits at least one of these categories. And it must be unusual.

A caller says, "I don't want to give you my name, but you should look into what's happening at the Zebra Club. The treasurer embezzled $200,000 and ran off with the president's wife.

"The children's hospital we support is about to run out of money because of the theft. There's a big internal fight now, on whether to prosecute the treasurer, who — by the way — is a priest."

Now, *that's* news. Crime, corruption, crisis, conflict, color.

Veteran politicians understand the conflict/crisis technique and use it to get news coverage. The people they attack understand the game. They get on their soap box and fight back, and their point of view gets time on the air, space in blogs and the newspaper.

Nothing personal. A lot like attorneys who seem to have a grudge match going in court, but play golf together every Sunday.

Conflict/Crisis Announcement

If you want the media to cover your issue, publicly announce that some revered institution or program is under attack (conflict) or faces disaster (crisis).

This is done routinely in state and national capitals worldwide. A member of Congress predicting that Medicare or Social Security is about to go bankrupt because of some element in the program will guarantee broad media coverage.

The opposing political party will be obligated to denounce the doomsayer. Trying to be fair, the media cover that side of the conflict, which extends the coverage and the debate.

Conventions No Longer News

Because the primaries now determine who will run for President in the United States, the national party conventions that once chose those candidates have lost their critical news elements.

They are simply rubber stamps. Old news. No crises, no major conflicts.

They were once given the same level of coverage as a Super Bowl. But because we usually know what the result will be now, covering them has become a kind of public service chore.

Crank Up the Coverage

If your association's conferences are rarely covered by the media, here's how to change that:

Bring opposing points of view to the speaker's platform for a hair-pulling, eye-gouging debate. The Q&A session after the debate will lead to great quotes and pictures. This must be done very skillfully.

If reporters suspect they are being manipulated with a phony issue, the technique can backfire.

Conflict is the key ingredient that makes most novels and movies work. It is a guaranteed way to get news media attention. It is a game, very much like professional sports. To communicate effectively, you need to learn how to play the game.

One reason sports gets so much coverage is that it incorporates these basic elements. **Conflict** is central, with a **crisis** every game. If they lose, will there be **changes** in the coaching staff?

Catastrophe when the star quarterback is injured. **Color** stories about **celebrity** players are a staple. And much too often lately, stories of **crime** and **corruption** off the playing field.

Manufactured Conflict

The most damning criticism of America's invasion of Iraq in 2003 was the assertion that this was a manufactured conflict. Critics said the White House accused Iraq of holding weapons of mass destruction to get media coverage of that issue, to mask the real motives for the war.

In news, the game is life and death, success and failure, the come-from-behind underdog vs. the powerful champion.

In his book, *Breaking the News* (Pantheon Books, 1996) magazine editor James Fallows made a powerful argument that the media's obsession with conflict is undermining democracy in America. In a series of real-life anecdotes, Fallows recounts how journalists avoid society's critical issues. They spend their time and space covering conflict instead. Conflict sells.

Community Size & Timing

"My civic club elected officers last night, and I knew you'd want to do a story," the caller tells the city editor. In large communities, there are hundreds – perhaps thousands – of civic club elections each year. Not news.

In a small, rural community, with two or three civic clubs, the election of a new Rotary president may be a major story. News often depends on where it happens.

Timing can be everything, when it comes to news coverage. On a slow news day, they still need to fill print and website pages and newscast minutes.

If there is still empty space on the page as the deadline approaches (a "slow news day") a personality profile of the Water Buffalo Lodge president becomes more attractive to the editor.

The day two bombs explode near the finish line at the Boston Marathon, a five-alarm fire may get only two sentences.

Weekend Strategies

Newspaper editors need a lot of copy to fill the big Sunday edition. So Saturday can be a good day to release a story.

Because government and business are closed for the weekend, broadcasters have difficulty finding stories for their Saturday and

Sunday newscasts. The same is true for Monday morning's paper. It may be easier to place a story then.

The downside is that both newspapers and broadcast stations work weekends with a skeleton staff. The weekend staff may be newer, and less talented. Fewer people watch TV on weekends.

Embargo Until Sunday

One solution: Release the story on Friday, with an embargo. The media must agree to hold it until Sunday.

Before their decline, some newspapers traditionally had a large "news hole" on Wednesday or Thursday, because that's the day the grocery stores bought entire sections of display ads.

If you expect to sell stories to your local news media, you need to know local editors. So that when you call or e-mail to offer a story, they'll know your name. They'll know you have a sense of news value.

On many story tips, you should notify the editor in advance. (See **News Releases**) Follow up with a phone call or e-mail the day before the story breaks.

Pitching to Broadcasters

For the assignment editor at a radio or TV station, the slack time is mid-to-late-afternoon, the day before the story. The call or e-mail should be something like this:

Editor: This is Tom Tipster. I sent you a news release earlier this week about the environmental protest we're planning in front of Koffalot Chemicals. We expect to have about 500 people there, willing to go to jail, if necessary. Just wanted to see if you need any other information.

Be careful not to push too hard. A good story doesn't really need to be sold. Selling too hard makes the editor suspicious that there may not be real news there. Make any unusual element clear.

Timing for Newspapers

You'd make a similar call to the editor of an afternoon newspaper about 1 or 2 p.m. the day before the story will break. By that time, the last deadline has passed. Time to work on tomorrow's early morning assignments.

For a morning newspaper, the call should be between noon and about 2:30 p.m. the day before. Just after lunch, the city editor has issued most of today's assignments. The afternoon editors' meetings that decide which stories will be in tomorrow morning's paper haven't begun yet.

The call may also lead to a story in tomorrow morning's newspapers, giving readers a preview of what's going to happen. In the evening, you can tip the night city editor, who leaves notes for the early morning staff.

Radio & TV Needs

Radio assignment editors need to know the day before, and may appreciate updates through the day.

Remember – television needs more advance notice, because they have to collect video to cover everything the reporter will write about. They may need to plan a live shot, with a reporter on the scene to interview one of your people.

Look for News Pegs

You need to contact the media while the issue is hot. If a national story develops on any subject, local editors and news directors look for a local angle. They call it a local "news peg" or a "news hook."

It is a reflexive response. If you're the first to call with a suggestion, you'll usually be the person they interview and include in their story.

When there is a mass shooting at a school or workplace, that triggers thousands of local, "pegged" stories all over the nation on local security measures, gun ownership, and mental health issues.

The Easiest Sell

A local news peg is the easiest story you'll ever sell to an editor. The national or international story has already established the story's importance.

Editors and news directors put the localizing of stories very high on their agenda. But call quickly. Your competition may beat you in tipping the local media, and get the coverage.

If you work in a hospital or medical research facility, there will be many national health stories you can "peg" to.

Call the editor and say, "There's a story this morning in *The New England Journal of Medicine* about fingernail transplants. Did you know we've been doing that here for years? We invented the technique."

If you're a bank executive, there are daily financial stories for which you can suggest local news pegs. Many companies can peg to stories about new technology.

Personal Interest

First Amendment issues – "The People's Right to Know" – get a lot of news space and time. That's because reporters and editors have a personal interest.

So if you want to get coverage for your issue, look for a journalist who has some personal connection to your cause, and let him/her know about your story idea.

If your issue is the search for the cure for a certain kind of disease, you might want to find a journalist who has a close family member with that disease.

A story about foster homes will be very appealing to a reporter or editor who grew up in foster care.

If your story involves a hobby, like photography, sailing, woodworking or antiques, check with clubs whose members have those interest and ask if any journalists belong. Contacting that journalist to suggest your story will have a better chance because of his/her personal interest.

Lobbying Your Issue

When legislation is pending, or the courts hand down a decision affecting your special interest, you need to let local people know how that law or decision will affect them.

Media coverage at the local level has a powerful grass roots effect. In Washington and the state capitol, officials who will decide the issue are much more influenced by local media stories reaching their constituents than by coverage in the capital city.

But local editors may not be aware there IS a local peg unless you call them. For most people, a hometown person is more believable, more compelling than a national or state figure. The local authority puts it in perspective for local people.

You'll Become a Regular

Once you develop a reputation as someone who understands difficult issues – who can decipher them, so ordinary people understand them – you'll discover reporters come back to you for future stories. You become an expert they can rely on.

In **Webcam Interviews**, I show how you can become the "Expert on Call," available 24/7 as a resource about your specialty. This new technology is incredibly cheap and effective.

The payoff for you (in addition to effectively arguing your point of view) is a subtle form of public relations for your organization. It won't hurt your role as community leader, either. Or your standing with your supervisors.

Stereotypical Stories

There are other types of stories that are absolutely predictable. They make it easier for you to place your stories.

Editors have an unusual, aberrant gene which compels them to publish and broadcast some kinds of pictures and stories. Stories that all of us want to hear, see and read. Because these stories are so formularized and repetitive, they're easy to sell.

Anniversary Stories

The anniversary story is a news media staple. On New Year's Day, almost all news media run the Year in Review. The anniversary of a disaster or a major crime will be marked by thousands of news stories. At first, the stories will be revisited annually. Anniversary stories usually disclose very little that is new.

The anniversary story traditionally recurs at the five-year mark, the 10-year mark, then jumps to 25- and 50-year commemorations.

There was massive media coverage of these 50-year anniversaries in 2013 and 2014:

- Martin Luther King's "I have a dream" speech
- Expansion of nightly network news from 15 to 30 minutes
- The assassination of President John F. Kennedy
- Arrival of The Beatles in America

If you have a point of view – an angle you'd like to see published or broadcast – several weeks before the anniversary will be an excellent time to sell that story idea to an editor.

The Editing Hierarchy

Here's the hierarchy at the local news media, to help you choose who to contact when you have a story to pitch:

At most newspapers, the top editor overseeing daily news stories is the **MANAGING EDITOR** or **EXECUTIVE EDITOR**. This editor is the final word on almost everything that happens in the newsroom; supervises all other news editors; and may even have authority over the editorial page editor. At many newspapers, the news and editorial pages are kept separate. This kind of organizational chart is designed to make editorial writers more independent. It is a reminder that editorial writers express their opinions, and news reporters should not.

Newspaper Publisher

The managing editor answers to the **PUBLISHER**. At large newspapers, the publisher has almost nothing to do with daily news coverage. The publisher's function is to represent the owners and give overall supervision to keep the newspaper financially healthy.

Some publishers write a weekly column. The publisher is often the newspaper's representative in community affairs and civic clubs. At "throwaway newspapers" the publisher is frequently the owner and editor-in-chief. As daily newspapers decline, these free newspapers (usually published weekly) are becoming much more important for local news coverage.

General Manager

At small newspapers, the publisher may also be the **GENERAL MANAGER** who oversees circulation, advertising, and the mechanical portion of the paper. General managers traditionally have no voice whatever in news content. This avoids the suggestion that advertisers can influence news coverage.

City/Metro Editor

Local news is supervised by a **CITY EDITOR** or **METRO EDITOR**. The city editor is responsible for the local staff, and coverage within the immediate city and nearby suburbs.

Many morning papers also have a **NIGHT CITY EDITOR**, to supervise the local staff from the time the city editor goes home in the evening until the last deadline, sometime after midnight.

State News Editor

State news (news within the state, but outside the local community) is the responsibility of the **STATE EDITOR**, who may also double as **POLITICAL EDITOR**, since the reporters at the state capitol bureau are within the state editor's geographic area.

Business Editor

There's probably a **BUSINESS EDITOR** at your local newspaper who handles most financial stories. Business news coverage has increased dramatically in recent years. Partly because most workers now have an IRA that is supposed to help finance their retirement.

The stock market, interest rates, banking policy, inflation and unemployment statistics have become much more newsworthy to those investors.

Many newspapers have a special business section, published on the same day every week. That section has a voracious appetite for detailed stories on local firms and the people in them.

There are also groups of local papers totally focused on their local business community that cover these stories intensely (and often better than the daily newspaper).

Editorial Page Editor

Editorials, syndicated columns, letters to the editor, and other material printed on the page opposite the editorial page (they call it the **Op-ed Page**) are usually under the control of the **EDITOR** or **EDITORIAL PAGE EDITOR**.

The editor and editorial writers make up the **EDITORIAL BOARD**. At some newspapers, a representative from the newsroom also sits on the editorial board.

Editorial Board

It is the custom in many communities for political candidates, government officials, and leaders of major causes to visit with the newspaper's editorial board. It is like an audience with the President or the Pope, in which you appear, hoping for their blessing.

You make the board aware of your cause or point of view and subject yourself to cross examination. The goal is to garner support or endorsement for yourself or your issue. At most newspapers each editorial writer is assigned specific areas, based on experience, interest, and expertise.

Features Editor

The **FEATURES EDITOR** supervises long-term reporting projects that are normally not produced on deadline.

Stories like profiles of people in the news; an extensive look at controversial issues; magazine-length pieces where writing style is encouraged and enhanced.

The section devoted to feature stories is now given a variety of names, like Style or Lifestyle.

With the advent of gender equality, the old "Women's Section" was abandoned. Many of the stories that would have once been in the Women's Section are now in the features section.

Favorite topics are human interest stories, personality profiles, animals, marriage and family issues, diets, medicine, moral conflicts like abortion and assisted suicide.

A few newspapers with long traditions of investigative reporting have an **INVESTIGATIONS EDITOR** who supervises a team of specialists. At most papers, investigative projects will be directed by the editor who would normally supervise other stories in the same area.

Radio and TV News Director

At radio and television stations, the person in charge of all news operations is the **NEWS DIRECTOR**. The news director is roughly the equivalent of the managing editor or executive editor at a newspaper.

The news director works closely with, the **GENERAL MANAGER**, who reports to the station owner.

Broadcast Assignment Editor

The **ASSIGNMENT EDITOR** is the person who decides how reporters and photographers will be dispatched to cover stories. If you'd like to have radio or TV coverage of something you're involved in, you need to let the assignment editor know about it.

In today's world of major staff cutbacks, the work of assignment editors has often been given to the news director.

Assignment editors are the most harried people in television news. The typical assignment editor sits in the center of the newsroom, totally immersed in noise and confusion.

On the desk, a bank of telephones are constantly ringing. With one ear, the assignment editor must monitor several squawking police and fire department radio scanners. E-mailed news releases constantly arrive.

Noise and Confusion

On top of that, a dozen camera crews out in their cars need directions to addresses they can't find.

They are reporting by radio every few minutes to say their camera or tape recorder has broken down; they arrived 30 seconds too late to catch the bridge collapse; the convention they're supposed to cover doesn't begin until next week, that the massive protest against police brutality is actually a little old man who hand-delivered a letter to the mayor's secretary.

No Respect

If the assignment editor happens to get a crew to the right place at the right time, and they come away with a great visual story, the reporter and photographer usually get the credit. If the assignment edi-

Winning with the News Media

tor misses a story, the news director has a nasty habit of screaming, banging on the desk and shouting obscenities.

Good assignment editors are born. Those that aren't sometimes come apart. During my years in TV news, I saw one assignment editor have a nervous breakdown; another ask to be demoted because he could no longer cope with the stress of the job.

Show & Story Producers

The **PRODUCER** of the newscast decides the length of stories, their format, and their placement in the newscast. Producers are the equivalent of a page or section editor at a newspaper. The stories gathered at the direction of the assignment editor are turned over to the show producer.

Network TV crews have a **FIELD PRODUCER** who travels with the correspondent and photographer, does most of the research, and manages the details.

The field producer may also do interviews, but is rarely seen or heard on the air. Local stations will occasionally assign a field producer to a crew for a major series or documentary.

Since there are several newscasts each day, the producers of each show may be supervised at larger stations by an **EXECUTIVE PRODUCER,** who also serves as deputy news director.

Virtually every TV station had a **PUBLIC AFFAIRS DIRECTOR** back when the FCC required licensed stations to dedicate air time to items that served the "public interest."

Public Affairs Programs

The standard format for public affairs programming was a weekly talk show, in which a guest was invited to discuss a current event or project. Those shows were polite and often boring.

A completely different breed, compared to today's talk shows (Transvestite Mothers Who Seduce Their Children's Pediatricians! Don't miss this afternoon's guests on *Wired and Weird*!).

With the deregulation of broadcasting, many stations have phased out their public affairs departments. The old talk show format, however, is still a Sunday morning staple on network television.

CNN invented today's redesigned talk show on public issues which speeds the pace, increases conflict, and sometimes invites viewers to participate by telephone or the Internet. (See **Talk Shows**)

Editorials & Commentary

Broadcast editorials and commentary are written, produced and performed by the station's **EDITORIAL WRITER** or **COMMENTATOR**. They are usually supervised by the station's general manager or public affairs director. At some stations, the editorials are delivered on the air by the general manager.

Ride-Alongs

When the Navy's Blue Angels team of jet fighter pilots come to town for an air show, the first stop is every local newsroom. We can take one person up for a ride, they tell the editor.

The result is almost always a huge story, with dramatic pictures or video and breathless copy. Syndicated reality TV shows like *Cops* use this technique. If reporters and photographers ride along, you'll get more favorable stories.

Journalism magazines have even warned reporters — Beware! If you ride with them, you'll like them. You'll lose your objectivity.

The traveling circus invented the technique. Circus animals are paraded from the train yard to the place where they'll perform. Reporters and photographers are invited to ride the elephants — perhaps perform in the show as clowns to do an "inside" story.

The secret of good coverage is often to bring reporters into your life or work. Let them ride in your cockpit — walk a mile in your shoes. Only then can they see and report your perspective.

Do It When You're Under Attack

And the very best time to bring them in is when you're under attack. It goes against your reflexes to do it then. The normal reaction is to barricade the building; avoid reporters at all costs.

But there are many cases where reporters switched from attack dog to awed reverence, once they experienced, first-hand, the problems insiders were coping with.

Targeting the Audience

When people buy advertising, they shop for the medium that can best reach their target audience. You don't sell cemetery plots on a hard rock station. Or acne ointment in a magazine for retirees.

Advertising agencies know the number of people who read, listen to, and watch local outlets. They have the demographics. In some cases, through market research and focus groups, they practically know what the audience had for breakfast.

Advertising Agency Data

If you need to sell stories on a regular basis, visit a local advertising agency and learn more about the audiences for each local media outlet.

In today's world, huge amounts of data are collected and sorted to create targeted advertising. Especially on the Internet. When I shop for a new electronic gadget online, within hours pop-up ads appear in my browsing that are trying to sell me what I was shopping for earlier in the day.

At a cooperative advertising agency, you can find out how many subscribers, listeners, viewers each local news outlet has. How old is their audience? What's the male and female breakdown, the income and education levels?

Association Newsletters

Virtually every association publishes some kind of newsletter. You may not realize how many associations there are in America. Professional, business, neighborhood associations. Associations that cater to hobbies or issues.

Groups that promote the use of dairy products or reverse-threaded wing nuts. Nationwide, there are tens of thousands. An Internet search for associations aligned with your issues will surprise you. And they're always looking for stories to fill their newsletters.

The Encyclopedia of Associations lists more than 150,000 associations. It's available at most public libraries, or online. The American Society of Association Executives is headquartered in Washington, D.C.

Association Directories

The state association of association executives will usually be located in your state capital. Most of them publish an annual directory. Obtain a copy so you'll have a specific name and address to call when you have a story idea that would appeal to their members.

Remember, too, that most newsletters are now distributed by e-mail. A Google search of "e-mail newsletter" as this book went to press brought back nearly TWO BILLION results.

Don't forget the local and state-oriented magazines that are always looking for fresh ideas involving local people and issues. Many local and state chambers of commerce publish magazines that concentrate on business, finance, and community development.

Think Pictures That Sell

Your success in selling a story idea to a radio or television assignment editor will often hinge on your suggestions for sound and pictures. In many cases, you can supply the sound and pictures.

Unfortunately, much of government and business is dull, by comparison with other, more visual stories. How do you show a smooth-running water department?

How do you photograph a record stock dividend? So much of government that has been traditionally covered by newspapers is almost entirely ignored by television.

Photo Opportunities

PR agencies and government PIOs have created a new event — the "photo opportunity." This is an event generated specifically for news media pictures.

It is neither spontaneous nor unrehearsed. In many respects, it is phony. But the appetite for pictures is so great, the media play along. Your success in selling a story may depend on your ingenuity in creating a photo opportunity.

Television and radio newscasts miss many stories simply because they don't know about them in time to get a camera or microphone there. They depend on newspapers, and on listeners and viewers who call to tip them to stories. TV stations in large cities usually have specialists, like newspaper "beat" reporters once did.

The most common television beats are medicine, consumer reporting, business, politics and crime. Some stations in larger markets have investigative reporters, but they are increasingly rare as large media corporations cut costs.

Don't Cry Wolf

Public relations firms have a bad habit of trying to sell stories that really aren't newsworthy. Once an editor gets burned by a story tip that flops, he'll hang up on you when you call to report you just found Jimmy Hoffa hiding in your basement.

If the story is not an event that needs to be photographed, you sometimes have to decide whether to give it first to radio, newspapers or TV. Or to all at the same time.

It is very rare to choose radio as the medium that will get it first on an exclusive basis, largely because coverage will be brief. It will not reach nearly as many people.

The Newspaper-TV Feud

Another element few people outside the media understand is the intense dislike − hatred, really − among newspaper people for television news. This can affect how your story will be covered.

For many years, newspapers tried to ignore television. If television beat them to a story, they wouldn't touch it. It was an ego thing. Newspaper people looked down their noses at TV and the people who work in it.

Television, in their minds, was fleeting, shallow, delivered by people who were actors hired for their looks, not their ability or intelligence. They thought TV was showbiz, not journalism. They also resented the fact that TV was largely responsible for the decline of newspapers.

If television got it first, it was hard for newspaper editors and reporters to admit they were beaten by the medium they spend so much time criticizing. So days or weeks later, they would revive the story with a new twist, trying to make it look like they found the story and broke it first.

Those days are gone forever. Most newspaper newsrooms now look like ghost towns. With so few staff members, they'll pick up a story however − wherever they can.

It Isn't Old for TV

Television is not so concerned about competing with newspapers. News directors will kill to beat a competing TV station to a story, but they know that most of their viewers do not read newspapers. Just because it was in the newspaper this morning doesn't make it old news for the TV audience.

And then the Internet became a primary conduit for news. Because it was instantaneous, there were no deadlines or schedules or time and space restraints.

The old competition to be first made established print and broadcast outlets race to put their stories on their websites. That changed everything.

STRATEGY

TEN COMMANDMENTS

Basic Techniques for Better Media Relations

Unless you've been caught in the crossfire of a pitched media battle, you will have a hard time understanding what it's like. It may be the most difficult experience of your life. The combat scenes from *Apocalypse Now* and *Saving Private Ryan* will give you some idea of what to expect.

In the *Apocalypse* attack on a Vietnamese village, the air is thick with helicopters. They swarm like dragonflies. Napalm is exploding. There is gunfire from all directions.

In the Normandy invasion scenes in *Private Ryan*, everything is noise and total confusion. It is virtually impossible to keep focus and perspective. You know the incoming fire can suddenly target you. Death and disfigurement are whistling by, very close. People around you – people you know well – are being torn apart.

An All-Out Media Attack

That's what it feels like at the center of a national or international story. The invasion force is hundreds of reporters and photographers. They come in, from all over the world, in helicopters and private jets, armed with tons of exotic, space-age equipment.

They surround your office, your home, your church. They camp there, round-the-clock. Think back to a recent major story. How many interviews took place in somebody's driveway? It happens because the target cannot move without running the gauntlet of microphones and cameras.

If you are their target, you may be followed everywhere you go for weeks at a time. You will be a captive. Your life, your career, the stability of your home and family will suddenly be at great risk.

Fight or Flee Syndrome

That's the worst-case scenario. But the Fight or Flee Syndrome will also seize you when a reporter shows up, unannounced, and begins to ask questions. If it is a television crew, stage fright will be added to the stress.

To help you cope, I developed the Ten Commandments of Media Relations. Some of them are just basic, common sense. But your fear of the media often leads you to do strange things. These commandments should help you develop some regular routines and policy for coping with reporters, editors and photographers on an everyday basis, as well as in the center of a national story.

The Ten Commandments

1. **Be Open and Cooperative – Never Lie**
2. **Personalize the Organization**
3. **Develop Media Contacts**
4. **Take Good Stories to The Media**
5. **Respond Quickly**
6. **Never Say, "No Comment"**
7. **It's OK to Say, "I Don't Know" (But I'll Find Out)**
8. **If You Screw Up, Confess and Repent**
9. **Use the Big Dump**
10. **Prepare, Prepare, Prepare**

Let's go over them, one at a time.

1 - Be Open and Cooperative

When you close the door in the face of a reporter, or refuse to provide a document, you may not realize the visceral reaction you trigger. Particularly if the reporter has a legal right to enter that door, or see that document.

As a young reporter, I quickly realized I was too sensitive covering stories that involved death and human tragedy. The emotions got in the way of my objectivity. They prevented my seeing and hearing everything.

So I set out to desensitize myself. I attended executions. As a college student, I covered a shooting one afternoon. The sheriff's deputy asked me if I'd like to attend the autopsy that night. I ate a big dinner and then watched the coroner open the skull and chest cavity of the shooting victim. I knew my exercises were succeeding as I watched, fascinated, with no sense of nausea.

Those exercises were extremely valuable to me later in my reporting career. I was caught in the middle of several riots. In separate incidents, I just happened to be very close when two major industrial accidents occurred.

Each of them killed half a dozen people and injured many others. I was able to walk through the carnage, cool and deliberate, taking notes, shooting pictures. Surgically recording what was happening, so I could give my readers or viewers an objective, clear account.

You Challenge the Reporter

And yet, after 30 years of conditioning to be unemotional on a story, I sometimes felt an adrenaline rush that made my pulse jump and the hair stand up on the back of my neck. It happened whenever someone told me I could not enter. Or that I could not look at a public record.

They challenged my skill as a reporter. They sharpened every combative instinct I possessed. They were hiding something. It was my job to find what they were hiding and tell the entire world.

I was no longer Clark Kent. I stepped into the phone booth and came out – SUPERMAN! Fighting for truth, justice, and the American Way. I usually found what they were hiding and wrote a much larger story about it. I was able to obtain a copy of the document they hid, and put it, full-screen, on the next newscast.

Nixon's Private Meeting

Richard Nixon thought I bugged him during the 1968 Republican Convention. I didn't. But he pulled the trigger that challenged my reporting skill. He announced he would hold a private meeting with all the Southern delegates to discuss his personal position on school busing.

School busing to end racial segregation was a big issue that year. The night before the private meeting, John McMullan, my managing editor, called me over to his desk. "Jones," he said, "You're a good reporter. I want you to find out what Nixon says tomorrow morning about school busing."

Ancient Equipment

I had already infiltrated other meetings at that convention, but I couldn't get into this one. The guards on the door were too good. So I stood out of earshot, looking for delegates I knew. I was carrying an audio tape recorder in a leather case. I wanted someone with credentials to take my recorder into the room.

A portable recorder in those days was heavy. Much too large to hide.

Two delegates refused to help me. The third grinned and said, "Sure. Show me how to turn it on." He slung the tape recorder over his shoulder, in plain sight, flashed his credentials at the guards, and waltzed in.

When Nixon began speaking, my secret agent turned on the recorder. He brought me back a studio-quality tape. The next morning, across the front page of *The Miami Herald*, we stripped the story, then jumped inside for the complete transcript. Nixon had violated the First Commandment – he had tried to lock reporters out of his meeting with the Southern delegates.

1A - Never Lie

There is a sub-commandment here. Never lie. The lie, in the Good Guy/Bad Guy scale, is usually worse than the sin you lie about.

As an investigative reporter in TV, I did whatever I could to get you to talk to me on camera. If you were the villain I thought you were, you would lie. And I could use the lie to destroy you.

In the past, people who lied to reporters could later claim they were misquoted. No longer. With audio and video recording, we hear exactly what you said, and your denial that you said it.

You do not lie once. Your lie is posted on the Internet. You lie on cable television news in every hour's cycle. Again on the local and network news at 6 o'clock; at 11 o'clock. Once more on the morning shows; and again at noon tomorrow.

We may hear the lie played over and over as long as you live. Even after you die. How many times have you seen and heard Richard Nixon say, "I'm not a crook?"

Break some of the other commandments, but don't lie.

2 - Personalize the Organization

Americans do not like big government or corporations. They have a negative mindset for almost anything that smacks of bigness and bureaucracy. They carp about the phone company, the military, lawyers, doctors, public schools – you name it.

But their attitude about any large group changes when they get to know someone inside.

The medical profession is just a big bunch of quacks, my next-door neighbor says. You go in for surgery, they cut off the wrong leg.

The dandruff prescription gives you cancer. Except for my cardiologist. A saint. He saved my life.

Who Are You?

To be successful with the media, you have to become very creative at showing us real people in your organization. All public relations boils down to one simple concept. You need to communicate effectively: Who are you? What do you do?

The media have created myths about virtually every profession and job. The stereotype in Joe Sixpack's mind may be very distorted. That will change only when reporters watch people in your group, close-up, being who they really are — doing what they really do.

People Stories

Virtually all news stories today are people stories. When hurricanes strike, earthquakes rumble, forest fires roar, major rivers flood, we are told the story, one person, one family, one business at a time.

Over the shoulder of the TV correspondent, we can see the townspeople filling sandbags, trying to protect the country store in the Midwest. They've been at it for two days now. One of the people interviewed drove 75 miles to help. Doesn't know the store owner. Just wanted to do something to help.

But the river creeps higher. Then, the sandbag levee breaks. The water rushes in. People run up the hill as the floodwaters surge into the store. The store owner and his neighbors weep. That's just one business, the correspondent tells us somberly. There are a thousands of others whose homes or businesses have been destroyed. As viewers, we understand the story's impact.

3 - Develop Media Contacts

Let's be frank. You develop personal relationships with reporters, photographers and editors so you will get better coverage. As you cultivate the contact, you know that. They know that. But you never say that. It is a strange game in which you collect poker chips which you will someday cash in. But it is done without a word.

As a young reporter, I covered federal court arraignments every morning. I wrote small stories about the procession of car thieves, pimps, moonshiners, draft dodgers and occasional bank robbers who appeared to enter a plea and have their bail set. This tells you how long ago this was. Pimps were prosecuted under the "White Slave Act" that outlawed taking prostitutes across a state line.

Narcotics was not yet on the federal justice system's agenda.

My Doctor, the Defendant

I walked into court one morning, glanced over at the group of defendants, and my jaw dropped. In the group was a prominent local surgeon whom I knew very well. He had corrected my hernia a few months earlier.

Before I could check the docket to see what he was arrested for, his attorney scurried over to me. I knew the attorney, too. He was a state senator I had covered on a daily basis during legislative sessions at the state capitol.

"I'm here representing your doctor," the senator said earnestly. "Please, please don't write a story. It will destroy him."

Now my curiosity was really aroused. What did they get him for?

"Please, Clarence, no story."

Why is he here, senator?

"The game warden caught him. He was hunting with his family. They shot too many ducks. He took the fall."

A Strange Ethic

Normally, I would not have written a game warden arrest story. But that day, I was compelled to. Why? To prove my relationship with the defendant and his attorney could not influence my unbiased, objective coverage. In retrospect, it is a strange ethic.

How do you develop contacts? I used to say, invite them to lunch. But today's news operations are so stretched, most of them go through a fast food drive-through and eat on the way to their next assignment.

Now, I tell clients: If a reporter writes a really good story about you or your organization, it is imperative that you send an e-mail that goes something like this –

That was a superb story. You got everything exactly right, and the story could not have been more fair. Thank you. If I can help you in covering future stories, please let me know.

Good Reporters Need You

Good reporters have many contacts. They depend on them. Contacts call with story tips. Volunteer inside information they know will help on today's major story. And when it's time for a story about your profession or organization, you'll be the one who's quoted. It enhances the positive image of your group. And it won't hurt your career, either.

Remember, all stories are not black and white. Reporters have tremendous power in deciding which stories will be written, and which will be thrown away. Stories take a slant or tone by the choice of a word or a phrase.

Knowing You Changes the Story

When you're having problems, the reporter who knows you personally — respects your competence and integrity — will write a very different story than the reporter who is a stranger.

After you develop contacts, they call you when they get tips suggesting something's wrong at your place. Rumors — and the stories they generate — die when you assure your reporter contact the rumors are false.

When the rumors are true, you must NEVER, NEVER suggest that the reporter owes you something. If you do that, the game is over. You lose all your chips, and a good media contact. You will go directly to the front page or the top of the newscast.

4 - Take Good Stories

The side dish with many American dinners is a generous helping of blood and guts. Night after night, we watch bodies dragged across the screen. Our TV sets are smeared with blood.

If not a massacre, then a plane crash or a terrorist bomb. From every corner of the world, we see tears, pain and human suffering. Clock radios wake us each morning with news of the latest human catastrophe.

Why Always Bad News?

Why do they always bring bad news? Because people *want* to hear and see it. Because they *need* to know.

It is not just morbid curiosity. It is part of our instinct for self-preservation. We *need* to know there is a killer stalking children so we can protect our children. We *want* to know about the design defect in a new airplane so we can take a different flight.

We have always pictured ourselves as caring people who value human life. But because most of us never venture into the ghetto, we do not think about inadequate or unenforced building codes until we see children die there.

We have become so isolated from each other, so insulated from our own neighborhoods, we do not notice problems unless there is a disaster that grabs our attention.

The Media Set the Agenda

Once the news media bring those issues to our attention, we put them on our agenda. The reform of drunk driving laws in the United States swept across the nation in the 1980s as local and national media focused on the terrible toll of death and permanent disability caused by drunk drivers. The same thing happened with environmental pollution, the AIDS epidemic, and child labor laws.

The latest as this is written is a national campaign to stop texting while people drive.

We do not believe a problem exists unless we *see* that problem spotlighted in the news media. And if you are a problem-solver, we will not believe you are doing anything until we *see* you working to solve that problem.

It can be very hard to get your issue on the media's agenda. Until some unexpected event spotlights it. When that happens, you need to respond very quickly. (See **Selling Your Story**)

We Are Insulated from Life

There is another theory, too, about the crowds that gather to stare at people dead, or dying, in the street. In this sterile, high-tech society, most of us have never seen the struggle and wonder of birth, the anguish of a nervous breakdown, the pain and loneliness of old age. Most Americans have never seen someone die.

We hide life's basics in hospitals and nursing homes, or in a code of behavior that says we must never, never let anyone know what we are feeling, or who we really are.

We are terribly alone, and often bored, in our sanitized lives. We need to touch reality. And so we are drawn to – fascinated by – death and violence, human triumph and tragedy.

That is one reason cops, reporters, doctors and lawyers are the central figures in so much of contemporary television drama. Their jobs put them in touch with humanity. We want to look over their shoulders. We envy their opportunity to experience life with the wraps off.

How Much Gore?

In newsrooms everywhere, there is constant debate over just how much to show. How much blood should they let seep into your living room? How close should the camera zoom in on the face of the dead child? In 2013, when the American version of Al Jazeera news began to appear on cable networks, there were columns written about their coverage being much more gory than U.S. audiences were accustomed to.

In American newsrooms, the history has been a gradual increase in how much they show, until the audience begins to complain. Editors and news directors then write memos ordering less blood and gore, and the cycle repeats itself.

The media in this country are always trying to sense just the right balance. Enough to satisfy the viewers' cravings – not so much to disgust them and make them stop watching, listening, or reading. Enough to inform and motivate without turning them off.

We Forget Good News

There is another phenomenon here. We remember the BAD NEWS stories and forget the rest. In every newscast, newspaper or magazine, there are lots of GOOD NEWS stories. Many local stations have their local version of the classic _Charles Kuralt On The Road_ series.

Newspapers were doing it long before Kuralt. Folksy visits with little old ladies who still chop wood for their kitchen stoves. Trained pigs that bring in the newspaper. Kids who have defeated birth defects through sheer courage and determination.

But we forget the story about the cop who saved a life, and remember the one who sold his badge to the dope peddler.

Looking For a 'Kicker'

At the networks, and in more than a thousand TV newsrooms across America, they are searching right now for tonight's "kicker." By decree in the television news industry, every newscast must have a kicker.

The kicker is the last story in the newscast. It is a warm, fuzzy, feel-good, overcome handicaps, success story. It is a story that picks us up and makes us feel that people are basically good, despite what we've been told in the previous 28 minutes. It reinforces the maxims our mothers taught us.

The kicker concept was devised years ago by TV news consultants who interviewed focus groups on their reaction to TV news.

Maybe We Shouldn't Watch

"You know," people in the focus groups would say, "We watch the news every night while we eat dinner. And after all that blood and pain and tears, we get indigestion. We've talked about watching reruns of _Gilligan's Island_ instead of news."

The consultants came up with an easy cure – run a kicker as the last story, and the audience will forget the blood and pain and tears. They'll feel good, and come back tomorrow night. And so virtually every newscast in America ends with a kicker.

Bad News Leaks

The bad news almost always leaks out. You assume that good news leaks, too. It doesn't. Gossips inside your organization take bad news to the media. It is a phenomenon of natural law.

To get positive coverage, you must create a system where everyone in the organization is sensitive to good stories. There must be a way for those ideas to reach the person who is responsible for public relations. It is that person's job to try to sell the good story. Thousands of good stories die every day simply because nobody told the media about them.

5 - Respond Quickly

If you are under attack, YOU MUST RESPOND IMMEDIATELY.

Your lawyer can be a real problem here. Lawyers have learned in the judicial arena that delaying as long as possible will usually help them win. Good legal advice can be horrible media advice. (See **Lawyers & Lawsuits**)

Crisis management used to counsel: Don't say anything until you know as much as possible, and then say as little as possible. With Internet news bulletins, all that has changed. (See **Crisis Management**)

Tylenol's PR Victory

When someone planted cyanide in Tylenol capsules in Chicago, the attorneys at Johnson and Johnson counseled CEO James Burke to say absolutely nothing. The giant corporation would surely be sued for billions of dollars. Whatever was said could come back to haunt them in court. Tylenol was responsible for a third of the corporation's revenue.

Burke thanked his lawyers for their opinion, and then did exactly the opposite. The doors of the corporation were flung open to any reporter who called. Burke went on *The Phil Donahue Show* and took questions from the audience and anonymous callers. Mike Wallace and a *60 Minutes* camera crew were allowed to cover a top-level executive meeting at the height of the crisis, with no holds barred.

Most people in the public relations business consider Burke's gutsy decision the most successful PR coup of the 20th Century. If Burke had followed the legal advice, the company might have gone belly-up.

Scheduling Media Trials

The media do not grant continuances, as the judicial system does. Once the allegation surfaces, the trial starts with an online bulletin. More will come out on tonight's newscasts. The longer versions will be posted online and printed in tomorrow morning's newspaper.

Let's look at what happens when you stonewall. The nightly newscast opens with the anchor saying, "Well, there's more trouble at Widgetworks tonight. Frank Ferrett, our investigative reporter, has been following that story and tonight he has the latest development. Frank – "

Ferrett now assumes the role of prosecutor, or plaintiff's attorney. His opening statement to the jury lays out the charges and allegations. He calls several witnesses to the stand.

In those interviews, they are not cross-examined. Ferrett puts several documents into evidence. We see them on the screen, with key portions circled or enlarged for emphasis. They are not challenged or questioned.

The Prosecution Rests

Then Ferrett rests.

If you have attended courtroom trials, you know that the prosecution or plaintiff presents their case to the jury first. Then the defense has its turn to dispute the allegations.

In this media trial, by stonewalling, the defense does not present any witnesses, or introduce a single piece of evidence. "Officials at Widgetworks refused to talk to us," the script says, as we see them going into their offices, closing the door, covering their faces.

Ferrett now makes his closing argument. He sums up all the evidence, which has not been challenged. The defense chooses not to make a closing argument. Their attorney says curtly, "We will have nothing to say at this time."

Guilty On All Counts

The case goes to the jury. This is a speedy trial process. It is now one minute and 40 seconds since the trial began.

The jury has already decided the verdict. Guilty on all counts.

Several days or weeks later, the attorneys go to the Widgetworks CEO. Let's ask for a rehearing in the media. A new trial. We now have the evidence to prove we are absolutely innocent.

The media court has different rules of procedure. New trials are extremely rare. Once you are cast as the villain in a story, it is difficult – often impossible – to change that image, no matter what you do.

6 - Never Say No Comment

Never say, "No comment."

Why? It violates Commandment Number One. We hear something else. We assume you are hiding something. Evading. If you haven't done anything wrong, why not talk to us?

In reality, there are times when you shouldn't talk to the media. If the detectives tell us too much about the kidnapping, the child may be killed. If the CEO discusses the proposed merger, the negotiations can fall apart.

The grand jury witness who tells reporters what happened in the jury room will be held in contempt and jailed. Your company may have decided that certain policy issues should only be discussed in the media by certain people.

So what do you say when reporters ask questions you shouldn't answer?

I'm Not the Expert in That Area

One of the best ways to dodge a media question is to profess your own ignorance.

"That's a legal question, and I'm not a lawyer."

"That's a medical question, and I'm not a doctor."

"That's an accounting question, and I'm terrible with numbers."

"That's a political issue, and voting is about the only contact I have with politics."

But I Can Take You to the Expert

When you beg off, BE SURE to tell the reporter you can steer him/her to the real expert who CAN answer the question. Another way to use the Home Depot technique I mentioned earlier.

When you do it this way, you save the reporter a lot of time in finding someone to quote in the story. And you carry out the directive within your organization – putting the reporter in touch with the designated spokesperson for that issue.

Other Reasons to Not Talk

Sometimes neither you nor anyone else in your organization will be able to answer because the law forbids it. Explain the law. Give the reporter a copy of the law.

Another reason – Media Morality. Reporters claim to value truth, fairness, the public good. Use those reasons in your response. Explain that because so little is known at this time, you don't want to be inaccurate or unfair.

Explain in great detail how you plan to investigate and find the truth. How partial facts can lead to unfair impressions. How great public harm can result if too much is released now.

I'd love to tell you more about the negotiations, but if I do, this city could lose its chance to host the Super Bowl.

We may not know the cause of this crash for months. It would be a terrible injustice if anyone blames pilot error at this point. We need to keep an open mind if we're going to learn the real reasons for this disaster.

I'll Get Back to You

Close the conversation with a promise that you'll get back to the reporter with a full answer just as soon as you can – as soon as the investigation is completed; the negotiations finished; the arrest made; the contract signed.

Be sure you keep that promise. In real life, if you are skillful at the media game, you will also learn how to talk to reporters in confidence. (See **Off-the-Record**)

7 - It's OK to Say 'I Don't Know'

If you don't know the answer to a reporter's question, don't try to fake it. Don't assume your employees did what they were trained to do. Don't use statistics unless you're absolutely sure of the numbers. Reporters don't expect you to have the Google data base in your head. But they do expect you to know where the information is, and to be able to retrieve it quickly.

Include Staff in the Interview

I recommend that you include one or more staff members in any complicated interview or news conference. (See **Interviews** and **News Conferences** chapters) It is the staffers' job to answer complicated technical questions in their area of expertise. Or to fetch the records that can answer the reporter's question.

"I can't remember the exact figure," you tell the reporter.

(Then to the staffer) "But Bill, if you'll get the 1996 committee report, that'll have the number in it. (Back to the reporter) We can give you those numbers before you leave the building."

In this way, you appear helpful, open, cooperative.

8 - Confess & Repent

There is another attitude deeply rooted in our tribal psyche. We respect those who take responsibility for their mistakes.

We will forgive you for a multitude of mistakes if you admit them, say you're sorry, and tell us what you're going to do to make things right.

How different our heritage would be if George Washington had said to his father, "Cherry tree? What cherry tree?" In deciding who is the good guy and who the bad guy, the lie, the cover-up, the insensitivity are greater sins than the crime itself.

Political Confessions

Richard Nixon was disgraced and lost the presidency because of the Watergate cover-up, not the original crime. No evidence ever surfaced that he was involved in planning the burglary itself.

Bill Clinton denied "having sexual relations with that woman" for almost a year before he finally confessed an improper relationship with Monica Lewinsky. But that still did not get him off the hook. *He failed to say he was sorry* for what he did.

And that he would not be unfaithful again.

Five days before the election in 2000, the story surfaced that George W. Bush had been arrested for drunk driving in 1976. His confession and repentance within hours was a classic.

George Bush's Confession

"I've told the people I made mistakes in the past," Bush told a news conference. "And this was a mistake. What I did was wrong, and I've corrected that."

He detailed once more his 1986 decision to become a teetotaler. He talked about counseling his children to never drink and drive.

Bush said he admitted he had been drinking to the Kennebunkport officer who stopped him, then paid a $150 fine the same night. His Maine driving privileges were revoked for a short time.

He followed the classic formula: Confess, repent, accept your punishment, say you're sorry, do what you can to make things right.

Cong. Anthony Weiner's Confession

Democratic New York Cong. Anthony Weiner was accused on May 28, 2011, of sending text messages to women that included photographs of himself in his underwear, sexually aroused. The story first broke in a conservative online blog.

Weiner at first said his Twitter account must have been hacked; that he could not say for sure whose private parts were in the photos; that allegations of his having online erotic contact with women outside his marriage were "outrageous." The story went national.

On June 6, 2011, Weiner held a news conference to confirm that he had "sexted" with more than one woman, but would not resign his seat in Congress.

The news stories continued, and 10 days later, he did resign, promising to go into therapy to correct his behavior "so that my wife and I can continue to heal from the damage I have caused."

Weiner's Race for NYC Mayor

On May 22, 2013, Weiner announced his candidacy to be mayor of New York City. The news media quickly learned that Weiner – despite his promise to quit – had continued to have erotic online contact with other women after he left Congress.

Some of the women were identified, and gave detailed interviews about their relationships with Weiner. One took advantage of the publicity and produced a pornographic video that went on sale. It did not include her with Weiner. In interviews designed to promote her video, she said she had only had phone and texting sex with Weiner.

The Clinton Connection

The story stayed on the front burner of national media partly because Weiner's wife was a close friend of Hillary Clinton; worked for her when she was Secretary of State, and was at the time a staff member for Clinton's probable Presidential race in 2016.

His wife stood by Weiner for a time, then no longer appeared in public with him. Weiner's campaign became a media circus as he was confronted by voters during campaign stops. Some of the shouting matches were recorded on video. They made their way to You Tube, cable comedy shows, local and network newscasts. He steadily dropped in the polls.

In the Democratic primary, Weiner ran last among the five candidates, drawing only five per cent of the vote. As he was driven away from his "victory party" on election night, he gave news photographers the finger.

The Statute of Limitations

My confess-and-repent commandment has a statute of limitations. You cannot confess the same sin too often. The Weiner case demonstrated that there is a limit to the public's willingness to forgive the same sins repeatedly.

9 - Use the Big Dump

When you have bad news to dump, dump it all at once.

Don't let it dribble out. That prolongs the stories and multiplies the damage. Once you decide to confess and repent, you may be tempted to confess only part of your sins. That's human nature.

But then the media will find follow-up stories and repeat the original allegations as they add tiny bits of new information. With each new story, the damage increases.

Months or years from now, a tiny detail that has not previously surfaced will be discovered by an enterprising reporter. **New Evidence Uncovered**, the anchors and bloggers scream. You appear to have hidden evidence of your guilt. Obstructed justice.

Tear Gas at Waco

Before the FBI's final assault on the Branch Dividian compound near Waco, Texas, in 1993, agents fired three rounds of tear gas at a bunker about 75 yards from the living quarters. Hours later, the compound burned to the ground, killing about 80 people. In the investigations that followed, the FBI did not reveal the gas.

Six years later, the failure to disclose was discovered. That led to the appointment of Special Counsel John Danforth, who ruled in 2000 that the tear gas did not start the fire. He concluded:

> *Although the government did nothing evil on April 19, 1993, the failure of some of its employees to fully and openly disclose to the American people the use of pyrotechnic devices undermined public confidence in government and caused real damage to our country.*

But the late disclosure made most news consumers believe the special investigation was simply a cover-up.

No Time or Space

Often, much of what you dump will not even be written if you dump it immediately. Its news value expands if you wait.

In breaking coverage, there will not be time on the air or space in print to cover everything you dump. The leftovers become old, stale, insignificant. You can move on past the problem. As a consultant, I have had remarkable success with clients who used this technique.

Dirt that you disclose is always less newsworthy than dirt reporters dig themselves. So long as the news media believe there is more to be mined, they will continue to dig. That's their job.

10 - Prepare, Prepare, Prepare

Most organizations have carefully-prepared disaster plans. They conduct fire drills, tornado drills, earthquake drills, hurricane drills. They buy insurance and prepare for the worst.

It is much more likely that you or your organization will experience a media disaster before you have a fire or an earthquake or a tornado. Yet few companies or government agencies have prepared for that more likely hazard.

A first step is a written media policy. Key spokespeople ought to be trained to deal with the media. They need to practice those skills often. Otherwise they get rusty. They lose their reflexes.

Rehearse Major Interviews

All major interviews should be rehearsed, preferably on camera. Get staff or friends to play the role of reporters.

You need to see and hear your responses to the tough questions. And get honest critiques of your performance.

Never, never do a major news conference without a rehearsal.

What Would We Do If?

To prepare for future, predictable media crises, hypothetical incidents should be created and studied by your command staff. Like:

- **What would we do**, in terms of media coverage, if a major internal embezzlement was discovered?
- **How will our police department react** if one of our officers makes a major mistake and kills an innocent person?
- **What will our hospital say** if a major slip-up occurs and a famous patient dies?
- **How will the bank explain** an employee who is charged with helping drug smugglers launder money?
- **What will the judge say** when he releases a career criminal, and that man murders a little girl within a week?
- **How will we cope** with hundreds of reporters and photogra-

phers if an employee we fired returns with an assault rifle and begins shooting?

- **What will we say** if government officials fail to order an evacuation in time, and a forest fire, hurricane or flood destroys dozens of homes and kills a lot of people?

All these things happen with some regularity. We are human. Our systems are imperfect. If we have not prepared for disaster, it can easily destroy us.

Oh, That Won't Happen Here

You may believe that you live far from the madding crowd. That you will never have to go through the torment of being at the center of a national/international story.

I'm sure that's what the sheriff in rural Union County, South Carolina (population 10,000) thought before Susan Smith strapped her kids in their car seats and pushed her automobile down the boat ramp into a lake in 1994. Then the media tsunami hit.

The Sandy Hook Massacre

Officials in Newtown, Connecticut were not prepared, either, for the news media tidal wave that overwhelmed the community after the Sandy Hook School slaughter in December, 2012.

The only bright spot in these kinds of tragedies is that the media attention leads to studies of how government coped, and how it could have been handled better.

At Columbine High School in Colorado in 1999, first responders waited for backup while shots were still being fired inside the school. That was standard, recommended law enforcement policy at the time.

But lives might have been saved if they had gone in immediately and confronted the shooters. That is now the standard for law enforcement in these kinds of situations. And it has already saved some lives.

Media Coverage of Major Cases

No court case before had ever been covered as massively and intensely as the 1995 O.J. Simpson murder trial. There were so many reporters and photographers, there was not enough room for all of them to stand along the pathways that led in and out of the courthouse.

So they built two and three-story platforms with construction scaffolding to accommodate the hundreds of journalists.

I participated in a three-day study of the media's trial coverage that was organized later by a California judges' group. They wanted to find better ways to handle future trials that will draw that kind of massive media coverage.

They Invade From All Directions

When these kinds of stories break, no matter where you live, several hundred reporters, photographers and technicians will be on your doorstep within about three hours. There can easily be more than a thousand by the next morning.

They come by helicopter, by chartered jet, by boat, by motorcycle. They use disguises to get in close. And they are equipped with the latest electronics to gain an advantage over their competition.

During the coverage of a series of murders at the University of Florida, police at one of the crime scenes thought a reporter across the street was using a portable satellite dish.

It was actually a parabolic microphone, which could pick up conversations inside the area where reporters and photographers were not allowed.

When an officer walked over to check it out, the reporter fled.

The Transport of Last Resort

"I don't think the media have arrived by parachute yet, for one of these gang bangs," I told a seminar group several years ago.

"Wrong," a woman in the class said. "A photographer tried to parachute into Madonna's wedding to shoot pictures for the tabloids."

I stand corrected.

SKILLS

DEFENDING YOURSELF

Ambush Interviews And Other Traps

It may be a bright spring morning. You will have no warning, no inclination to be cautious. As you leave your house and unlock the car in the driveway, you probably will not notice the van parked halfway up the block.

Even if you are wary, you will not see the hidden camera recording everything you do. As you come out of the driveway, the van follows, a discreet half-block behind.

You Will Not Suspect

You drive to your usual parking spot. You do not notice the same van, parked nearby. Two people jump out the rear door. One is shouldering a video camera. From behind, they come at a trot. You never hear them.

The reporter steps out in front of you, blocking the sidewalk. At that instant, the photographer bursts ahead. With a start, you see them for the first time. The reporter says, "Good morning, I'm Mike Wallette from Channel Seven. I'd like to talk to you about your company's financial crisis."

A Difficult Time

It is a difficult time, no matter how cool you are. The surprise of the ambush is a jolt. You look frightened. Pulse racing. Breathing short and hard.

You have only an instant to decide what to do. You may act reflexively. Here are five options:

Ambush Interview Options

1. **Punch out the reporter**, swing your briefcase at the camera, and run like crazy to get away.

2. **Keep walking,** but duck your head and put your hand in front of the camera lens. The photographer will stick with you. The reporter will fire non-stop questions, into the lobby, all the way up the elevator, into the reception area of your office. Somewhere along the way, you will probably utter a "No comment" as you grit your teeth and stare straight ahead.

3. **Stop dead in your tracks**. "I have no idea what you're talking about. Now if you'll excuse me, I have to get to work."

4. **Say: "Good morning, Mike**. Gee, if you wanta talk to me, come on up and I'll see when I can squeeze you in today. If you'd called, I woulda been glad to give you an appointment." In this scenario, the reporter will still keep the camera rolling, and fire questions all the way to the office. He is afraid you will renege on the appointment.

5. **Say: "I'll be glad to give you an interview,** but let's talk first, off camera. If you're sincere in wanting to talk to me – in doing a fair, accurate story – and not trying to make me look like some kind of criminal, turn off the camera and come on up. I'll get us a cup of coffee."

They Win, You Lose

The ambush technique has been used, and abused, throughout the history of investigative reporting on television. Radio and print reporters ambush their targets, too. On radio, we can hear the fear in your voice.

We can't see your terror in print or radio. But reporters in those media will tell us, in their own words, how frightened and guilty you looked, then give us your response.

Reporters know they can usually count on the ambush to make the target of their story look bad. At the same time, they're carrying out their obligation to get your side of the issue. It's heads they win, tails you lose.

Some veteran reporters who ambushed their targets for years now question its fairness. The late Mike Wallace of *60 Minutes* (probably the most-feared reporter in America) said late in his career that he would use the ambush technique only if the target refused to give him an interview.

The audience has become more sophisticated. Part of the rethinking involves not wanting to look like a TV bully picking on a defenseless little guy. The audience believes television has enormous power. If reporters and camera crews abuse that power the audience will side with the target.

They Will Persist

But television is words and pictures – mostly pictures. If they are to write words about you, they must have your picture. Good investigative reporters take great pride in their persistence. If they truly want your picture, they will get it. Unless you lock yourself in your basement for the next year. Even then, there are ways to get to you, or smoke you out. So the only question is, what do you say when they catch up with you?

Let's go back and examine your options in an ambush.

- **Punch out the reporter** – This makes great video. You can be sure every moment will be played on the air. At least three or four times. You will enhance your reputation as a hoodlum. Few people will side with you. They will decide you are guilty, as charged. If there is another side to the story, it won't be told. The reporter can have you arrested for assault and battery. There are excellent grounds for a civil suit. The proof for both criminal and civil action is all on video. You will boost the reporter's career immeasurably. The video will follow you to your grave. It will be resurrected and replayed as part of your obituary.

- **Refuse to talk, keep walking** – In most cases, this will also make you look like a nasty guy with something to hide. Remember – television, like politics, is often a matter of impressions, not exact words.

- **"Excuse me, I have to get to work"** – Here, you've said *something*. The audience knows you're human. But you'll still seem cold, elusive, probably guilty. This option has many modifications. If you don't want to give a full interview or answer questions, you can take this opportunity to get at least a brief statement on the air. Saying nothing at all, or "No comment" is like taking the Fifth Amendment. Many people will assume you're guilty. Otherwise, why not talk to the reporter? (See **Ten Commandments**)

His question has suggested there are financial problems in your company. You can say something like:

We've become concerned about a cash flow problem in the last week or so, and we're working on it. I'm confident the company is not in danger. We're negotiating now with some new investors, and I'm sure we'll work it out. But that is a delicate thing. I really can't say very much about it. If you'll give me your name and phone number, I'll be glad to call you when we come to an agreement.

This answer will guarantee a string of questions, that you can politely refuse to answer, repeating your reason for declining. You may want to answer some of them.

- **Make an interview appointment** – If you're polite, the reporter tends to return the courtesy. In making the appointment, try to find out as much as you can about the story. You may have to do some research to answer some of the questions. Delaying for several hours will give you time to prepare. (See **Interview Guidelines**)

- **Let's talk first, off-camera** – This is usually the best choice if you're concerned about getting a fair shake from the reporter. News people work a lot on instinct. From experience, they tend to be suspicious. Anything you do that appears to evade, to delay, to deceive or cover up will feed their suspicion that you're a bad guy.

Lay It All Out

During that off-camera talk, if you're not guilty, lay all your cards on the table. That may be the end of the interview, and the story.

The off-camera interview gives you a better opportunity to fully explain your side of the issue. The reporter may not have all the facts. Collect documents and bring in staff, if that's necessary for a full presentation.

There is another element of self-defense that you should keep in mind. If you are a public official or public figure you cannot collect in a libel suit unless the media publish or broadcast something false about you *with malice.*

The U.S. Supreme Court says you must prove they had "reckless disregard for truth." (See more about damage to you, and how to prove it, in **Libel**)

Libel Suit Strategy

As a public official, you must not only prove it was false – you must prove the reporter did a sloppy job; had information showing the story was false, but ignored it.

If you meet with reporters or editors to refute their suspicions, make sure you can prove what you told them. Tape record the meeting. Have a reliable witness present. Get a receipt for any documents you provide.

Keeping Reporters Honest

If you are concerned about the integrity of the reporter who asks for an interview, it might be a good idea to take the same precautions. Have a staff member sit in on the interview. Keep track of the records you provide. Make your own audio or video recording of the entire interview.

Let the reporter know you're recording it. Reporters who know you have the recording are much more careful in quoting you. With a transcript of the entire interview, you can make a major dent in the reporter's career if the story is not fair and accurate.

Editors are very concerned these days about reporters who can't write truthfully. They're a $20 million lawsuit, just waiting for the right assignment.

If, in asking for the off-camera conversation, you say you'll talk later on camera, or for quotes, don't back out. If you'll lie about giving an interview, surely you'll lie about more important things.

Reporters are always afraid to delay on-camera and on-the-record interviews. Too many people change their minds.

The Lie Will Never Die

Remember: Reporters and cameras are excellent lie detectors. Like the polygraph, the camera can sometimes be fooled.

But if you're caught in a recorded lie, the media will never forget. It will be played over and over again. You can't say you were misquoted. The lie is there, to haunt you forever.

The audience is also smart enough to know when you're blatantly evading a question. In many cases, it's better to say you can't answer — and why — than to sidestep the question.

A good reporter, like a good courtroom lawyer, usually knows the answer before the question is asked.

Police investigators go to school to learn how to decipher body English so they'll know when suspects are lying, or have guilty knowledge of a crime. Reporters learn the same skills through experience.

Almost unconsciously, they constantly monitor your fidgets and eye-blinks; what you're doing with your hands; whether your breathing is relaxed or shallow; whether you're sweating more than the temperature calls for; how tightly your legs are crossed; whether you avoid eye contact.

A real problem for TV interviews is fear of the camera. Stage fright gives the same physical symptoms as guilt and deception. You may be signaling that you're Public Enemy Number One, when you've really just got a bad case of stage fright.

Print's Hidden Cameras

Print reporters usually don't have a camera in their hands as they conduct the interview. But they have a camera in their heads.

As they sit there, making notes, they're often not writing what you're *saying*. They're writing what you're *showing*. Body English. Eye contact or movement. Fidgets. Sweat. How you reacted to that last question.

They will go back to their keyboards and create a picture of you with *words*. And that can be more distorted than video.

Take More Control

I urge clients to take more control of the interview – print or broadcast. If the room is hot and you're sweating, suggest that you take a break, turn off the TV lights, and let the air conditioner catch up. If you realize you made a mistake in something you said several sentences back, tell the reporter:

You know, I told you a couple of minutes ago we're planning to spend $54 million on that project next year. My memory was bad. Ask me that question again and I'll give you the correct figure. Or –

I told you we are planning to spend $54 million on that project next year. I'm not sure of that figure. Let's stop a minute while I check the numbers. Or –

My answer to that question you asked about next year's budget was awfully wordy and convoluted. If you ask me that question again, I'll try to give you a better, shorter answer.

Deciding whether to talk to an investigative reporter is very complex unless the charges are absolutely false. If the reporter has been misled – if an understandably false conclusion has been drawn from the evidence – then you should definitely talk.

Not Guilty: A True Story

A real-life example: An anonymous caller once told me I should investigate why a federal agency paid the city attorney twice as much for his house as it paid the owners of other, identical houses that were condemned for a government project on the same block.

That should be easy to prove, I thought. So I went to property records at the courthouse and discovered the tip was accurate. The lots on the block were all the same size.

The houses were all similar, built at the same time, carried on the tax assessor's rolls at virtually the same value.

Yet, when the government agency bought the entire block, it paid the city attorney – who had good political connections – twice as much as anybody else. It seemed to be an open-and-shut case.

I went to the city attorney to get his response – the last step before broadcasting the story.

The Target's Response

"Yeah, they paid me twice as much," the city attorney said. "But I didn't get the money. You see, I'd leased the house to a color photo processing company.

"The lease said if they ever had to move for any reason during the term of the lease, I would have to pay for their relocation and build them another processing plant. I've got a copy of the lease in my file, if you'd like to read it."

Oh. Three days of research down the tubes. No story.

When You've Goofed

If the story the reporter is pursuing involves your making an honest mistake, it's almost always best to say so.

Past the point of admitting an honest mistake, the decision on whether to be interviewed for quotes or on camera gets stickier. It depends on how serious the accusation, and your involvement in it. In a sense, you're on trial.

The reporter will present the charges, and the evidence against you, to the readers/audience who serve as the jury.

If the defense decides to rest with no evidence, no witnesses, we have been conditioned to believe that is a concession of guilt.

Conning the Reporter

Looking guilty by refusing to talk to a reporter may be better than taking the stand and convincing the audience you're not only guilty, you're a liar as well. Career con men often amazed me by agreeing to a sit-down interview. It was a heady challenge, to see if they could out-smart, out-talk the reporter. But difficult to win. Reporters always have the last word.

If there are people and documents that support your side of the controversy, the reporter may not know about them unless you disclose them. Refusing to talk will ensure a one-sided story.

What Are You Hiding?

It's hard to draw lines for every situation. But generally, reporters believe people have something to hide if they try to keep them out of offices, or meetings, or records. The more open you can be with reporters, the more honest and fair they tend to be with you.

Remember – whatever the reporter does that is underhanded, or belligerent – any kind of behavior that might raise eyebrows – will never be broadcast or written. Anything you do that is less than flattering will be preserved for all the world to see. We will see it, hear it, read about it many, many times.

There are other kinds of surprises reporters spring. They call and ask permission to shoot video in your business or office. "Just general footage to go with a story we're doing." Or reporters who say they need a general briefing on a benign subject. Once inside, you discover they have entered by subterfuge.

Sandbag Questions

In the middle of what you thought would be a friendly interview, the reporter gets nasty. Springs a completely different subject on you. A sort of verbal ambush. The sandbag question.

"Didn't your corporation fire four women last year simply because they were pregnant?" the reporter snarls. You may not have the foggiest idea.

Too often, people who don't know the answer to a surprise question will try to answer it anyhow, saying what they assume or hope is true. Later, when it turns out they're wrong, it looks like they were lying or trying to cover up.

If you don't know, say so. And tell the reporter you'll get the answer.

Become More Aggressive

If the reporter's question is a complete fishing expedition that unfairly or inaccurately impugns your character or motives, you should become very aggressive and adamant in your response. If you're not insulted by a completely false, damaging suggestion, the reporter will believe the allegation is true.

Controlled anger is the key here. Never give an interview when you're truly in a rage. You'll say something you'll later regret. Let us see a seething resentment that the reporter would stoop so low. A clear, positive statement, delivered with great intensity –

This company is not a sexist company, and I defy you to find a single shred of evidence that would even suggest such a thing.

Or –

I have never beaten my wife. I have never abused my wife, either physically or mentally, and I resent your throwing that kind of question into this interview. You are completely off-base, and I'm sure your viewers/readers/listeners will come to the same conclusion if you report such a scurrilous question – and have the integrity to include my answer.

How Are Things Going?

If a reporter asks you how things are going in your company or department, be careful. The landscape is littered with the carcasses of executives who proudly said everything was hunky-dory, not knowing the reporter already had proof of a massive problem, getting worse by the minute.

Typical of this kind of mousetrap was a TV interview with a hospital administrator, bragging that his institution ran a model program to deal with infectious waste.

In his office, he gave a lengthy lecture, telling how waste was carefully controlled within the hospital until it was incinerated at another site. The temperatures there, he said, would destroy any infectious virus or bacteria. Nobody could possibly be harmed.

The TV reporter asked him to do the interview on the loading dock outside the receiving department because the light was better there.

On the loading dock, as the administrator was talking, he was unaware the camera was zooming over his shoulder to a red bag of bloody waste, lying untended in the open. ZAPP!

If the question is a general one, about how things are going, the best answer is, "Pretty good, but I'm always trying to make them better. Do you have any specific area in mind?"

That will make the reporter, who knows something you don't, rephrase the question, getting closer to the real issue. If a reporter surprises you with an allegation that is news to you, you should say something like:

I'm not aware of that, but if that were true, I'd be very concerned about it. If you know something I don't, please tell me, so I can do something about it.

Unload Everything

If you knew about the problem and have been quietly working on it, this is the time to unload everything.

There aren't any secrets now, so you might as well look impressive as a manager or executive who makes things right. If you say you're working on it, but don't say how, the reporter will suspect you began your work 30 seconds ago.

An accurate statement of your position can be written in a way that telegraphs the reporter's suspicion –

The CEO said he's been investigating the allegation for two months, but refused to say who is conducting the probe; how they're doing it, or what they've found.

You may want to make a deal with the reporter, to keep things quiet a little longer. This will involve a confidential agreement, in which you persuade the reporter to delay the story.

To do this, you'll have to trade something. The price will usually be information that would not be available without this special agreement.

Beat Them to the Punch

Once you learn that you have a problem, you may be able to solve it before the story is published or broadcast. The story is not nearly as damaging if the problem has already been solved.

Call the reporter and announce what you've done, with thanks for bringing the problem to your attention.

If you really want to zap the reporter, hold a news conference and give the entire story – problem and solution – to the competition before the investigative report can be printed or aired.

I call this counter-punching. (See **News Conferences**)

Air Your Own Dirty Linen

You will almost always look better announcing internal problems before the media find them. If they find them, they tend to make the story bigger and more sensational. It's a way to pat themselves on the back. If you announce it, they are inclined to downplay it because they should have found it themselves. It makes them look slow or incompetent. A problem that no longer exists is not a very good news story.

Answering Allegations

When there is an allegation that is damaging to you or your organization, here is a generic response that can be modified to fit almost any situation. This should be done quickly, to include your point of view in the first story. You need to tell the media:

- **Your concern about the allegation**. You try to run a first-class operation here. Any complaint or allegation is a major concern.

- **What you're going to do about it**. Here, I suggest you give as much detail as possible. If you're launching an immediate investigation, tell us how many people will be involved. How will they conduct their investigation? Will outside investigators be brought in?

- **A general timetable**. If you can't be sure how long the investigation will take, make it clear that this is only an estimate. You may find more to investigate than you expect. If you see you won't finish by that time, tell the news media well in advance, with a clear explanation of why it's taking longer than you expected. A timetable will prevent some of the nagging calls from reporters – "Are we there yet?"

- **Your personal investment in finding the truth**. Here, your reputation for being open and fair with the media is critical if you are to be credible.

- **A reminder that the allegation may be false**. Unfortunately, the reporting of allegations in the media are often heard and read as a conviction. The reputations and lives of innocent people can be destroyed.

- **You will disclose the truth when you find it**. Investigations are meaningless if the public never knows what you found.

- **You will see that justice is done; any problems corrected**. If the allegation is false, the suspended employee will be reinstated. If it is true, you will personally help the prosecutor.

- **You will review procedure and training.** Sometimes the system is at fault, not the people in it. Sometimes they have not been trained to handle a crisis. The system should be blamed, not those who were caught up in it.

SKILLS

GOOD GUYS/BAD GUYS

Saints and Sinners
As the Media See Them

I often tell my seminar audiences I teach human relations more than news media relations. How you deal with a reporter in the first few minutes will have enormous impact on how you are portrayed.

Reporters claim to be unbiased and objective. But no matter how hard they try to meet that goal, they are inevitably affected by personal experience and their impressions of you.

Morality Plays

Since the morality plays of ancient Greece, the central theme of drama in most cultures has been: Good Guys vs. Bad Guys.

The news media in modern America have developed their own version of the morality play. The story usually does not say outright that you're a Saint or Sinner.

But the trivia that is noted in words or images will make the point very clearly. A lot that is communicated in news stories is written between the lines that are written; and in the cutaway shots of video news.

Reporters' Radar

Reporters develop a kind of personality radar. A sixth sense that quickly judges you and casts you on one side or the other.

Some media consultants claim reporters make that critical assessment less than a minute after first contact with an interview subject. I think I did that as a reporter.

Reporters usually know something about you before they arrive. From research, they may know a great deal about you. So they arrive with a preconceived attitude. Then they watch you very closely. Your facial expressions, your body language, the words you choose can quickly confirm their suspicions.

The Snowball Effect

Of course, they're sometimes wrong. But that impression will be passed on to their readers, viewers and listeners. Other journalists see the story, or dig it up as part of their preparation for your next interview. They arrive, already believing that you are who the previous stories said you were.

The snowball gathers speed. Can the political candidate really be as dumb as the media make him out to be? Is this movie star really as difficult on the set as the tabloids say? Is this mutual fund manager as brilliant as *The Wall Street Journal* reports? This rock star as promiscuous?

Once something has been written about you, other reporters observe and listen to you very closely, looking for some nuance that will corroborate what has already been reported.

Perception Becomes Reality

In a media-driven society, the first reporter's perception can rapidly become reality. Conventional wisdom.

In the cowboy movies of the 30s and 40s, Good Guys wore white hats; Bad Guys, black hats. There were no shades of gray. Good Guys did not smoke, drink or swear. They were chivalrous, brave, honest, idealistic. No matter how dusty the trail, their rhinestone-studded outfits looked like they'd just come from the cleaners.

Bad Guys smoked foul cigars, slugged down rot-gut whisky and muttered oaths behind scowling eyebrows.

They slapped women around, were bullies and cowards (it always took two or three to duke it out with one Good Guy), cheated and stole from their partners and their mothers. You knew immediately, who was a Good Guy or a Bad Guy.

The news media have set up a very similar morality play. I've isolated eight traits – good and bad – that reporters will look for, and judge you by. Notice how each trait dissolves into the next. There are others, but these are the most common.

 # 1 - Sensitive and Caring

Good Guys care about people. They forget about costs when they can ease human pain and suffering. They place human and family needs above profits or career.

Bad Guys lust for money and power. When was the last time a movie or novel portrayed the president of a multinational corporation as a warm, loving, sensitive individual who cares about employees, children, puppies, clean air and water?

Isolated Executives Out of Touch

American mythology says CEOs care only about:

self/power/career/company/stockholders/profit.

Michael Douglas' role in the movie *Wall Street* is the stereotype. CEOs like the character Douglas played reach the top by stabbing colleagues in the back, climbing up the pyramid of dead bodies to the executive suite.

This is one of the myths that can be easily reinforced by news media stories. In television or online, it can be done without saying a word. The edited video speaks eloquently. An example:

In his documentary *Roger and Me,* reporter Michael Moore intercut back and forth between video of General Motors CEO Roger Smith celebrating at a company Christmas party while on that same day, tearful GM employees who had been laid off were being evicted from their homes.

Reporters Tend to Be Liberals

Are most reporters liberals? Yes. Why?

Reporters tend to identify with society's victims. Victims are at the center of many news stories. Victims of natural disasters, medical malpractice, corporate policy, government bumbling.

The victims cooperate with reporters, because the story may help them. Young reporters spend time with them, get to know them as human beings. Imprinting takes place, just as it does with other young animals.

Reporters' vision of the world is formed in those early years. Most young reporters have never spent even an hour with a corporate CEO, a general, a governor, a cabinet secretary, or the director of the CIA.

The Imprinting of Young Reporters

To young reporters, power people seem distant, two-dimensional figures who are too busy to make themselves accessible to the media. Reporters never see their human side.

They become easy targets. Reporters grow up and become editors. Media stories continue to reinforce society's myths.

2 - David vs. Goliath

Good Guys are today's Davids battling Goliath. That value was planted in our genes when the scraggly colonists who founded the country dared to declare their independence and go to war with England, the most powerful nation in the world at that time.

We admire the town marshal in the Wild West who would go out alone to face the outlaw in the street. We love today's soccer mom who fights City Hall; the dark horse who wins the Kentucky Derby or the political campaign.

Show me two kids whose lemonade stand is shut down by the Health Department, but come back and argue with the health inspector, and I will show you a You Tube video that goes viral.

Bad Guys are bullies. They take advantage of little people. They abuse their power and get great pleasure doing it. They boast about their position and wealth. Too much money, too much power are never enough.

Donald Trump plays into this stereotype, like a wrestler who creates a character the crowd will love to hate. The news media help him promote the illusion.

Ralph Nader - Media Saint

In his heyday, the young Ralph Nader was probably our most revered media saint. Nader, the poor, bright eccentric who did not even have a car, a driver's license or a telephone, wrote *Unsafe at Any Speed* in 1965 – a book attacking General Motors.

The book contended that GM cars had deadly design flaws because the company was more interested in shaving costs than saving lives (Bad Guy Trait # 1).

In news stories and Congressional investigations, Nader was portrayed as a modern-day David, carefully choosing the stones for his slingshot while Goliath GM set out to destroy him and discredit his book.

With a lot of help from the news media, Nader hit GM squarely between the eyes. The corporate giant was staggered. Corvairs went out of production. Seat belts and head rests become standard equipment.

The bigger they are, the harder they fall.

Years later, when Nader tried to have home smoke alarms banned because they are radioactive, the media gave him a pass. Reporters did little to explore his claims or his numbers. As it turned out, you would need to wear a smoke alarm on your head for about 200 years to absorb the same amount of radiation you receive in a dental X-ray.

3 - Risk-Takers

Good Guys are risk-takers. Adventurers. They live on the edge. They thumb their nose at the boss, or company policy, if it feels good.

They are particularly valued by the media if they are willing to risk their own job security to help someone else (Trait # 1 again). They are not afraid to fail. They are confident they can find another job if they lose this one.

Bad Guys will sit silently and watch terrible atrocities take place. This is a side effect of Trait # 1. Bad Guys are security-centered. More interested in keeping job, power, money, status than in doing good. They are job cowards.

Fire Me, I Don't Care

Newspaper reporters have historically been paid so little they had very little fear of losing their jobs. At an early age, they become fiercely independent. They have great contempt for the executive who puts job above convictions, whether in government or the private sector.

I would never have left my job as Washington Correspondent for the *Miami Herald* to go over to television news if I had not been so desperately poor. Within a year, I had doubled my salary in a city with lower costs of living.

Looking forward to retirement is not a part of most reporters' personal value system. People who do, in their thinking, are burned out or incompetent. If you work in government, reporters will walk in with a bias.

In TV, Firing is No Disgrace

Television news is one of the few professions where being fired is not a disgrace. It comes with the territory. When ratings stall or begin to slip, management shuffles people, looking for a winning combination. The shuffling is constant. Television people, unlike those in newspapers, work on short-term contracts. Some of television's brightest, most successful stars were fired from TV jobs early in their careers.

4 - Rugged Individualists

Good Guys in media stories are often rugged individualists who do things their way. They are rebels with glorious causes. They hate red tape, and will find ingenious ways to short-circuit the system to get things done. They love to tweak the nose of pompous authority.

Eccentrics who run for public office or inventors working on the Original Perpetual Motion Machine often get warm, amused, but-you-have-to-admire-them coverage.

Reporters identify with them because good reporting requires a lot of individualism. Reporters in the field have very little close supervision.

Reporters develop tough skins. If reporters are hated and despised, they consider the source and wear it as a badge of honor.

Consider the Source

One of my early TV investigative reports showed a series of checks that had been cashed by a public official. They came from a man he had appointed to a political position, and were cashed regularly about the same time the appointee drew his government fees.

The local newspaper picked up the story, and quoted the official as saying, "I'd hate to be a guy like Clarence Jones, who goes around looking under toilet seats for stories."

My response was, "Where else do you find assholes?"

Good reporters are self-starters. Those who are innovative, willing to try anything, often get the story. They leave their habit-bound competitors in the dust.

Bad Guys Are Conformists

This is a side effect of traits # 1 and # 3. Bad Guys are often people who do things by the rules, no matter what the cost in human terms. They believe that one broken rule can lead to the breakdown of the entire system. They are anal. Obsessively cautious.

Bad Guys wallow in red tape. During the Cold War, this part of life in the Soviet Union was frequently reported as a way to deride communism. It is still popular in reporting about new, inexperienced officials in Third World countries.

Journalists sneer at this value system. They believe that those who follow it are corporate drones, cannon fodder, bumbling bureaucrats. Bad Guys slavishly follow the rules because they are not bright enough to turn out the lights without a company manual.

This journalistic prejudice often appears between the lines in stories dealing with religious zealots, union organizers, law enforcement and military officers.

5 - Idealists

Good Guys are often portrayed as idealists who sight on a personal star and never waver. They are persistent. Dedicated. To get gold stars in media coverage, the reporter does not have to agree with your ideals, so long as you truly believe them.

Bad Guys are quickly tagged in media stories if they have no real conscience or moral value. They do whatever the job, the boss, the party require. They swing from one position to another, twisting in the political or corporate winds.

They don't seem to notice that the position they embrace today was yesterday's anathema. Or to realize that *The Daily Show with John Stewart* has an incredible library of video that will quickly show and satirize their hypocrisy.

6 - Candid and Open

Good Guys are candid and open. They have nothing to hide. Their lives and organizations are open books. One of the most disarming tactics you can take with a reporter who seems antagonistic is to offer access to everything. It jams the media morality radar.

Good Guys sometimes make mistakes, but they're big enough to take responsibility for the mistake and put it right. Rather than blame somebody, or invent an alibi, the Good Guy boss also takes responsibility for the errors of those he leads. Like Harry Truman's famous desk sign in the oval office: **The Buck Stops Here**.

Gov. Christie Takes Responsibility

In September, 2013, the Port Authority of New York and New Jersey closed two of the three lanes that lead to the George Washington Bridge in Fort Lee, New Jersey. That led to days of massive traffic jams in Fort Lee as drivers tried to use the bridge to go into Manhattan.

Democratic members of a New Jersey state legislative committee began to investigate rumors that the traffic jam was engineered by Republican Gov. Chris Christie to retaliate for the Ft. Lee mayor's failure to endorse Christie in his fall campaign for re-election. Christie had persuaded other Democratic mayors to endorse him in his landslide win, but not the Ft. Lee mayor.

In early January, 2014, the committee released a series of subpoenaed e-mails indicating the lane enclosures had been arranged by Christie's deputy chief of staff and one of the governor's appointees at the Port Authority.

Christie's Agonizing Apology

In a highly unusual news conference that lasted for two hours, Christie condemned the traffic jam and repeatedly said he had nothing whatever to do with it. But as the boss, he said he had to accept blame for the political revenge arranged by his staff. He fired the staffer. Until this emerged, Christie was the leading contender among Republicans to run for President in 2016.The agonizing apology was his desperate effort to be the good guy in the scandal and maintain his viability as a Presidential candidate.

Bad Guys are secretive and evasive. They do not want their pictures taken. They run. They refuse to disclose information about themselves or their organization. They sic their bodyguards or attack dogs on journalists.

To be truly memorialized as a Bad Guy, put your hand over the camera lens and push the photographer out of your office. When I expected my target would do this, I always asked for a big photographer who loved contact sports. He could keep the camera rolling while a bouncer was shoving him out the door.

Bad Guys try to cover their mistakes and blame somebody else when things go wrong.

 # 7 - A Sense of Humor

Good Guys take things in stride. They can laugh at their own mistakes. They tell the uptight people around them to chill. Good Guys can take a ribbing. It means somebody likes them.

Bad Guys are so full of themselves they can hardly fit on the thrones they've built to make sure the world understands how important they are.

Their employees are afraid to tell them the truth about anything that would challenge the boss' self-serving perceptions. A joke about the boss can be a firing offense.

 # 8 - Expect to Win

Good Guys are fierce competitors, even when they're at a severe disadvantage. They pick themselves up and charge once more against enormous odds. They expect to win. They never give up.

Bad Guys portrayed in some stories see themselves as losers. Wimps. They're burned out. They don't even try any more. Reporters believe it is their duty to put losers out of their misery.

Deception was the deadly sin that destroyed Richard Nixon's presidency and forever changed his place in history. There has never been a shred of evidence to suggest that Nixon participated in hatching the plot to break into the Democratic Party office in the Watergate Building. Or that he knew about it in advance.

The cover-up *after* the burglary was the deadly sin Nixon committed that could not be forgiven.

The investigation of Bill Clinton by independent prosecutor Kenneth Starr quickly switched from the finances at a failed savings and loan association to Clinton's dishonesty under oath about sex with White House intern Monica Lewinsky. That became the major thrust of the House impeachment proceedings.

Sin # 3 - Insensitivity

Insensitivity is the sin of not caring what happens to a helpless victim. Particularly to a child or an animal. The lack of human compassion. Some of history's worst monsters were portrayed in the media as having no sympathy for those who were suffering.

War criminals are guilty of insensitivity. Otherwise, they could not participate in the atrocities. They are portrayed as evil personified – the Nazis during World War II; the slaughter of civilians in Viet Nam; the "ethnic cleansing" in Bosnia and Rwanda, the alleged use of chemical weapons in Syria in 2013.

One of the most chilling stories that made Saddam Hussein a monster in the public's eye was a video that showed him speaking to an auditorium full of military officers. Hussein told the audience that he was about to unmask the traitors in the room. Then he would call out a name and tell the man to stand. A group of soldiers would go to the officer. As Hussein watched with a sadistic smile, the trembling man would be led out of the auditorium and then shot.

Civil disobedience, as practiced by Martin Luther King Jr. and Mahatma Gandhi, goaded military and police forces to act harshly against defenseless demonstrators. Both King and Gandhi understood that the quickest way to change bad law is to force government to carry it out.

They knew they would eventually win the battle if they could set up situations that showed the insensitivity of government officials as they enforced racial segregation laws.

It is a powerful, perennial human interest story to show wealthy, powerful people who do not seem to care about the poor and hungry.

Police brutality is another form of insensitivity often spotlighted by the media.

Sin # 4 - Abuse of Power

Power can be abused in many ways. It is a wonderful media story because it often combines hypocrisy, deception, insensitivity.

By definition, this is a venal act of the powerful. Those in public office. In the public eye. The wealthy. Those we trusted with our votes, our money and/or the lives of those we love.

The sexual molestation of children by Catholic priests in their parishes, and the bishops' doing little to stop it, became a worldwide media story because of this cardinal sin.

Sometimes the story is the bribery of public officials. Sometimes it is misuse of semi-public money. The conviction of William Arimony for misusing United Way funds was that kind of case, where he spent money that had been donated for the poor on luxurious trans-Atlantic travel and his girlfriends.

Betraying Clients' Trust

Bernie Madoff's swindling of investment clients who trusted him with their life savings was one of these stories.

It broke in 2008, and was followed by a long string of similar frauds that were uncovered all over the country. Once this kind of story breaks, ANY similar offense gets more coverage than it would have in the past.

Stories about outrageously expensive conferences and bonuses for IRS employees began to surface in 2012, followed by the disclosure that some IRS offices had targeted applications for tax-exempt status if those in the organization had ties to the Tea Party.

Reporters are especially sensitive to influence peddling. Special treatment for friends of the powerful. It brings out a sense of outrage in readers, viewers and listeners.

The reporter who uncovers the abuse of power becomes a very powerful figure. A folk hero of sorts. A slayer of dragons.

Sin # 5 - Waste

Waste also involves a kind of power abuse. Usually the waste of money, resources, or human lives is done by someone in power. Damage to environmental resources that belong to the public and cannot be recovered is now a deadly media sin.

Stories about government and military purchasing often involve this sin. Five-hundred-dollar hammers. Expensive, ergonomic paper clips designed by industrial engineers and consulting firms will always get massive media coverage.

Politicians have learned to target these same sins because it gives them massive media exposure. One of the first to capitalize on the idea was the late U.S. Sen. William Proxmire of Wisconsin.

He became a major media figure in the 1970s by periodically giving a cynical "Golden Fleece" award for wasteful government projects. He continued the awards until he retired in 1988.News media outlets of all kinds love the concept, and continue Proxmire's mission.

Sin # 6 - Incompetence

The news media love to show how stupid people and procedures in large organizations can be. Government and the military are favorite targets for stories that feature bumbling bureaucrats.

Once the media focus on an agency that has stumbled badly, the system demands a scapegoat – a sacrificial lamb to appease the angry media gods. The media get credit for the kill; politicians get credit for cleaning up the mess; but the basic problem is still there, waiting for someone else to make the same mistake.

Sin # 7 - Job Cowardice

Bravery under fire has always been the highest value within the military. To run from battle during most recorded military history was considered a capital offense. In the past, many military codes of conduct gave superior officers the authority to shoot cowards who refused to fight.

Members of Congress are typically portrayed now as clowns who will do anything to get re-elected. Including the selling of their souls to lobbyists who finance their re-election campaigns.

Profiles in Courage

Then-U.S. Sen. John F. Kennedy won the Pulitzer Prize in 1957 for his book, "Profiles in Courage." It was a collection of essays about past senators who had taken unpopular positions at great personal and political risk.

In recent years, both political and media voices have deplored the lack of similar courage in current politics. The media code of honor has historically made heroes of those who risk their careers for a noble cause they believed in.

Whistle blowers were sometimes awarded the Media Medal of Honor. Particularly if their disclosures cost them their jobs.

Mega-Leaks to the Media

So the massive leaks in 2012 and 2013 of WikiLeaks, Army Private Bradley (Chelsea) Manning, and National Security Agency contractor Edward Snowden put many media outlets in a bind.

The information disclosed by the three was widely published by the media worldwide, but many news outlets could not bring themselves to praise the whistleblowers.

Why not? Because government and military sources said the intelligence leaks created huge national security problems. The news media were torn between conflicting ethics:

- The public's right to know
- Serving the public good, and
- Helping the whistleblowers commit crimes by distributing information that was classified and may not have served the public good

SKILLS

INTERVIEW GUIDELINES

Quotable Quotes That Won't Be Misquoted

When reporters want an interview, the most basic rule is:

If possible, **Give Yourself Time to Think Before You Speak.**

The quotes that people regret are usually said reflexively, in the traumatic surge of anger or shock that follows a rude surprise or sudden loss. If you can stall for even five minutes, you'll do a better job of speaking for yourself or your organization.

If Your Pulse Races, Pause

The rule is especially critical if the reporter's first question makes your adrenaline surge or pulse rate jump. You won't think well in fight-or-flight mode. You need a little time to get back to normal. To get your thoughts together.

If the reporter shows up unexpectedly, find an excuse to delay for a few minutes. If the reporter calls on the phone, say "I'm incredibly busy right now." (Which is true. You've got a lot to do in the next few minutes to get ready for this interview.) "Can I call you back in about 10 minutes?"

In that brief conversation, get a grasp of what the story is about. Then hang up and spend 10 minutes getting ready.

Check With Staff

During that 10-minute reprieve before you call the reporter back, check with your staff. "A reporter just called. The lead they're pursuing caught me completely by surprise. Is there something I should know?" The delay rule isn't necessary if the reporter's request is for simple information that poses no threat. But if you react viscerally, buy some time.

One Sentence Without a Breath

Use the time to decide what you really want to say. Boil it down to one sentence you can speak without taking a breath. That one sentence should become the base of the entire interview.

Always go into an interview with one central idea you want to get across. And repeat it often. In normal conversation, if you repeat yourself, we wonder if you're getting senile. But in a news interview, if you say it often enough, at least one of those quotes or sound bites that states the central idea is more likely to be used.

In normal conversation, we build up to our conclusion. We lay the groundwork first, before we get to the point. In media interviews, the process is reversed.

Always give the conclusion first. Then tell us how you got there. This takes practice. It's like telling a joke, punch line first.

Telephone Interviews

Many of your routine interviews will be on the telephone. With today's shortage of staff, a lot of reporter time is saved. Be careful. A reporter on the telephone is less threatening than in person. Many people are less cautious when they can't see the reporter. They say things they later regret.

Try standing while you talk on the telephone. This keeps some people more alert and aware that anything they say may be quoted. One of my clients looks into a mirror during telephone interviews, because facial expressions affect the energy and tone of your voice.

Do Important Interviews in Person

If the interview is critical to you or your organization, *push to do it in person, if possible*. It's much easier for you to get a handle on the reporter and the story angle if you're face to face.

If you don't recognize the name or voice of the reporter on the phone and the story is sensitive, use the delay tactic. When you return the call, look up the number, to make sure the call is legitimate.

The number the caller gave you may bypass the switchboard. Private detectives, insurance investigators, business competitors and operatives in opposing political camps sometimes pose as journalists.

Are You Being Recorded?

You should know whether the reporter is recording the interview at the other end of the phone line.

In some states, you don't have to tell the other party you're recording. In states with more restrictive laws, failure to notify the other person is a crime. (See **Privacy**)

Ambushes on Radio

Some radio talk show hosts delight in calling people – particularly public officials – for an instant, live interview. FCC regulations require them to tell you you're on the air. Which means instant stress. It's radio's version of the ambush interview.

Review the ambush interview portion in the chapter on **Defending Yourself**. The suggestions for dealing with a TV ambush can easily be adapted for radio.

Once you begin a telephone or face-to-face interview, (after you've had time to think about what you want to say) the next rule is:

Conduct a Pre-Interview Interview

From the first contact, where you arranged to delay the interview for a few minutes, you know generally what the story is about. When you call back, or the reporter arrives, expand that inquiry.

Weave it into the social chat that begins most conversations. While a video photographer is setting up the camera and microphones, talk to the reporter about the story at hand.

If you understand what the reporter is after, you can save a lot of time and anxiety. In this conversation before the shorthand pad, camera or audio recorder is at work, try to learn some basics:

- What exactly is the story assignment, and who thought it up
- When the story will run, and the deadline for finishing it
- How much time or space the story will be given
- Who else the reporter has interviewed
- Other research that's been done
- The reporter's knowledge and preconceptions on this subject
- Some idea of the reporter's intelligence and experience

What is the Story About?

This is a very important thing, so you can judge whether the reporter is working on a preconceived concept that may be misguided. If that's the case, you'll have to work very hard to swing the story in another direction.

Particularly if the misconception came from the reporter's editor. The reporter doesn't want to go back empty-handed. If this story was the boss's idea, you'll have to work *very* hard to convince the reporter the story concept should be abandoned.

Are They Here To Hurt You?

Before the real interview begins, you should have a good idea about whether the reporter is here to gut you, or simply needs your quotes to fill out the story. To give it authority and credibility.

Young, inexperienced reporters are rarely given tough investigative assignments. If the reporter seems very sharp, and seems to know a lot about the subject, that can be a warning flag.

As an investigative reporter, the interview with my target was the last stop before I wrote the story. I wanted to know as much as possible before the interview, so I'd know if my target was lying.

Good investigative reporters can also con you into believing they're dumb and innocent, so you'll talk more freely. They'll respond with "no kidding," or "really!" to things they already know.

That makes you want to tell them more.

You May Need More Data

You may learn in the pre-interview interview that you need to gather some more written information to help you recall exact facts and figures.

If you discover the reporter knows very little about the subject matter, you have a great opportunity to steer the story your way. The way you structure the pre-interview-interview can strongly influence the questions when the real interview begins.

The room will sound like an echo chamber. The reporter will ask you questions that let you repeat what you said before the scribbling or recording began. That's all the reporter knows to ask.

Avoid the temptation to educate the reporter too much.

Pre-interview Ethics

It is considered unethical for a reporter to tell you exactly what the questions will be. The interview is supposed to be a spontaneous conversation. To rehearse either questions or answers is staging. But there is a fine line here.

Most reporters consider it proper to tell you the subject they're covering and broad areas they want to explore in the interview. Find out as much as you can. Remember, the reporter will also be sizing you up. And the impression you give in those first few minutes will be critical to the slant on the story.

Have Your Staff Handy

For stories that involve a lot of numbers or complicated, technical details, it's a good idea to have your staff experts sit in. They can hand you documents when you grope for the right number.

You can ask them to fetch details the reporter needs for the story. Having a friend in your corner may also make you feel more at ease and less threatened.

The Certain Question

I estimate that at least 35,000 people are interviewed by the news media in America every day.

This is hard to believe, but I already know *exactly* what the reporters are going to ask in the vast majority of those interviews. It doesn't matter where the interview takes place. Doesn't matter who the reporter is – who is being interviewed – doesn't even matter what the story is about. I know the key question:

How Do You Feel?

How do you feel?

The perennial question was institutionalized by a television news story formula – the Sony Sandwich. In some shops, it's called a "Package" story. (See diagram and other details in **Interviews-On Camera**) It has now spread to all news media.

The meat in the Sony Sandwich is the interview in the middle. It gives the story flavor, substance, emotion, humanity. It is sandwiched between the facts the reporter gives at the beginning, and the conclusion the reporter draws at the end.

The Sony Sandwich

The reporter sets up the basic facts for the reader, the viewer, the listener. Then we go to the central figure in the story.

How did you feel when you learned you have terminal cancer?

- **How does it feel to lose** after 24 years in the Senate?

- **How does it feel to win** the New York lottery?

- **How do you feel about** the Mayor's proposal?

The Top on the Sandwich

Then the reporter puts the top on the sandwich by drawing the conclusion, telling us where the story goes from here. Print reporters once laughed and made fun of broadcast reporters who always asked,

"How do you feel?" But you'll hear most newspaper and magazine reporters asking it now, too.

Television changed the format for all news media. Newspaper stories today are much shorter. They use more pictures and graphics. To compress their stories — just as broadcasters do — they've adapted the Sony Sandwich to print.

If you can learn how to speak media language, and give a formula response to the formula question, you almost guarantee they'll use what you said, exactly as you said it. No editing, misquoting or taking out of context.

Disguising the Question

Reporters are so aware of their trite question, they try to disguise it. But it is still the search for the human perspective.

Tell me — what were you thinking when the section of the airplane just ahead of you blew out?

When the officer walked in the door with your baby in his arms, what was that like?

Someday, we may go through that same experience. How does it feel to do what you did ... see what you saw ... hear what you heard? We want to know what it was like to be there.

What Was It Like to be There?

Since humans wandered the earth, passing on tribal history around a camp fire, that has always been the essence of storytelling. "You should have been there the day we killed the mammoth!"

If a ghost story is told skillfully, I shudder and look over my shoulder in the dark. Tell me the story of a blind child who can see for the first time, and I get a lump in my throat. When she tells me what she's feeling, I may cry.

Interviews inject the human perspective in news stories. Few people outside the news media understand this basic purpose for the question that will elicit the quote or the sound bite.

You're the Expert

Often, the person being interviewed is an authority, whose assessment of the situation is important to our understanding. In court testimony, witnesses are not allowed to express their opinions or feelings. Unless they are certified as expert witnesses.

Then they can tell the jury how they feel about the evidence.

When you become the subject of a media interview, it is often because you're the expert witness who can explain so ordinary folks can understand. Experts are needed to put things in perspective.

Verbal Shorthand

Words that express feeling tell us a lot very quickly. They are verbal shorthand — headline words that communicate like no others in our language. They get to the heart of the story, and set us up to hear and understand your reasons for feeling that way.

When the reporter asks how you feel about something, it can mean:

What do you think about this?

What is your reaction to the situation?

What is your opinion or prediction?

But we will understand your response much more clearly if you tell us HOW YOU FEEL. Backed up by WHY YOU FEEL THAT WAY.

News stories are so formularized, it is almost a paint-by-numbers process. I've collected a list of words, from which at least one will fit virtually any news interview. They're in alphabetic order. In the print version of his book, the words are formatted in columns. But e-book formatting can't handle columns or tables. So I've grouped them as best I can. The next time you're getting ready for an interview, take your pick.

Words That Say How You Feel

A Abandoned, Abused, Afraid, Aggravated, Alienated, Alone, Amazed, Ambushed, Amused, Angry, Anxious, Ashamed, Astonished, Astounded

B Besieged, Betrayed, Blessed, Bored, Bothered, Burned out

C Caught in the middle, Certain, Challenged, Chagrined, Cheated, Concerned, Confident, Conflicted, Confused, Conned, Cozy, Crazy

D Dazzled, Deceived, Delighted, Deserted, Disappointed, Dismayed, Disorganized, Distraught, Distressed, Doubtful

E Ecstatic, Elated Embarrassed, Encouraged, Energized, Enthusiastic, Envious, Excited, Exhausted, Exposed

F Fearful, Fed up, Forgiving, Frantic, Free, Friendly, Frightened

G Glad, Grateful, Gratified, Great!, Grief-stricken, Guilty, Gutted

H Happy, Harried, Hate (I hate it!), Haunted, Helpless, High, Hollow, Homicidal, Honored, Hoodwinked, Hopeful, Hopeless, Horrendous, Horrible, Horrified, Hounded, Humble, Humiliated, Hungry, Hurt

I Impatient, Impotent, Ineffective, Insecure, Inspired, Insulted, Intrigued, Invaded, Irritated, Isolated

J Jaded, Jealous, Joyful, Jubilant, Justified

L Livid, Lonely, Love (I love it!), Loser (Like a loser), Lucky

M Mad, Maligned, Marvelous, Misguided, Misunderstood, Mortified, Mystified

N Naked, Nauseated, Neglected, Nostalgic

O Offended, On top of the world, Optimistic, Out of touch, Outgunned, Outnumbered, Outraged, Overjoyed, Overwhelmed

P Paranoid, Parental, Peeved, Pessimistic, Pleased, Powerful, Powerless, Proud, Put down, Put out, Puzzled

R Ready, Recharged Regretful, Rejoice, Rejuvenated, Relieved, Reminiscent, Resentful, Responsive, Rested

S Sad, Safe, Sated, Satisfied, Saturated, Scared, Secure, Shocked, Sick, Skeptical, Sorry, Stupid, Supportive, Sure, Surprised, Surrounded, Swindled, Sympathetic

T Targeted, Terrible, Terrific, Terrified, Tired, Torn, Trampled, Traumatized

U Uncertain, Undaunted, Under control, Underwhelmed, Undone, Unforgiving, Unjustly accused, Unsatisfied, Unwanted, Unworthy, Used

V Victimized, Victorious, Vulnerable

W Warm, Weak, Weary, Weepy, Winner (Like a winner), Wonderful, Worried, Worn out, Wounded

Condition Words

Some of the feeling words in the list above are not real feelings. They are *conditions* that convey several emotions or strong feelings. When you say, "I feel betrayed," you tell us — with just one word — that you feel angry, sad, deceived, abandoned, badly used. If you feel "surrounded," you are feeling insecure, outnumbered, overwhelmed, vulnerable.

Interviews add flavor and spice to a story. Once the conflict, the catastrophe, the crisis is established, we want to hear the participants. We want to know how they feel about it.

Quotes they'll use for sure:

- **"I'm embarrassed.** The mayor has made a terrible mistake."

- **"It's frightening.** This guy is completely bonkers."

- **"I was terribly sad** just before we hit the water, thinking that I'd never see my son again."

- **"Fantastic.** After the surgery, I feel years younger."

A Word of Caution:

There are a few rare times when showing too much emotion on camera can be hazardous to your career. We don't expect a homicide detective to break down at a murder scene. Unless the victim is his partner, or his own child.

Edmund Muskie may have lost his campaign for the Democratic presidential nomination in 1972 when he became teary during a speech in the snow in New Hampshire.

He was defending his wife after a newspaper editorial defamed her. In those days, we expected Presidents to be tougher. It was part of the macho model.

The Rules Have Changed

But society's expectations of Presidential candidates are changing. I trace the beginning of that trend to the televised 1988 Presidential debates. Democratic nominee Gov. Michael Dukakis — an opponent of capital punishment — was asked how he would feel on that issue if his wife was a rape or murder victim.

Dukakis showed no emotion. His answer was academic, distant, unfeeling. People in the audience thought: *What sort of man is this, who doesn't react to the idea of his wife being raped or killed?* His nickname became "Zorba the accountant."

A Kinder, Gentler President

In that same campaign, George Bush's media experts asked focus groups what kind of President they wanted. A woman in one of the groups said she would like a "kinder, gentler President." Based on that research, Bush used her exact words when he promised during campaign speeches to be a "kinder, gentler President."

In television interviews, Bush began to talk about his family as sensitive, caring people. The Bushes, he said, show what they feel. Sometimes the men are not afraid to cry. He was drawing a sharp contrast between himself and Dukakis.

During Thanksgiving dinner with the troops in Saudi Arabia in 1990 – before the ground war was launched in Kuwait – Bush wiped his eyes as he talked about the young soldiers he would soon send into battle. Some of them would not come back.

Schwarzkopf's Tears

One of the most dramatic demonstrations of how the rules were changing came during Barbara Walters' *20/20* interview in Saudi Arabia with Army Gen. Norman Schwarzkopf. It was 1991, shortly after the Persian Gulf War ended.

"Stormin' Norman" talked about how much he missed his family, half a world away, and the tears welled in his eyes. When Walters asked about his dead father, (who had also been a general) the tears came again. "I'm sure he'd be proud of me," Schwarzkopf said, his lower lip trembling.

There was a long pause in the interview. "You know," Walters said, "The old picture of generals – is that generals don't cry."

"Sure they do," Schwarzkopf shot back, naming Civil War generals Ulysses Grant and William Tecumseh Sherman. "And these were the tough old guys. Lee cried at the loss of human life, the pressures that were brought to bear. Lincoln cried. Frankly, any man that doesn't cry scares me a little bit. I don't think I would like a man who was incapable of enough emotion to get tears in his eyes every now and then. That's not a human being."

September 11, 2001

The real sea change of attitude about showing emotion publicly in America came after the terrorist attacks of Sept. 11, 2001. Police officers, firefighters, and reporters wept openly on television as the news media covered the carnage and its aftermath.

And so did those watching the story unfold. Americans became more human, more able to express their caring and their grief.

It is common as this book goes to press to see fathers cry when they talk about sons and daughters killed in mass shootings. Soldiers break down remembering buddies they lost in Iraq and Afghanistan.

Each night during the CBS coverage of the massacre at the Sandy Hook Elementary School in December, 2012, anchor Scott Pelley often seemed close to tears.

And we sometimes see Barrack Obama wipe his eyes when he talks about horrific events. It has finally become OK for men in this culture to be human and express their feelings.

Gender Conflicts

But gender conflicts remain. In their childhood, men who are now middle-aged or older were taught not to show their feelings. Men don't cry, we were told. Men don't show fear, or pain or love.

Women are caught in a crossfire as the culture shifts. Cry at the office and the men in power are likely to invoke the old standards that said showing emotion was a sign of weakness. "Just like a woman," they mutter under their breath.

America still has many double standards for men and women. An angry man is called aggressive. Bold. An angry woman may be called shrill. Bitchy. Emotionally unstable.

That's why seeing yourself on video is so important. Everybody has a different threshold in expressing how you feel without appearing to go overboard.

Show Your Humanity

I don't want you to cry in every interview. My goal for you is to show your humanity. If you do, by crafting quotes that tell us how you feel, those quotes will be used, and used *exactly* as you spoke them. In context. No misquotes.

The formula that reporters use in choosing quotes and sound bites is so predictable, I make a bet with my seminar groups:

Send me a transcript of your next media interview. Print, radio, television. Doesn't matter. I'll bet you dinner I can pick the quote or sound bite the reporter uses.

It will always be the quote that tells us how you feel. I've made that bet with more than 100,000 people. Haven't lost yet.

SKILLS

INTERVIEWS - BROADCAST

It's a Conversation While The Camera Eavesdrops

Listening to one end of a telephone conversation, you can usually tell who's on the other end. If it's long distance, most people tend to talk louder. Subconsciously, they think they have to speak up to be heard clearly a thousand miles away.

We slow down if we sense that the person at the other end of the line is old, or has a foreign accent. We change the tone of our voice if we're talking to a child, or a lover. The same kind of subtle changes take place when people talk in front of cameras and microphones.

An Audience of One or Two

If they know they're being recorded, many people reflexively talk as if they're making a speech at a civic club. There may be half a million people – perhaps more – out there listening. With a crowd that large, you want to make sure the people in the back row hear what you have to say.

But they're not all in one, humongous auditorium.

The broadcast audience is one or two people. It is Joe Sixpack and Aunt Millie, sitting in the living room or kitchen, six or eight feet from the TV set. The online audience, watching an on-camera interview as it plays on a computer monitor or smart phone, is usually only one person.

Radio listeners are very close. Probably in a car. One of the secrets of broadcast interviews is to keep that tiny audience of one or two people in mind.

Recorded interviews are very intimate. The zoom lens on a camera invades your zone of privacy, moving even closer than a person would, to focus on a drop of sweat, the flared nostrils, the gritted teeth. Radio's microphone puts the person speaking at our shoulder. Sometimes, it whispers in our ear. In the best of these interviews, the people talking seem unaware that we are eavesdropping.

Think of the Living Room

To prepare for a radio or on-camera interview, change your mind-set so you're talking to that small, intimate audience. It may help you to think of a real living room, and real people.

In your mind, think of the reporter as someone else, and that may help. Your spouse, a neighbor, the cashier at the restaurant where you have lunch, the bartender who knows you well enough that you no longer have to order. In your head, talk to *them*, not the reporter.

Changing your mind-set will change your body language. In the noise and confusion of a political rally, a candidate holds up his arms and flashes a big grin to communicate warmth and charm as he tries to woo the crowd.

He uses a very different kind of smile and body language later that night if he's trying to seduce a beautiful woman sitting across the table in a quiet restaurant.

If you think of the large broadcast audience, you will instinctively project your voice to reach them. You don't need to do that. But it takes a lot of practice to squelch that natural inclination. Today's microphones are so sensitive they can pick up a whisper across a room.

The Camera Spots Phonies

The camera detects phonies. Bring to the conversation the real person inside you, not a front. Let your emotions show, if they're real. You can be angry, or sad, pleased with yourself or your organization, shocked or dismayed at what you've just learned.

The reporter does not want many facts or figures when you are on camera. There is not enough time. You probably don't have the skill to boil down the facts extemporaneously.

Even experienced reporters have trouble doing that. To condense them to 20 or 30 seconds may require a half-hour at the keyboard, eliminating a word, rewriting a phrase to save another three or four seconds.

A famous quote, attributed to several people: "I'm writing you a long letter because I didn't have time to write a short one."

The Sony Sandwich

Most on-camera interviews wind up as the meat in a Sony Sandwich. What you say in the story – the "sound bite" – will be sandwiched between a reporter's introduction and the reporter's summary or conclusion.

The purpose of the interview is to add the personal, human perspective. You are being interviewed because you were THERE and can tell us what it was like. Or because you're an expert.

In virtually every interview, the reporter at some point will ask "How you feel about .. ." The broad, trite "How do you feel?" question seems absurd and intrusive if you have just witnessed a disaster, or learned that a loved one is missing. Or dead.

"How do you think I feel?" grief-stricken people sometimes shriek. The reporter may apologize. They are habit-bound by that one-size-fits-all question. But it really does work for most interviews, because it can mean so many things. Like:

- **What is your assessment**/ prediction/ analysis of this?
- **How are you coping**?
- **What is your reaction** to this?
- **Take us inside**, where you are/ were/ plan to be.
- **What was it like** to be there?

Building the Sony Sandwich

The beginning of the Sony Sandwich is the bottom half of the bun. The reporter quickly sketches the scenario. It is a summary of the story. We hear the reporter's voice over video of what he is describing. If it is a hotel fire, he tells us about it while we see the flames and smoke.

The Meat of the Sandwich

The meat of the sandwich – the interview – will be with the fire chief, the hotel manager or – best of all – a hotel guest who escaped the fire. It is the interview that gives the story excitement, emotion and drama.

Now we know what it was like inside the burning building, and how the guest was rescued.

The reporter may edit a series of interviews together – different people giving their reactions to, or perspectives on, the same incident. Sometimes the interviews may pit one point of view against another.

Editing Distills Conflict

When sound bites are edited against each other, the conflict is distilled quickly and effectively. Instead of watching a ten-round boxing match – mostly dancing, feinting and clinches – we get to see and hear just the knockdowns.

Occasionally, if the sound bite is very strong, it will be placed at the beginning of the reporter's story. In this position, it is usually very short. Then a longer portion of the interview, expanding that opening bite, goes in the middle of the story.

Job Conditioning

People in certain professions are interviewed more often than others. The ones who get the hang of it find reporters coming back to them on future stories.

They make the reporter's job so much easier. Unfortunately, the experience and training for some careers tend to make some people poor interviewees.

Doctors, lawyers, scientists and accountants are often terrible on camera. They speak their own, professional jargon, as though we, too, had Ph.Ds in their specialty.

They provide dry, lengthy, logical, step-by-step reasoning, with lots of footnotes. The subject matter is complicated. The simplest question takes three minutes to answer.

This kind of interview is a horror to edit. The people interviewed call the next day to complain that they were quoted out of context.

Human Synthesizers

On camera, police and military officers often become voice synthesizers spouting official reports.

The cop who just caught two armed robbers after a shootout speaks very normally until the camera is rolling. Then he says something like:

My unit was dispatched to 4481 Ocean Street at nineteen hundred hours. As I approached, Code Three, I observed two white males rapidly exiting the dispatched location in an easterly direction with weapons drawn. When the perpetrators observed my vehicle, they commenced firing. One projectile impacted my vehicle. I then returned fire.

What Did He Say?

What did he say? I think he said:

"As I rolled up, these two guys with guns were running out of the jewelry store. They saw the patrol car and started shooting. When the first bullet hit the windshield, I jumped out and shot back."

Which leads to the reporter's question:

"You ever been shot at before?"

"Nope."

"How did it feel?"

"Scared the hell out of me."

Guess which section of the interview is certain to be included in the Sony Sandwich. Police officers, doctors, lawyers, accountants have been conditioned to talk like robots by writing too many reports, and by testifying in court.

On the witness stand, you are not allowed to express how you feel. Just the facts, please.

What Are We Afraid Of?

Survey after survey has shown that stage fright is America's biggest fear. Bigger than war, cancer, divorce, unemployment, dying in a plane crash. What are we so afraid of onstage?

I think we're afraid of looking stupid.

People in front of a camera often talk non-conversation because they're afraid they'll make a mistake and look dumb. They're not sure the boss will like the idea of their talking to a TV reporter. So they cram and memorize, to avoid mistakes.

Walking Encyclopedias

They want to be walking encyclopedias. Instead, they look like stupid drones. The one thing they fear most.

Other people deal with the stress by drawing themselves into tight little knots, making their voices small and flat, as they speak every word very carefully. They pause a lot. On TV or radio, they are deadly. More than five seconds, and everybody in the audience will be snoring.

What Does It All Mean?

The closing section of the Sony Sandwich is also formularized. The reporter sums up the story. Tells us what to expect next. Here's the form:

What does it all mean? Only time will tell. I'm Tom Trite, Channel Four, Action News.

Listen to how TV reporters almost always build their closing standups around this basic blueprint. The close to an interview with the Speaker of the House may say:

Does this mean the tax bill is dead? We won't know until the conference committee issues its final report – probably tomorrow. I'm Claudia Cliche ... yada, yada.

Or this close to a story about a plane crash:

Was the explosion aboard the plane caused by a bomb, or was it mechanical failure? Safety Board sources say it will take months of meticulous detective work before they know for sure. I'm Bill Bromide ... yada, yada.

Inverted Pyramid Formula

The old news story formula developed by newspapers in the 1800s was called the inverted pyramid. At the beginning of the story – into the first paragraph, if possible – the reporter tried to cram all the important facts. Who, What, When, Where, Why.

From that broad beginning, the story narrowed down to a point at the bottom where unimportant details were thrown in. Pure trivia.

The inverted pyramid had several practical purposes.

Correspondents in faraway places (St. Louis was the edge of civilization in those days) sent their stories to New York or Washington by telegraph.

Practical Reasons for the Pyramid

The telegraph was not very reliable.

So if the telegraph failed sometime during transmission, the home office would at least have the important stuff. If the entire story reached the newspaper, readers knew they could drop off in mid-story and not miss anything critical.

Easy to Edit

Each page of the newspaper was designed by an editor, using rough word counts to measure each story, and how it would fit on the page. In those days, newspaper stories were set in lead type.

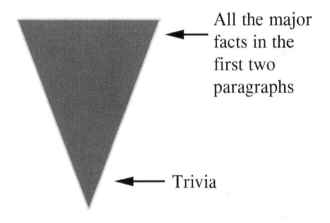

All the major facts in the first two paragraphs

Trivia

Down in the composing room, fit each line of type into a page form, as the editor had designed it. But the word count measurement system was not very precise.

If a story didn't fit, the employees in the composing room were told to cut from the bottom until it did fit. Just throw away the last paragraph. Maybe two paragraphs. There were huge barrels where the lead type was thrown to be recycled.

They were not editors. They were craftsmen. As a result, stories sometimes seemed to have been edited with a meat ax.

The Sandwich Spreads

Because the Sony Sandwich works so well, both radio and newspapers have adopted it for their own use. Almost all radio stories that include an interview will be in Sony Sandwich form.

Newspaper stories have become much shorter, and the Sony Sandwich has been adopted by newspapers, too.

Examine the stories in *USA Today*. A quick summary of the facts in the first paragraph or two, setting up the quotes of the person interviewed in paragraphs three and four. Then two or three paragraphs to tell us what it all means, and that only time will tell.

The Sony Sandwich formula will help you craft a quote that will be used exactly as you said it – without editing – in newspapers, radio or TV.

If you can learn to do this, you'll seldom be misquoted or taken out of context. You'll find your interviews go very quickly. As soon as the reporter hears the magic, formula quote, it's time to pack up and move on to the next assignment.

The FACE Formula

I invented the FACE Formula for the first printed edition of this book in 1983 to help readers remember what kind of quote the reporter is looking for. If you're the subject of the interview, we're going to see your face on TV, and probably your picture in the newspaper. In radio, we'll imagine what you look like. Keep these factors in mind:

- **F** eelings
- **A** nalysis
- **C** ompelling C's
- **E** nergy

The F-Word Question

I ask those in my workshops to guess what F-word will be in the reporter's question during their next interview. They often guess "facts."

Yes, I tell them, the reporter is going to ask you about the facts, but the facts will usually not appear in quotes.

What appears in quotes in newspapers – and what we hear you say in radio and TV – will *almost always* be your response to "How do you FEEL about ... "

There's more about the feeling question in **Interview Guidelines**, and a long list of feeling words to insert in a sound bite.

Let's look at each factor in the FACE formula:

Feelings. Let the audience know what you're feeling. From time to time, review the Sony Sandwich formula to help you reflexively craft quotes that begin with how you feel. That first phrase sets us up to receive your reasons for feeling that way.

Analysis. Sometimes you're asked for your assessment of the situation. In one phrase or sentence, tell them what the bottom line is. The audience wants your expert opinion on the subject. That's why the reporter is talking to you. But to avoid the cutting room floor, the expert must be able to translate into everyday language.

If you use numbers, they are meaningless unless you put the numbers in perspective.

Many experts speak in strange tongues. After the reporter has said there seems to be no danger from the accident within the nuclear power plant, an internationally recognized expert says on camera:

We've put the effluent through exhaustive electron microscopy plus radiofluorocarbon laser analysis and we come up with a count of point four, seven, zero micro-mini roentgens.

Translated, with perspective:

You'd get more radiation sitting in front of a television set for two hours than you would if you took a bath in the water that leaked out.

Compelling C's. Most news stories revolve around at least one of these basic elements. Notice the feeling words:

- **Catastrophe** "I'm afraid. We're facing a global disaster if we don't change the way we dispose of toxic waste."

- **Crisis** "I'm astounded by their stupidity. The tidal surge will sweep across the highway and cut off their escape route if they don't leave now."

- **Conflict** "I hate him and everything he stands for. I'll fight him to my last breath."

- **Change** "I'm confident things are going to be different around here when we control the Legislature."

- **Crime and Corruption** "I grieve for the victims of this horrible crime. I will not rest until we find who did it."

- **Color** (We used to call it human interest.) "I'm really amused. Anyone who believes that also believes thunder curdles milk."

- **Celebrities** "I'm awed by his technical skill. He can manipulate a computer the way LeBron James controls a basketball."

Energy. There is one major difference in talking on camera and talking to your friends in their living room. To be effective on camera, your conversation must project energy. Like a salesperson who must believe in the product, you must show that you truly believe what you're saying.

Since so many stories for television news involve conflict and imminent danger, you must convince us – through the energy you invest in what you're saying – that we ought to be concerned, too.

Executive Cool = Dull

Some executives in high-pressure jobs adopt a cool, clinical personality that says to their employees, "I know exactly what I'm doing. If the building were on fire, I could lead you to safety." That deliberate, slow, calculating style can appear, on TV or radio, to be boredom, disinterest, or a mask for insecurity.

I constantly tell my clients that they need to see themselves on camera to know what they really look like. In our minds, we have imbedded high school yearbook photos of ourselves.

That image distorts our perception of ourselves. The mirror lies. The person I see when I shave is about 20 years younger and 20 pounds lighter than the person I see onscreen.

The TV Time Warp

There is a major distortion when we watch the replay of recorded interviews. Time slows down.

Five seconds of dead air seems like a minute. Unless they inject energy into what they say, our perception of people talking on camera is that they are incredibly dull and boring.

Why does that happen? I think I have the answer. Have you ever been in a life-threatening crisis where everything seemed to go into slow motion? I've questioned hundreds of people in my workshops about these experiences.

It seems to be universal.

Crises in Slow Motion

In the moments before the automobile accident, they watched the oncoming car spinning gracefully, edging closer, as they carefully analyzed right up to the moment of impact whether it would hit them.

A pilot told about losing an engine on takeoff. It seemed to take half a day to turn the plane and get it back on the ground.

A scuba diver ran out of air and made a desperate attempt to reach the surface. He drowned, but was rescued by his buddies and resuscitated. The time between his realizing the air tank was empty and unconsciousness seemed like hours.

Shooting As He Fell

A cop was shot. The bullet knocked him on his back. As he fell, he was able to pull his pistol and fire three times before he hit the ground. One of his shots hit his assailant in the chest. Normally impossible in that time frame. But he had plenty of time, he said, because it seemed like he was suspended in mid-air for several minutes.

The technical name for the phenomenon is tachypsychia. Part of it is caused by the sudden dump of adrenaline into your bloodstream. Another part is total focus on the threat to your life.

Our Perception Changes Time

It is my theory that when we watch video replayed, we are focused just enough to change our perception of time.

I see this happen regularly in my seminars. I record an interview and then we have instant replay. The person who seemed to be speaking in a normal voice just a few seconds ago now seems to have lost energy and conviction.

I believe the recorded image and audio are accurate. It is our perception that robs the interview of energy and passion.

By studying video of yourself on camera, you can learn to inject just the right amount of energy to make our perception of you on replay match what we see in real life.

Forget About Memorizing

In preparing for an interview, don't memorize, or write out what you intend to say when the camera or audio recorder is rolling. It makes the interview seem staged and rehearsed. Statements read at live Presidential news conferences are about the only prepared statements that make the air, unedited.

I recommend that before the interview, you go over in your mind the main points you'd like the story to include. You need to have a central theme in your head, and some sub-sections that connect to that central idea. No more than three. If you're afraid the stress of the interview will make you forget, write yourself a cheat sheet, the same way students cheat on exams.

Using a Cheat Sheet

The cheat sheet should be one-word cues – bullet points – that will refresh your memory if your mind goes blank. Put the cheat sheet where you can glance down at it if you need to.

The trick is to look thoughtful, pause and glance down as if you're thinking deeply, then come back slowly to eye contact with the reporter to finish the thought. This is a natural head movement in normal conversation. Nobody will know you cheated if you do it carefully. For radio, you don't even need to hide the cheat sheet.

Writing the key points helps you remember. Having the cheat sheet handy is an assuring psychological crutch. If it's there, you probably won't need it. Remember – unless it's a 30-minute talk show in the studio, you have to *condense, condense, condense*.

In public speaking courses, the instructor gives you a subject and forces you to make an immediate, extemporaneous talk. The exercise teaches you to think and talk on your feet. It's called an "elevator speech." What you want us to know in the time it takes an elevator to go up one floor.

Some Training Exercises

To train yourself for broadcast interviews, try to say how you feel about a difficult subject – and three reasons why you feel that way – in 12 seconds or less. Pick tough, complicated subjects and practice with a tape recorder or video camera. In one sentence, say how you feel – and why – about difficult subjects like:

- **Legalized abortion**
- **Gun control**
- **Capital punishment**
- **Prayer in schools**
- **Immigration reform**
- **Replacing the income tax with a flat sales tax**

There is no quick miracle drug, no magic diet, no futuristic exercise machine to make you an instant success. It takes tough, conscientious mental calisthenics if you want to be truly good at it. This exercise, practiced regularly, will develop your mental agility for condensing what you know and feel about complicated subjects.

Congressional Pros

The real pros of on-camera interviewing are congressional leaders who've been interviewed several times a day for 20 years. They develop stopwatches in their heads. Before the red light on the camera glows, they discuss the story with the reporter. They get some idea of how their comments will be used.

"How much time do you need?" the congressman says, clearing his throat and brushing his hair aside.

"About 10 seconds," the reporter tells him.

"OK. I'm ready"

"Rolling."

The congressman speaks for 10 seconds. Perhaps nine. And then he stops. He has learned the language, and the game. He edits himself. There can be no distortion. He is rarely quoted out of context.

You Can Do It, Too

Most of those who've learned to speak in sound bites did it the hard way, through trial and error. For many, it became a self-defense tactic. The news media are kinder to some people than others. One person's slip is never aired. Another, similar stumble becomes the comedy element in tonight's news.

Watch and listen to TV and radio news. Make notes on the people who are effective in their interviews. Learn from the mistakes and blunders of other people.

Watch the Process

If you're in a position where you expect to be interviewed regularly, ask for a guided tour of the local newsroom and editing facilities. If you can, spend a day with a TV reporter and camera crew. Watch them shoot, write, and edit a story. The more familiar you become with the entire process, the easier it will be to adapt your speaking style to the medium.

Learning to speak Media Language requires some concentration and hard work. But it's a lot easier than Spanish or German.

Do On-Camera Interviews Early

If you set up an appointment for an on-camera interview, try to make it at least four hours before the newscast. The closer to air time, the more harried the crew. They'll do a better job of lighting, shooting and editing if they're not pressed against their deadline.

Choose Your Turf

Choose a place that's comfortable for you. If possible, one that fits the story. If you're a doctor, and you'll be talking about a new surgical technique, do the interview with a backdrop that says *medicine.*

If you're a computer programmer, let us see a monitor and keyboard behind you. It's a real advantage if viewers who turn on the story in the middle of the interview know at a glance this story has something to do with doctors or computers.

If you're more comfortable standing while you talk, suggest that to the camera crew. Standing keeps your diaphragm open for easier breathing, especially if you have a touch of stage fright. When some people sit down, it appears – on screen – as if they've let the air out. They go flat. Their entire speech pattern changes. You'll have to watch yourself on camera to see if this happens to you.

Don't Cram

For the interview, you don't need to do any cramming. If you, the expert, can't remember, how do you expect viewers to retain what you say? The reporter doesn't want statistics on camera.

Go over the numbers before the interview. Most people can't absorb spoken statistics. They *do* remember analogies and perspective. "The money we'll spend this year treating this disease would buy everybody in the state a new Lexus."

Provide Graphs & Charts

If the audience is to retain numbers, the story will have to be told with graphs and charts that put them in perspective. Seeing the numbers on the screen helps people remember them.

Most reporters in major cities would not think of printing or broadcasting a news release exactly as you wrote it. But they will often use your graphs or charts with no editing whatever. Virtually every computer word processing program has graph and charting capability. Your providing graphics will help the story immensely.

TV Crew Pecking Order

You should know there is a rigid pecking order within a TV news crew. In most places, the photographer works under the direction of the reporter. The sound technician or grip (almost extinct with the advent of lighter, more compact equipment) is considered the photographer's assistant.

For network interviews, the story producer often accompanies the correspondent. The producer may come ahead of the correspondent to gather information, scout interviews and shooting locations.

The correspondent makes more money and technically has more authority than the producer. But the producer often does more reporting than the correspondent. For some stories, the producer even does some of the on-camera interviews. The producer and correspondent then work jointly later, editing it all together.

Help – Don't Push

If the reporter doesn't introduce the other crew members to you, introduce yourself. Remember, the photographer is the one with the power to make the shot flattering, or downright ugly. It never hurts to be on good terms.

You can suggest a place for the interview, but leave the final decision up to the crew. There may be some technical problem with the spot you've suggested. Never make them think you're telling them how to do their job

If the crew is using a small "peanut" mike that clips to your clothing, try to hide the cord. Run the wire inside your shirt or blouse to the waist, then inside your waistband to one side

There's always a clumsy moment when a crew member tries to clip the mike to the interviewee's shirt or blouse. Feel free to help, so you don't feel like you're being groped; and to prevent the clip-on the mike from damaging your clothes.

If they're using a hand-held mike, the tendency is to lean down, or toward the mike. You don't have to do that. It makes you look stooped. Forget about the mike. Picking up good sound is their job. If you're not speaking loudly enough, they'll tell you, or move the mike.

Interviewees will often try to take the mike away from the reporter, because they've seen reporters, actors and singers holding their own mikes. If you do that, the reporter will know immediately you're a rank amateur.

Talk to the Reporter

During the interview, talk to the reporter, not the camera. The camera is there, listening to the conversation, but it doesn't ask questions. If you answer into the camera, the audience reacts. The reporter asked the question – why are you giving *me* the answer?

Actors in commercials look into the camera to make their pitch to the audience. A news interview shouldn't look like a sales pitch.

Choose Which Eye

Another fine point – look at the reporter's eye that is closest to the camera. In normal conversation, we switch back and forth between the eyes of the person we talk to. But if the camera zooms in very tightly, we will see your eyes darting back and forth. You make us think you're shifty. Scared. Guilty.

By looking at the reporter's eye nearest the camera, we'll see more of your face, but you won't be looking at the camera.

Try not to blink too much. That can also be interpreted as a sign of stress or deception.

Sit Up and Lean Forward

Don't lean back in the chair, whether it's hard or soft. Leaning back changes your body English. You tell us, without words, that you're not very enthusiastic about what you're saying.

Sit on the Edge of the Chair

In this still frame from an ABC World News show, Correspondent Bianna Golodryga talks to anchor Diane Sawyer. Anchors and correspondents are trained to sit on the edge of the chair while they're on camera. It conveys a sense of energy and interest, and straightens the spine. I teach witnesses in trials and legislative hearings to sit the same way. It adds authority. Try it.

If the interview is not live, take your time. If you start a sentence that gets tangled and confused, start again. That's what editing is for.

If you don't understand the question, say so.

If you're nervous and your mouth is dry, stop for a drink of water. Keep thinking of the living room and the friend or neighbor you're talking to. That will relieve the nervousness. If their lights heat up the room and you begin to sweat, suggest that you take a break to let the air conditioner catch up.

Once the camera is rolling, most people give up all control of their lives to the camera crew. Don't do that. Take more control. Like:

You know, I gave you an answer several minutes ago that took me much too long to get to the point. If you'll ask me that same ques-

tion again, I think I can give you a better, shorter answer.

Short and Simple

Try to talk in short, simple sentences. Lawyers and professors have a tendency to speak in outlined, organized form – firstly, secondly, thirdly – or to label their points A, B and C. Suppose the reporter is only interested in your third point, and you've run the words together, so they can't edit out "thirdly." They may have to throw away the entire section.

Other common phrases like "first of all" and "as I said earlier" can create editing nightmares. There may not be enough time in a news story to let you say it twice, or to include your "first of all" point. If you drop the "as I said earlier" in the middle of a sentence, the entire sentence may have to be dumped.

Talk to the Jury

Some of the best on-camera interviews are with trial lawyers who've spent their entire careers summing up complicated cases for jurors.

They keep it short and simple, conversational and colorful. They're good at one-sentence conclusions jurors will remember and repeat to each other in the jury room.

For the main point, they let their feelings show. Jurors are very much like those people sitting in front of the television set after a hard day's work. They're easily bored. They want it simple. They want it interesting. They want to know what it was really like. How did it feel?

Avoid Parentheticals

Any kind of parenthetical thought can make a sentence too long for radio and television.

Example – the senator says:

I've come to believe, as most of my constituents do, who've had any experience with firearms, that every person in this country has the God-given right to own a gun.

It can be edited much easier if the senator says:

I believe every person in this country has the God-given right to own a gun. I'm sure most of my constituents who have any experience with firearms feel the same way I do.

With this version, the reporter can use either sentence, or both. The two sentences can be separated to punctuate different points in different parts of the story.

Anticipate the Why

Another technique that can help the editing process:

QUESTION: Then you will not vote, Senator, to outlaw Saturday Night Specials?

ANSWER: No.

QUESTION: Why?

ANSWER: The Saturday Night Special is a phony issue.

QUESTION: Why do you say that?

ANSWER: Most police officers, and most store clerks are killed with expensive weapons. Why should the poor homeowner be denied a weapon he can afford to protect himself and his family?

If you give a "Yes" or "No" answer, it will almost always be followed by "Why?" Anticipate the Why. This answer will enable the reporter to cram the entire response into about two-thirds as much time:

QUESTION: Then you will not vote, Senator, to outlaw Saturday Night Specials?

ANSWER: I will never vote to outlaw Saturday Night Specials. They're a phony issue. Most police officers ... etc.

Incorporating the question into your answer allows the reporter to drop the sound bite into the story without having to set up what you were asked.

Don't Date What You Say

Try not to date what you're saying, particularly if the interview will not be used today. If you talk about something that happened today or yesterday, or predict what will happen tomorrow, it won't be accurate if the story runs on the early morning news tomorrow, or next week.

Show Me While You Tell Me

What the audience *sees*, if you're genuine, may communicate more than what they *hear*.

Years ago, advertising agencies learned how to use visual signals in print. A lot can be said in a picture that doesn't require words. Because of television's time limitations, that technique has become a science. The real message is visual, not verbal.

Luxury car commercials tell us about the wonderful engineering or handling of the automobile. But the more powerful message is what we see.

The driver is pulling up to a home that cost several million dollars. Sliding behind the wheel at the country club, or at the airport, with a corporate jet in the background. And, of course, there is a trophy wife or husband in the passenger seat. The key visual message: If you're rich, sophisticated, influential, sexually attractive, you'll drive this car.

Visual Shorthand

Politicians have learned to use visual symbolism to communicate with their constituents. After a flood or earthquake, it is now a tribal ritual for the governor – dressed in fatigues and combat boots – to survey the damage from a National Guard helicopter.

Is that really necessary? Can't governors get reports from experts who are better equipped to assess the damage? Yes, but we've come to expect a personal visit. If we don't see the governor, the president or the vice president at the scene of a major disaster, we think they don't care.

I've done a lot of law enforcement training. Chiefs and sheriffs worry about what they will say the day an officer is killed in the line of duty. I tell them I'm much more concerned about what the public will *see* you doing, than in what you will *say*.

You need to be seen at the scene, at the hospital, at the officer's home. And if you're not at the funeral, kiss your job good-bye. *Being there* speaks volumes. *Not being there* also delivers a powerful message.

The Great Communicator

Ronald Reagan's popularity was helped immeasurably by his understanding of the camera and the need to be seen *doing* something rather than talking about it. Do you think he really liked to chop wood on his ranch in California?

More likely, his media managers decided it would convey other, unspoken messages about him if he were photographed, early in his first term, clearing brush and chopping firewood. They frequently arranged for him to be photographed on horseback. The John Wayne image never hurt a politician.

Clothing Messages

The clothes you wear are part of the visual shorthand. When he was president, Jimmy Carter liked to be interviewed in a plaid shirt and sweater. To enhance his "just plain folks" image, Carter often carried a piece of luggage when he was embarking from Air Force

One or a helicopter – even though a small army of aides and Secret Service agents were there, empty-handed.

Richard Nixon wanted to suggest a more regal kind of presidency. You sometimes wondered if he slept in a coat and tie.

Barack Obama on the campaign trail rarely wears a coat and tie. In the White House, he does. But out among the common folk, he often ditches the coat to shake hands or speak in his shirt sleeves.

Fatigues Among the Brass

Retirement festivities for admirals and generals are normally a sea of dress uniforms, gold braid and ceremonial swords. Because I had coached his wife before a network TV interview, I was invited to attend General Norman Schwarzkopf's retirement ceremony at MacDill Air Force Base in Tampa. Almost all the guests were splendid in their spit-and-polish best.

But not the retiree. Schwarzkopf wore his desert fatigues and combat boots – the same uniform we had seen him wear all through the recent Gulf War.

There was a message there.

Coats, Ties and Tailored Suits

A CEO wearing his coat and tie behind an immaculate desk tells us, subliminally, that he is a figurehead who is aloof, unfamiliar with his employees, and rarely gets involved in the nuts and bolts of running the company. A paper shuffler.

The same message can be conveyed if the female CEO is in a sharply tailored suit. Everything about her clothes and makeup seems perfect. Not a hair is out of place. Another distant, aloof paper shuffler.

It is hard to draw a line for women's clothes as easily as it is for men. Men's suits are a kind of uniform. Women's clothes have much more variety.

Let's design another scenario.

The desktop has some papers scattered on it, with a computer at one side. That same CEO has his coat off, tie loosened, sleeves rolled up. The female CEO's hair is a little tousled. Now we get the impression that either is hands-on, hard-working, personally involved.

I suggest to my clients that if they normally come to work in business clothes, they should also keep some more casual clothes at the office, for interviews in the field where office attire may be out of place.

Business Casual

Many offices in America have now amended their dress codes to business casual. Even high-end law and accounting firms.

Watch how campaigning presidential candidates and the CEOs of large, multi-national firms dress when they're speaking to an audience. Men rarely wear coats and ties.

There is now a demeaning term for those who dress too well – "the suits." If most Americans no longer wear more formal clothes to work, the message you give them if you're wearing a coat and tie or tailored suit may be that you're old, out-of-date, uninvolved in the real work your company does.

In Early TV, Blue Was White

In the early days of television news, men were told to wear blue shirts. That's because they were shooting black-and-white film. A white shirt glowed in the harsh light and high-contrast film. A blue shirt *looked* white when the film was broadcast.

With today's color cameras, white looks white, and blue looks blue. But the automatic sensor in those cameras reads the general light level coming through the lens.

Light clothing makes the aperture of the camera lens constrict, just as the iris in the human eye does. Dark clothing widens the camera aperture.

Dark or Light Clothing & Skin Tone

The general rule is: people with light complexions should wear light colors to make their skin look healthier. People with very dark complexions should wear dark colors, so the camera will open up to better light their faces. This is particularly important for African-Americans.

Generally, your clothes for television should be subdued. Plain, solid colors are best. Stay away from stripes, checks and bold prints. Broadcast-quality electronics can make busy patterns ripple and pulsate.

Make the clothes fit the story and the place where you're being interviewed. A power business suit for an interview in your living room will seems as out of place as a tuxedo or evening dress at Burger King. One of my simple suggestions:

If we remember what you were wearing, you wore the wrong thing.

Don't Get a Haircut

If you know the camera is coming, don't go to the beauty salon or the barber shop. We will probably be able to tell that you spruced up for the interview. Remember, this is a spontaneous, unrehearsed conversation, not a formal portrait or glamour shot.

Flashy Jewelry Distracts

The goal: Don't let anything about your appearance distract from what you're saying. Large expensive jewelry is so distracting we may not pay attention to what you're saying. Take off your Rolex watch. Ditch the flashy necklace. Stay away from earrings that are larger than a quarter.

Wear Your Eyeglasses

If you normally wear eyeglasses, wear them for the interview. Without them, your eyes will have to work harder. You'll squint. There will be a crease through a man's sideburns and depressions in your nose where the glasses rested before the interview.

But Not Sunglasses

Don't wear dark glasses for TV interviews. In this culture, you're supposed to look people in the eye when you talk to them.

The stereotyped movie hoodlum wears dark glasses during conversations – perhaps to hide the evil thoughts his eyes would reveal if we could see them.

Prescription glasses that darken in sunlight will also turn dark in bright light. If you have light-sensitive lenses – and know you'll be talking on camera often – buy another pair with regular lenses.

Anti-Reflective Coating

If you're going to do a lot of TV interviews, have your optician treat the lenses with the invisible, anti-reflective coating that television reporters and anchors use.

If you're being interviewed in bright sunlight, it is almost impossible not to squint. Modern-day cameras don't need bright sunlight. Tell the photographer your eyes are unusually sensitive to bright light. Can we shoot in the shade?

A suntan makes you look healthier and younger. A *sunburn* makes your skin shiny and puffy.

For field interviews, women should wear the same makeup they'd wear to work.

In-Studio Makeup

In a TV studio, the light will be much brighter and harsher. Use heavier makeup, with eye shadow and cheek blush a little darker.

Outside the studio, men don't normally use makeup. If you're balding, wipe rubbing alcohol across your shiny forehead just before the interview. Give it time to evaporate, so you don't smell like you've been drinking it.

Interviews in the studio use many of the same techniques as field interviews, but are also different in some ways. You need to understand the differences. For a preview of what the TV studio is going to feel like and the difference in techniques, see **Talk Shows**.

Live Remotes

The most difficult of all TV interviews is the live remote. This involves your having a conversation with an anchor, back in the studio, whom you can't see. In this format, you talk to the camera lens. To the audience, it looks like you're talking to the anchor.

You'll have to wear an earphone to hear the anchor. Television reporters have their earphones custom-molded, like a hearing aid, to improve the quality of the sound.

But they'll give you a clumsy ear "bug" with a bent wire that hangs it loosely over your ear. It will be hard to hear what the anchor is saying. You often see live shots where the person on the street has one hand pressing an ear, head tilted. They're pushing the earphone tighter, straining to hear.

If you know you're going to be interviewed regularly in live shots, a custom earphone is a good investment. They're made at hearing aid shops. Call local news directors to get any special technical requirements used in your community.

Reading the Details

As a television reporter, I developed the technique of ad-libbing live remotes, with pauses to read exact words from an important document. It adds authority and credibility.

If three legislators had been indicted for bribery, I'd do the live shot in front of the court house, with the indictment in my hand. I'd summarize what had happened, then say, "Let me read for you what the grand jury said." I'd have a sentence marked; read it, then continue off-the-cuff until I reached another section where I wanted to use the grand jury's exact words.

If your interview is a live shot, the pressure to condense is greater than in any other interview form. There's no chance to edit, and very little opportunity to use cutaways and other video techniques that can keep viewers visually interested while you talk.

If you talk too long, they'll cut you off.

SKILLS

INTERVIEWS - PRINT

No, You Can't Talk To My Psychiatrist

By print, I mean news stories whose content will be read, not viewed as video, or heard. They can be on paper, or a blog that's read on a computer screen. They're different because the reader cannot weigh the nuances of facial animation, body English and voice inflection.

Compared to audio and video recordings, print interviews can be a very lengthy process. To compete with broadcasting's immediacy and time limitations, newspapers, magazines and websites have more time and space for the story.

The Luxury of Time

They sometimes go overboard with detail. Intimate, minute trivia is showcased. It is common for print stories to tell us what brand of cigarette the interviewee smokes and just how the smoke is inhaled. The designer of the dress. How many times the phone rang during lunch, and who called. Everything that was ordered. Whether it was eaten.

They do this partly to compete. For a major story, print reporters have a luxury that broadcast reporters rarely have – the luxury of time. Lots of time to research and write the story. Writers at newspapers like *The Wall Street Journal* and *The Washington Post* may work on one feature story for weeks. Major investigative projects can take more than a year.

Another reason for this kind of trivia is an effort to draw pictures with words. One reason for the decline of newspapers, in my opinion, was that newspaper editors were word people. They simply did not understand the impact of pictures. When they had good photos, many of them didn't know how to display them to their best advantage.

As their budgets and staffs were cut, the number of pages in most newspapers were cut. The actual size of the paper was chopped to save the cost of newsprint. So there was even less space for photos.

Fire the Photographers

One of the most shocking events in the decline of newspapers (for old-time journalists like me) occurred in May, 2013, when the *Chicago Sun-Times* fired its entire photography staff.

The Associated Press story about the firing quoted a statement issued by the newspaper's management:

"Today, The Chicago Sun-Times has had to make the very difficult decision to eliminate the position of full-time photographer, as part of a multimedia staffing restructure." The statement noted that the "business is changing rapidly" and audiences are "seeking more video content with their news."

Depend on Readers for Pictures

Other stories said the staff was told the newspaper would depend on readers who take pictures at news events to provide them to the newspaper. Reporters were also issued cameras.

Unspoken in all this was the rapid decline of the newspaper's circulation and profit. And corporate ownership's need to show a profit.

The AP story said:

Like most major newspapers, The Sun-Times, which was bought by the investment company Wrapports in 2011, has been hard hit by the technological shift that has caused more people to rely on their personal computers and mobile devices to stay informed. As more readers have embraced digital alternatives, so have advertisers in a move that has been steadily siphoning away newspaper publishers' biggest source of revenue.

The Chicago Sun-Times ended September 2012 with a paid circulation of 263,292, according to the most recent statement filed with the Alliance for Audited Media. That contrasted with circulation of about 341,448 at the same time in 2006. Including satellite editions that operate under other names, the Sun-Times' circulation totaled 432,451 in September 2012.

Moving from Print to TV

I attributed my ability to move successfully from newspapers to TV partly to my lifelong love of photography. I had a darkroom when I was 10 years old. In my early newspaper jobs as correspondent in a distant city, I had to be both reporter and photographer. I understood how to tell stories with pictures.

In television, the reporter and photographer work closely as a team. Without pictures, the reporter has no story. Every word the TV reporter writes must have a picture to go with it. The reporter and photographer map out ahead just what they'll need to illustrate the story. The pictures often tell us more than the words.

Separate Words, Pictures

In newspapers, the reporter and photographer traditionally worked separately. Even at a breaking news story like a plane crash or building collapse, they would go to the scene in separate cars and have little contact with each other. They brought their work to an editor independently. It was the editor's task to merge the words and pictures.

I remember going to a shooting in a Miami Beach restaurant shortly after I went to the *Miami Herald*. I quickly cased the crime scene and discovered a pistol on the restaurant patio. The police had not yet arrived in force.

A still photographer ran up. I told him about the pistol. He hurried to photograph it. I was too new in Miami to realize that I had tipped a photographer from my competition. He worked for the *Miami News*.

Print reporters' obsession with trivia can be a real pain. They may want to just hang around and watch everything you do for several days. They'll want to talk to your spouse, your children, your boss, your employees, your parents and your psychiatrist.

Drawing the Boundaries

You may have to decide just how much time and privacy you're willing to give up. Early in your contact with the reporter, you should diplomatically draw some boundaries. Celebrities often do this to protect their families.

Remember – barring a door often whets the appetite of a reporter to get inside. But knowing very early how the reporter views the assignment – the talent and experience the reporter brings to the story – can help you make that decision

Print Is More Tenacious

Print reporters can be much more tenacious than broadcast reporters. The luxury of time permits them to doggedly stick with a rumor, trying to prove it's true. Broadcast reporters will usually be pulled off and sent to another story if they don't find what they're looking for quickly.

An Endangered Species

But in-depth reporting is an endangered species.

The profit margins at TV stations and newspapers are not nearly what they used to be. Owners are almost universally looking for ways to cut operating costs and restore their profit margins. Newsrooms are shorthanded. They look like ghost towns these days.

When people leave, their jobs are often left vacant for a long time. Maybe permanently

In the ongoing loss of audience for both newspapers and broadcast news, there's a real emphasis on pushing every employee to be as productive as possible. Too often, that rules out any serious investigative reporting or extensive research.

A Few Bright Spots

There are a few bright spots. I read the *New York Times* online every day. They work constantly to make their website easy to read; and easy to find a story you want to read.

They won a Pulitzer Prize in 2013 for a story titled Snowfall – The Avalanche at Tunnel Creek. Snowfall was an experiment that superbly combined words, photographs and video. It was much more effective in telling the story than pure print could ever be.

It will take that kind of innovation to keep newspapers alive online. Journalists also have high hopes for the *Washington Post* since amazon.com CEO Jeff Bezos bought it. His genius for innovation online may morph newspapers into a new form that will bring them back as a primary news source for most Americans.

Experts With a Specialty

Reporters at larger newspapers were historically better educated and more experienced than their broadcast competition. They were often experts who developed a specialty.

Like police reporters who did nothing but crime and law enforcement stories. Reporters on the school beat who knew more about schools than members of the School Board. That's rare these days.

When you know a print reporter will be interviewing you as part of a major assignment, it saves time if you can supply written material before the interview.

Collect data that will educate the reporter. Supply history and statistics. Arrange other interviews with staff who are technicians. When the reporter is ready to do your interview, this can save a lot of time.

Charming and Disarming

Good reporters – both print and broadcast – know how to be very charming and disarming. Newspaper and magazine reporters researching a major story will begin to seem like old friends.

They'll hang around a lot. Have meals, drinks and coffee with you. Their goal may be to get your guard down. Don't get defensive. Just be aware. That's their job.

In a confrontation with a newspaper or magazine, a written statement can be effective. But if we don't see you on TV or hear you on radio, it may seem like you're hiding.

Quotes from a written statement in print don't telegraph that same message. Even if the story points it out, few readers will care that you gave a written statement rather than an interview.

Questions in Writing

If you refuse to be interviewed for a print story, you can offer to answer written questions in writing. This can avoid a slip of the tongue in a touchy situation.

You may want to grant an interview with certain restrictions. Remember, the ground rules must be agreed on by both parties in advance.

You can't talk to a reporter, and later ask that part of what you said be trashed. (See **Off-the-Record**)

Newspapers keep mug shots in their libraries. Often they're old and unflattering. If you don't like the picture they're using, send a newer, better one. The cover letter or e-mail should say the old shot is out of date, and you're offering another. You can do the same with your organization's annual report. Send the latest one, just to keep in their files.

During an interview, if the reporter doesn't ask about shooting your picture, you may want to offer one. They're more likely to use a candid, informal shot, rather than a posed portrait.

While most daily newspapers won't print news releases verbatim, they'll often reproduce graphic material you give them. To emphasize your points in an interview, give the reporter copies of graphs and charts that illustrate your data.

Print's Comfort Deceptive

Most people feel more comfortable with print reporters because of camera shyness. While you're doing it, the interview seems less threatening. But print can often do a lot more damage.

Winning with the News Media

When we know we're being recorded for broadcast – both TV and radio – there is a much greater stage fright factor. As we speak, we think the entire world is listening and/or watching.

Not only are the print media more tenacious; newspapers and magazines have traditionally been much more vicious than broadcasting.

Another factor in the past was the longer life of print clippings. Old newspapers and magazines could be dredged up to hurt you. They were on file at the library. In earlier days, it was very difficult to retrieve a TV news story. No more.

Broadcast News Archives

There are now massive libraries of video news stories available online. For free.

Archived video is John Stewart's most effective weapon to skewer politicians on *The Daily Show*. I often marvel at his ability to dredge up old, forgotten video of interviews shot years ago that contradict what his targets said today.

As I said in an earlier chapter, HYPOCRISY is the greatest media blunder. Video replay is the most effective tool to prove that.

SKILLS

INTERVIEWS - WEBCAM

For Less Than $200 You Can Be Television's 24/7 "Expert On Call"

Here's a novel idea – for about $200 you can now set up a webcam studio in your home or office that will make you instantly available for on-camera interviews to news outlets all over the world. I call it becoming the "Expert on Call."

I've written another book detailing how to choose, buy, set up and use the equipment; and then how to develop the personal skills that make it work.

Webcam Savvy

That other book is "Webcam Savvy." It is available in both print and e-book versions. Essentially, you need the best computer and webcam you can afford, and a high-speed Internet connection. I won't duplicate that book here, but I'll summarize it.

Regular interviews on newscasts are worth tens of thousands of dollars in advertising for you or your company.

If you're a government agency whose employees are interviewed regularly, the constant availability cements the relationship between you and the video news outlets who cover you. It avoids the "could not be reached for comment" tag in their stories.

Major Efforts to Cut Costs

In the last few years, as networks and local TV stations lost audiences and profits, they made desperate efforts to cut costs. There were massive layoffs.

Networks shut down bureaus all over the world. Some returned to the "one-man-band" system, where reporters double as photographers.

And then there was the AH-HAH moment. Do interviews by webcam! As this book goes to print, ABC and CNN are using them almost daily. I predict the entire industry will soon swing that way. Why? Because they save a HUGE amount of money.

ABC Webcam Interview

In this photo, an ABC correspondent is interviewing someone on the other side of the world from the ABC newsroom in New York.

Normally, this kind of interview needs needs a reporter, a photographer, sometimes a producer, about $75,000 worth of equipment, plus travel time and costs.

The crew will not be available for other stories for a significant part of the day. Perhaps several days, if they have to travel a long way.

For webcam interviews, the correspondent simply launches Skype® or an equivalent program, then records the interview.

Notice the books under the laptop in the photo above, to lift the camera to the right height.

The skills needed for a webcam interview are a lot like an ordinary on-camera interview, but can be tricky. Because you're shooting yourself, eye contact and how the shot is framed need special attention.

Dreadful Quality

The problem with this idea has been the quality of webcam audio and video. Mostly it was DREADFUL. Because the people being interviewed didn't know how to set up their equipment, and/or didn't have the skills to do a good job on camera.

An Unflattering Example

Here's an example of an unflattering webcam interview on CNN. It is striking because the man at the left in this split-screen is also participating remotely, but from a TV studio.

Harvard Law Prof. Alan Dershowitz (on the right) appears to be using his laptop computer's built-in webcam.

The webcam is either out of focus or has very low resolution. Dershowitz is badly framed. There's a light behind him that affects the exposure, and another light seems to be directly overhead, so his face is in shadow.

The laptop screen is tilted so it reflects in his glasses. The camera is too low. The laptop is probably sitting on a table.

The average laptop webcam has a photo resolution of 1.3 MP (megapixels). By comparison, the stand-alone webcam I use has a Zeiss lens and captures 10 megapixels of detail. It is incredibly sharp. Online, it sells for about $75.

How to Improve Audio Quality

Most webcams have a built-in microphone. You can never get great audio quality if the microphone is more than about six inches away.

Think about what happens to the quality of the voice you hear on the telephone if the caller is using a speakerphone. The farther the distance to a microphone, the lower the audio quality.

So I recommend a clip-on accessory microphone or a headset for Skype interviews. Either will make a major improvement over the mike built into the webcam or laptop.

Ideally, the webcam will be at about the same height as your eyes. And it should be shooting horizontally, not up your nose. So it will probably need some adjusting. Because laptop webcams are built into the lid of the laptop, they can't be adjusted. The laptop may need to sit on something to raise the camera. The screen should be vertical, not tilted up or down.

Financial Analyst Diane Swonk

Diane Swonk (above) is so good at this, she is frequently interviewed on several different TV networks. She does these interviews from her office. Notice the clip-on mike at the bottom of the screen for optimum voice quality. And the lighting.

Where Do I Look?

She seems to be talking to a reporter, not the camera. In arranging a webcam interview, this is an important point you need to work out ahead of time. Where do you want me to look? If the interview is done live and the anchor is asking questions, they'll probably want you to talk to the camera.

If the interview will be edited into a "package" story, they'll probably want you to look slightly to one side of your webcam. You should also ask which side.

In the on-camera chapter, I said you should maintain eye contact with the reporter in the standard field interview.

This is where is gets tricky. During a webcam interview, you tend to talk to the reporter in the middle of your computer screen, just as you would in a normal conversation. But the camera is not in the middle of the screen. So at the other end, you appear to be talking to the reporter's navel.

This Will Take Practice

This is hard to do. It takes practice. Luckily, programs like Skype make it easy to record your own performance. You can study the replay and work out the kinks. Learning to do this and look like a pro will take a lot of practice.

You'll need to clear the clutter behind where you're sitting. In my *Webcam Savvy* book I show how to make a frame out of PVC pipe that's easy to assemble and break down.

You can easily clip a blanket or a large piece of fabric to it for an anonymous background that hides distracting clutter. The farther away the background from you, and the more out of focus, the better.

The easiest way to create better lighting is to bounce a floodlight off the ceiling. A utility light available at any home improvement store for about $10 can be clamped almost anywhere and will do this very well. Two bounced lights are even better. Notice the back fill light at the top of Swonk's head in the photo above. The main light is coming from the front. A second light from another angle gives depth and dimension to the shot.

If you do the interview from home, try get away from barking dogs, crying babies, and doorbells that might ring unexpectedly. Turn off your cell phone.

Check for Reflections

If you wear eyeglasses, check for reflections from your computer screen. Sometimes the light from the screen gives your face a blue color cast. You may have to turn the screen slightly to one side to eliminate the reflection. An auxiliary webcam, rather than one that's built in, makes this work better.

After you've fine-tuned your webcam studio and honed your skills, let the news directors at local TV outlets know about your expertise and your ability to do interviews on short notice. If they're interested, they'll want to audition you.

Don't expect to be paid for your expertise. At first.

If you're really good, they may make an offer to hire you as a "consultant." You'll become their "Expert on Call."

Stories That Need Experts

Here are just a few areas where TV news can frequently use experts to expand and improve their stories:

Medicine, Education, Finance, Travel, Cars, Aviation, Law Enforcement, Politics, The Environment, Legal Issues, Utilities, Highways and other Infrastructure.

If you've retired after years of training and experience, you can be a true expert who can speak without appearing to promote your personal financial interest. College professors have that same kind of independent status and respect.

If you're still working fulltime, interviews salted regularly into news stories are great endorsements for your services and the organization you work for.

SKILLS

NEWS CONFERENCES

Stage Productions
That Sing and Dance

News conferences are a necessary evil. Good reporters don't like them. Everybody will come away with the same story. Most reporters need to win. To beat the competition. To stand out from the pack.

But news conferences are efficient. It would take all day to give individual interviews to a dozen news outlets. You can do them all at once at a news conference.

News conferences are a way for you to take advantage of the fierce competition between the media. If the story is marginal, they may all use it to prevent their competitors from having a story they don't.

Neat, Convenient Packages

News conferences offer some real advantages. You can provide, in one, convenient place, the people that reporters would like to talk to. Properly produced, a news conference provides all the elements needed for a story in one neat, convenient package.

News conferences, when done right, give reporters *everything they need to write the story you want*. They should inspire reporters to write the story from your point of view.

Suppose you had to choose between a story that will take a lot of legwork and another that's easy. Both of them are fairly equal in news value. On most days, if you're the assignment editor or city editor, you'll take the easy one.

Now, the Disadvantages

News conferences also have some major disadvantages. They're much less intimate. At a news conference, you never know who they'll send. If you call a specific reporter to suggest a story, you get to pick the reporter.

In a news conference crowd, you can't give reporters you trust confidential background material. If you're under attack, and the mob of reporters and photographers smell blood, you can be overwhelmed and lose control.

News conferences should be called only for stories that all media will consider important.

BEWARE false alarms. If you call news conferences for stories that don't merit them, you'll seem like the boy who cried, "Wolf." Next time you call a news conference to announce a cure for cancer, nobody will come.

A Theatrical Production

You should think of a news conference as a theatrical production. It needs a stage, a script, a cast, costumes, a director, a program, props, a rehearsal, an audience, and a final curtain.

Choosing The Stage

Where you hold the press conference can be very important. Think about the way television reporters shoot their standups. If the story involves a trial, we see the courthouse over the reporter's shoulder.

Network correspondents who cover the President do their standups on the lawn of the White House. At space shots or political conventions, we see the launch pad or the banners in the background.

Place Gives You Credibility

This is a kind of visual shorthand that television has developed. It suggests, subliminally, that because you're there, you're an authority on the subject.

If you're an officer in the longshoremen's union, hold your news conference on the docks, so we can see the ships at the wharf behind you. If you're a school administrator, let us see a school in the background. If you're a cop, talking about street crime, go to the most violent neighborhood in your community, where it happens. It tells viewers you know what you're talking about.

That kind of field location is not always possible. TV cameras are magnets for kids, who swarm in front of the lens. Grinning, jumping, waving, yelling "Hi, Mom. Am I gonna be on TV?"

Requirements for the Room

If it's indoors, the room needs to be big enough to hold everyone you invite, and all their equipment. It needs electrical outlets and a good air conditioning system. But one that's quiet, so mikes don't pick up the noise.

Write a Script

Decide what you want to say. Not a word-for-word script. A bullet-point outline.

Somewhere in Media Class 101, they must have said that all news conferences should begin with the boss reading a statement. Dull. Deadly dull. Presidents do this, but their news conferences are carried live. The audience HAS to sit through the entire statement. Or switch to the movie channel.

Openings We'll Never Hear

In working with clients, I try to avoid having them read prepared statements at news conferences. Most executives do not read statements well. It's obvious they're reading something somebody else wrote, not expressing their own convictions.

I've also found that CEOs know the material extremely well. They don't need to read what they already know. If what they say appears spontaneous and unrehearsed, it is much more credible. I suspect some of those written CEO statements are job security for people in the public relations department.

You may want to distribute a statement as part of your handout material. Newspaper reporters don't need to hear you read it. If you *must* read, limit it to one or two sentences. It will be a lot better if you make that summary without looking at a script.

The electronic media will summarize the gist of the news conference and then look for two or three short sound bites. The sound bites they use will almost always be your off-the-cuff answers to questions.

Casting the Play

Movies, plays and TV shows have a cast of characters. Each is necessary to tell the audience what the author wants them to hear and understand.

To move the plot along. Each member of the cast is chosen carefully for talent, experience, and audience appeal.

In most organizations, protocol requires that certain people be featured at news conferences. They'll get their feelings hurt if they're not invited. If they're good spokespeople, that's great.

But they may not be.

It's embarrassing when the boss doesn't know the answer to a technical question, fakes it, and someone on staff later has to correct the error.

Generally, the boss needs to be there to speak about policy. But you also need someone there who is intimately familiar with the equipment or process. A technician.

If you're talking about a major event, where someone has made a breakthrough in research or saved a life, that person should be there to tell the world how it felt at the moment of triumph. Bosses can't tell us that. They weren't there.

Don't Do It Alone

For most news conferences, use two to three people, if possible. I recommend no more than four.

Never do it alone. One person rarely knows everything. If you're by yourself you'll feel terribly outnumbered in a room full of aggressive reporters. You can easily be overwhelmed. More than three or four can get clumsy.

A style for press briefing has become common recently, where a group of staff people stand behind the boss as he speaks. They are not introduced. They don't say a word. I'm not sure why they're there. For moral support?

It should work this way: If the boss is overwhelmed by questions, one of the other members of the cast can step in for the rescue. "Let me answer that question," the relief hitter says, "That's my area of responsibility." That gives the boss time to catch his/her breath.

But this probably won't happen unless the news conference has been rehearsed (below).

Costumes

Decide what the cast of the news conference will wear. Their clothes should fit the story. Business suits are out of place at a news conference that gives details about a disaster or an ongoing search and rescue operation.

The Director's Role

Like plays, good news conferences need a director. A stage manager who supervises the production; shapes both the content and the style; coaches the actors. The director of a news conference is usually the public relations director or public information officer.

The director's job also includes: notifying the media, preparing the room, distributing the handouts, establishing the ground rules, introducing the cast, and closing the news conference.

The Press Package

When you walk into a theater, you hand the usher your ticket and the usher gives you a playbill. A printed program. The playbill has a very specific purpose. It educates you about the history of the play, its author, and the cast. It gets you ready for what you're about to see and hear.

You should do the same thing for reporters as they arrive at your news conference. Give them a printed press package.

Avoiding Stupid Questions

Editors often send new, less talented reporters, believing news conferences don't require much skill or experience. You'll get some really stupid questions. The press package will educate them and, hopefully, avoid some of those dumb questions.

Include in the package the names and titles of those who'll be taking questions. That way, the names will be spelled right. Give reporters time to read and digest the information before you begin.

The press package should also include copies of things you're going to show and tell the audience. A copy of your formal statement. Graphs, charts, pictures – which the media can include in their stories – are powerful tools in shaping the story.

Good Props Are Vital

Trial lawyers have learned that juries are more convinced by evidence than by witnesses. The best witnesses may have personalities that irritate some jurors. Witnesses have faulty memories. No matter how sharp, under tough cross-examination, witnesses can become confused.

They can be sandbagged with the nitty-gritty of what they said earlier that appears to conflict with their testimony today. Witnesses may contradict each other

But hard evidence – documents, pictures, the murder weapon – can be touched and studied by the jurors. Evidence can be carried back into the jury room during deliberations for closer examination.

Reporters Are Like Jurors

If you're under attack, the reporters at a news conference are very much like jurors at a trial. They've already heard the plaintiff's or prosecutor's side. Now they're ready to hear your side. Persuade them with the right witnesses **and especially the right evidence.**

You need to use props all through the news conference. Refer to the charts and graphs. Hold up the murder weapon or the broken part that caused the accident so all the world can see it.

One of my favorite props is a poster board that summarizes with large type the points you want to make. You need to stand near it from time to time, pointing to the next item.

Use Poster Boards

The poster board is a visual element for the story which also serves as a cheat sheet to keep you organized and on track. With it, you don't even need a script. Newspaper editors will always choose the picture of you at the chart over the shot of you at a podium. The chart lists all the critical points you want to make.

As you design a news conference, you should create the picture for tomorrow's front page and tonight's newscast. What we see will be much more memorable than what we hear.

When you hold a news conference to announce the introduction of a new product or service, I believe it's important to let reporters play with that product. If your new copier or computer is faster than the competition, have both at the news conference.

Let Them Try Out the Device

When you've finished your presentation, invite reporters to test what you've just told them. Personal involvement by the reporters will *always* result in bigger, better stories.

Suppose your company is announcing a major medical break-through. A small pump to replace an ailing human heart. A device so small it fits in the patient's chest, powered by an inexpensive battery.

Show us the new artificial heart. Let reporters handle it. Bring the frisky German shepherd in whom the prototype was implanted three years ago. Let reporters pet him.

Make sure the cast includes the inventor who toiled in his garage for 20 years. Let us hear about the failures and disappointment, until the night the inventor woke out of a sound sleep, knowing immediately how to solve the critical problem. He ran to his shop and tried it. It worked!

Guaranteed question: "How did you feel at that moment?"

The Rehearsal

No group of actors would think of going on-stage, in front of a live audience, without a rehearsal. Lawyers carefully rehearse their witnesses by asking them the questions they know the other side will ask on cross-examination.

But most people hold news conferences with no preparation at all. Standard procedure is to choose one or more knowledgeable people and throw them on stage to be cross-examined.

When I'm hired to help a company plan a news conference, we hold two rehearsals, if there's time. The first rehearsal turns up graphs that are too complicated; cast members who are not skillful enough. We rework the graphics. Replace some cast members.

Who Answers Which Questions?

Part of the rehearsal is designing who should answer which questions. Cast members should know when and how to hand off a question to someone else, who has more expertise. Employees may be uncomfortable taking the ball away from the boss, unless the play has been carefully practiced.

My choice of timing for the dress rehearsal is late in the afternoon the day before the real performance. It seems fresher the next day. As with all rehearsals, don't over-do it. Remember, these people are not professional actors. To much rehearsing can make them appear insincere. Regurgitating a canned script. The audience/jury should get the impression that what they say just occurred to them.

If possible, alert the **City Editor** at the newspaper and the **Assignment Editor** at radio and TV stations − normally with e-mail − a day or two in advance. Just a simple note. "We will hold a news conference at a certain time and place to discuss a certain topic." Say who will be there to answer reporters' questions.

Don't be vague or mysterious. There may not be enough staff to gamble on an unsure story idea. If your note clearly explains why this is a good story, they'll be there.

Call or e-mail the assignment and city editors the day of the news conference, to remind and update them.

The Earlier, the Better

If you want the story to break on the noon news and in the afternoon newspaper, call your conference no later than 10 a.m. Nine or 9:30 is better.

If you want the story to break on the evening news and in tomorrow morning's newspaper, call your conference no later than 3 p.m. One-thirty or 2 p.m. is better.

The Timetable

Let's look at the timetable. If you begin at three, the television crew may not be able to break down their gear and get away before four. A 30-minute drive back to the station gets the writing started at 4:30.

Script finished and approved by 5:15 means only 45 minutes to edit, during the worst crush of the day in the editing booths. If other stories are breaking late, your news conference may have a tough time competing.

In a crunch, a daily, 90-second news story can be slapped together in 15 minutes.

But it looks slapdash. Since a news conference can be called at any time, the earlier you set it, the more care and attention the story will get.

Avoiding Musical Chairs

Many news conferences are a major technical problem for broadcasters. A common setup puts five or six people at a long table, facing the reporters and cameras.

That format was created for press conferences – the printed press – before radio and television were invented. It just doesn't work for the electronic media.

So where do you put the microphones?

The sound problem can be overcome, if each person participating has a microphone that feeds into a central sound system, and each broadcaster can plug into that system. But that requires special equipment.

Do It Standing Up

If you don't have a sophisticated sound system, do your news conference standing up, with a podium for the microphones. Those participating in the conference stand close to the podium. Reporters can ask questions of specific people, and they can easily move to the mikes to answer, then step back.

Most people who don't have a lot of experience (and many who do) are much more effective standing than sitting. They invest more energy in what they're saying.

If you're expecting 100 reporters and photographers, you'll need a sound system to be heard at the back of the room.

Have backup people there who can, hopefully, rush out and get material you may have overlooked, and supply it to the reporters before you adjourn. If you can't get it in time, tell the reporters how they can get the information later in the day.

Keeping It Under Control

Like dogs and horses, groups of reporters can smell fear. They sense it when you're losing control. Once it happens, the mob mentality takes over. The first drop of blood puts sharks into a feeding frenzy.

It's *your* news conference. They're there at your invitation, and they need to understand what the rules are. *In advance.*

If you've said you won't take questions until your presentation is finished, stick to that.

When half a dozen reporters all shout questions at the same time, you need to be firm in saying you can only deal with one question at a time. Ask reporters to hold up their hands and be recognized before they ask a question.

If things get really wild, enlist the reporters' help in controlling their unruly colleagues. "I'm sure that some of you need the information we're trying to give you. But if you can't persuade your colleagues to be more civilized, we'll have to end the news conference."

The Final Curtain

If you're under attack and try to close the conference in midstream, you look like a coward who couldn't take the heat.

If you expect a stormy session, have a staffer announce in advance that you can only give the reporters X minutes. That staffer should then be the timekeeper who announces the time is up and gets you to your next appointment.

At that point, if things are going well, you can always be the good guy. "I'll take just one more question." You can take one more question all afternoon. You're in control. If things are going badly, you can escape without appearing to flee.

If you're briefing reporters in the middle of a breaking disaster, you may want to announce at the beginning that you will not answer questions until you know more. You should also say when you'll come back with more details. In that kind of situation, brief them often.

Careful With the Names

In a one-on-one interview, it's sometimes a good idea to use the reporter's name in your answers. "I'm doing this, Sally, because I think the school system is in deep trouble." But be careful about appearing to be too cozy with the reporter. Or trying to con the reporter.

In a news conference, your recognizing one reporter by name may prevent the competition from using your answer. That's how competitive they are.

Don't Leave Too Soon

Good reporters who know a lot about the subject of the news conference may want to interview you privately after you finish. They don't want to disclose their exclusive by asking key questions that would tip their competitors.

So don't leave too soon, before those more knowledgeable reporters have a chance to buttonhole you, one-on-one.

Again, the theater analogy. Special members of the audience get to go backstage and talk to the actors after the play.

SKILLS

NEWS RELEASES

Save the Forests & Digital Space –
Stop Sending PR Junk Mail

America would have more forests if public relations firms would stop cranking out so many news releases. Editors consider them an insidious form of spam or junk mail. Most are never read.

But PR people continue to blanket the nation with news releases to justify their jobs or their fees. Look what I did, they tell the boss or the client. I've been churning them out, but those editors are really stupid. They wouldn't know a story if it hit them in the face.

The boss's name is in the release. Probably in the first sentence. Words written for the boss are quoted extensively. Good stuff, the boss thinks. *The PR people are right. Local editors are truly dense. They don't appreciate my golden words. Even if I never said them.*

Historic Artifacts

For major news outlets, the written news release *in news story form* has been obsolete for years.

The news release was invented long, long ago to cater to lazy newspaper people. Since it was written in newspaper style, a sluggish editor or reporter could retype it, word-for-word, and put it in the paper.

In the bad old days, some sleazy reporters would even put their own by-lines on the news release without retyping it.

Public relations people loved it. They could not only plant stories, they could actually write them exactly as they appeared in print. It was better than free lunch in the old-time saloon. Times have changed.

Virtually all daily newspapers today consider it unethical to run an unedited news release. Some weeklies, however – short on staff and budget – will run them just the way you send them.

News Release Ethics

I guess the moral for people trying to get publicity is:

If you can still get away with it, do it.

But if they don't cover the stuff you tell them about, you need to re-think the whole process of news releases.

You can save a lot of time. The news release *written in news story form* takes a lot more time and paper than just a straightforward, quick summary telling an editor about a possible story.

Television news doesn't write a script until after the video is shot. The script has to be written around the video.

For radio news, if the story has actualities (recorded natural sound from the scene, or interviews) they, too, must write the script around them. So your effort to write a script for broadcasting is a total waste of time.

Advance Notice

What all editors – print and broadcast – DO need is advance notice so they can decide whether to cover the event. Most news releases today are sent by e-mail, but you should check with your local news outlets to find what they prefer.

In most cases, a simple, one-paragraph e-mail message will do, sent to the city editor (print) or assignment editor (TV and radio). Something like:

Mike Megawatt will speak to the Chum and Chowder Society next Tuesday at 12:30 p.m. in the Anthracite Hotel. He'll talk about the company's requested rate increase and the Power Company's petition to burn coal in the Smoky Hollow plant. We hope to have copies of the speech available shortly before the meeting begins.

Fact Sheets

If you're opening a new plant, send a simple fact sheet. Example:

The Wee Widget Company will open its new plant Monday. The new assembly line will be the most automated of its kind in the world. Robots will perform many of the jobs formerly done by humans. Production will increase by at least 30 per cent. Brief opening ceremonies begin at 9:00 a.m. A special news media tour begins at 9:30 a.m.

Plant construction cost – $ 46.3 million.

Building contractor – Saw and Hammer Corp.

Construction time – 21 months.

Building size – 92,500 square feet, all air-conditioned.

Special features – Employees' cafeteria, child care center, workout center, solar panels to heat water and generate electricity.

Expected production capacity – 6.6 million widgets per year; retail value, $134 million, to be sold throughout the world.

Better Questions

If the editor decides to cover the opening, the fact sheet will go to the reporter who's assigned the story. It will result in better questions. It will help a photographer plan what to shoot.

Fact sheets are especially helpful if you have a news conference. As a print and TV reporter, I covered news conferences where the only handout was a release in news story form that ran several pages. The facts, names and numbers I needed were hidden far down in the copy. Or simply weren't there.

TV News Is Pictures and Sound

Television is pictures and sound. Radio needs actualities.

Some major corporations know how to do it. And there is a glimmer of understanding in many government agencies. The modern news release for television can be a broadcast-quality video, sometimes produced by a professional studio. Local TV can use the video as an anchor reads a voice-over script. No need to even attend the event.

The print version of the release includes 300 dpi digital stills. Send them in color. They can easily convert to black and white if they choose. You need to be aware of their technical requirements and preferences, and how they'd like them transmitted.

E-mail providers have a limit on the size of attachments they can transmit. Files containing video and high-quality stills are large. Very large. So you may need to upload them to a website, where the news outlet can then download them.

Video/Photos as News Release

Video and photos of automobile crashes in laboratory safety tests are a good example of photographic releases. The tests take place over months, or years. Knowing that someday they'll want news coverage, they photograph the tests as they go along.

When they're ready for publicity, they supply video and still photographs of the crash tests, along with a fact sheet. If it's unusual, the fact sheet may provide technical detail on how the stills and video were shot.

The fact sheet notifies editors that laboratory officials and engineers will be available for interviews. Here again, both print and broadcast stories can be produced with very little investment in reporter and photographer time.

Video Cutaways

For TV news, the video can be used as cutaways to cover part of the interviews with the technicians. When a new airliner makes its inaugural flight, the manufacturer supplies video and photos of engineers at the drawing board, a model in wind-tunnel tests, the assembly line, the cockpit instruments, the plane's interior.

And finally, the plane in flight, outlined against a spectacular sunrise, with the company name prominent on the tail section. Hard to produce a story without using some of those pictures and video.

Video and Photo Libraries

The Pentagon has extensive photo and video libraries showing weapons systems, ships, planes, and troops in war maneuvers. When a reporter does a story that needs pictures, the public affairs office is happy to supply them. They make their people and their equipment look good. More corporations and government agencies need to build similar libraries.

Staff Photographers

Many police and fire departments now have broadcast-quality equipment and talented photographers who get to major disaster, fire and crime scenes before the news media do. They move in close, shoot pictures news photographers may not be able to shoot, then make them available to the media.

In the late 1980s, when I was training U.S. Coast Guard admirals, a Coast Guard cutter intercepted a boat loaded with drugs as it approached Florida. The boat refused to stop. Someone on the Coast Guard ship happened to have a personal camcorder.

Coast Guard Video

He shot videotape of the Coast Guard captain using a loudspeaker, telling the crew of the drug boat to move toward the bow of their boat.

He warned them that the Coast Guard was about to shoot out the smugglers' engine. And they did. You could see the tracers peppering the rear of the boat. It caught fire. The smugglers surrendered with their hands up. Great video, which was used by every TV network.

I suggested that all Coast Guard ships and aircraft should carry camcorders so their crews could video rescue and drug interception missions.

Think back to the TV coverage of Hurricane Katrina. Remember the videos of Coast Guard choppers lifting people off roofs? Similar video has become standard now in virtually every natural disaster.

The Coast Guard couldn't design a better way to build their image. I take credit for the idea.

If the public is going to know who you are, and what you do, we need to see you doing it. Words are no longer sufficient to tell your story.

Medical Research

Major medical research facilities do the same thing. In some kinds of pioneering surgery, the risk to the patient is too great to invite a news camera. So the hospital shoots the entire procedure.

If the operation is a failure, the video gets lost. If the surgery is a great success, the video becomes part of the announcement for the new surgery.

In these kinds of situations, if at all possible, shoot both stills and video.

Video Interview Releases

This is a true story of a pioneering breakthrough by a Miami attorney when I was still reporting –

Two cars loaded with teenagers collided head-on at 2 a.m. A 16-year-old boy in one of the cars received massive head injuries. The paramedics rushed him to the nearest hospital emergency room. The hospital refused to treat him, claiming they did not have a neurosurgeon on duty.

After a heated argument, the paramedics took the boy to another hospital, where he died. The first hospital's failure to treat the youngster was leaked to a reporter and became a major news story.

Day after day, the ethics of refusing medical treatment were debated in the media. You could smell the lawsuit coming.

Sure enough, a prominent attorney called a news conference to announce that he represented the parents of the dead boy, and had just filed a multi-million-dollar suit against the first hospital.

Control Over What is Said

He explained the basis of the suit and how he planned to pursue it. In closing, he said, "I know you would like to interview my clients, the parents. They have been through so much pain and suffering, I just couldn't put them through that ordeal.

"But – knowing you would want to hear their story – I videotaped an interview with them. I have copies here, for each of you."

In this real case, every local TV station used portions of the recorded interview. By making and editing his own video, the lawyer was able to completely control what his clients said publicly, while he shielded them from questions he wanted to avoid.

Now a Standard Technique

This is now a fairly standard technique. But isn't this just like the old written press release that editors feel uneasy using? Well, sorta.

But if the video is good stuff, they'll use it every time. They'll probably warn the audience that they didn't shoot it. They'll make clear where it came from. But they'll use it.

You don't have to own expensive video equipment. The quality of consumer-quality camcorders is incredibly good today. If you're in the right place at the right time, the news media will even pay for your video. News outlets now BEG the public to bring them their photos and video. There were some landmark events photographed by amateurs that led to where we are today.

The Zapruder Film

The 1963 assassination of President John F. Kennedy, captured on 8-mm film by Dallas dressmaker Abraham Zapruder is a famous example of amateur video broadcast and published worldwide. Now in the U.S. National Archives, the government in 1999 was ordered to pay the Zapruder family $16 million for the film.

Amateur news video really came into its own shortly after midnight on March 3, 1991, when George Holliday heard a commotion outside his apartment in Los Angeles. He had a new video camera in his hand as he stepped onto his balcony.

The Rodney King Video

Down below and across the street, Rodney King had just emerged from his car after a high-speed police chase.

The novice photographer turned on his camera and videotaped the entire incident as police shot King with an electric stun gun, then beat and kicked him repeatedly.

It made King's name a household word; led to the indictment and trial of the officers involved; the resignation of the police chief; and was instrumental in focusing the anger of the black community. That anger would explode in massive, deadly riots when the officers were later acquitted.

Disaster Photography

The most memorable photograph after the Oklahoma City bombing in April, 1995, was shot by Lester LaRue, the safety director for a gas company. It showed a firefighter carrying the bloody body of a small child from the debris.

This kind of amateur photography is commonplace today.

Radio Actualities

Local radio news is becoming extremely rate as station owners discover the profits to be made in completely automated stations. Most radio news is now bought from a national service.

But they're still hungry for anything that can make their station seem more enterprising. Local radio talk show hosts need variety in their programming. This provides marvelous opportunities for taped interview quotes when you're trying to get coverage for your issue.

Charts and Graphs

For both television and print, charts and graphs that make numbers meaningful are critical if you expect the public to understand your operation, your problems, or your solutions.

Big-city newspapers won't run the copy verbatim from your news release. But many of them will use your charts and graphs, unedited. You can easily create multi-colored graphics with virtually any computer word processing or presentation program.

You can provide low-resolution thumbnails embedded in an e-mail and attach the graphics files. The standard resolution for most print outlets is 300 dpi. They may also have a preference for bitmap, JPEG or GIF formatted files.

Security Camera Footage

As security cameras proliferate, we will see more and more of their footage on broadcast news. The national network of cameras covering almost every inch of major highways is already producing lots of video for the media that shows major crashes, traffic blockages and pileups.

If you have a security camera that has recorded a major crime, law enforcement will almost certainly ask for the video to use as possible evidence. There was a massive collection of security camera photography after the bombings near the finish line at the Boston Marathon in 2013. Some of it helped identify the bombers.

If you want credit for this kind of photography, you should think about offering it to the news media before you give it to law enforcement. Law enforcement has no obligation to give you credit for capturing the video.

And it would be very unusual to be paid if it is subpoenaed.

But you can get credit, and perhaps be paid, if you make that part of your agreement when you give it to the news media first.

SKILLS

OFF-THE-RECORD

Guerrilla Tactics for Leaking So Plumbers Can't Find the Source

A crucial skill for the media game is knowing how to successfully leak information. It happens every day in politics, government, and the corporate world.

Suppose your competitor has a major skeleton in the closet. If the media wrote about the skeleton, the competitor would be embarrassed or eliminated. But the media will never know about it unless somebody tips them off.

Tips Have Many Uses

Confidential leaks have other uses:

- **To brief** reporters in advance, so they can produce better stories
- **To negotiate** for the delay of a story
- **To correct a wrong** when the system seems powerless or disinterested
- **To bring reporters** into an investigation, so they'll feel more personally invested and put more effort into their coverage
- **To bring an outsider** in as an observer when you feel vulnerable and overpowered

When I begin to talk about off-the-record skills, occasionally an officer in one of my law enforcement seminars frowns at that idea.

"I'd never do that," the officer says. "I'm not a snitch."

Cops consider informers a necessary evil. They don't respect them. That's because informers are usually the kind of people who should be in jail. But to catch bigger fish, you have to give the informer a "walk."

Snitch = Traitor

Many in law enforcement think of informers as traitors who turn against people who trusted them. They'll sell their mothers if the price is right. Information from an informer is always suspect. In law enforcement, information is being sold − bartered − and informers may enlarge the truth to improve their bargaining position. They often get immunity for their own crimes if they testify against their buddies.

Media Sources Different

Confidential sources who leak to reporters, however, are usually very different kinds of people, with very different motives.

As an investigative reporter, I made off-the-record agreements with dope smugglers, gamblers, con men, bagmen, prostitutes and murderers. But they were the exception. My most frequent sources of confidential information were whistle-blowers. Conscientious cops, doctors, lawyers or government officials who became completely frustrated with injustice or incompetence and the system's failure to cope with it.

Setting the Agenda

They went outside the system, and their leak of information to me often led to stories that brought about sudden changes in the system. Prosecutors who had been blind to certain types of activity suddenly began personal crusades.

One of my most successful series involved a sleazy lawyer who had lied, cheated and bilked his clients in two states for 40 years. Officials at several levels had tried to put him out of business. They failed. He had an uncanny ability to weasel out of it − or a corrupt connection somewhere in the system. So one of those frustrated officials quietly came to me with a confidential file − the transcript of four days of secret, federal testimony. Despite that effort, the attorney was still in business.

Using the transcript as my springboard, I found the lawyer's victims. I interviewed them on camera, and gathered the documents that supported their accusations.

Amazing Things Happen

Once the story was broadcast, amazing things began to happen. The U.S Immigration Service, which had seemed impotent before, announced a hearing on the lawyer's qualifications to practice.

A federal prosecutor charged him with coaching a client to commit perjury about a phony marriage so an illegal alien could remain in this country. The lawyer was tried, convicted, and went to prison.

Interestingly, all of the details about the client who had lied under oath were in the original information leaked to me. It was available to the prosecution all along. But nobody did anything about it until my stories turned up the heat, and moved the case to the top of the agenda within the Justice Department.

Tobacco's Whistle-Blower

The tobacco industry had never lost a lawsuit until an insider leaked key documents to *60 Minutes* and *The Wall Street Journal.* Shortly after, there was a sea change in the campaign to curb tobacco sales and advertising.

Tobacco executives who had sworn before a Congressional committee they did not believe tobacco was addictive resigned or were fired within months. The leaked documents proved the industry had been aware for years of tobacco's addictive qualities.

States began to sue tobacco companies for medical costs they'd paid for patients with tobacco-caused illnesses. After several large settlements, tobacco threw in the towel and negotiated a national settlement.

In Florida, a civil court levied the highest punitive damages in history against the tobacco industry. All of this happened as a chain reaction to those original leaks to the media.

Honest Insiders Leak

In working stories on law enforcement corruption and medical malpractice, my usual confidential sources were other officers or doctors anxious to clean up their own profession.

I met people in unusual places at all hours of the day and night, with signals that would tip us to each other's presence. We used all sorts of maneuvers to make sure neither of us was followed or bugged.

Reporters Can Provide Protection

I was sometimes brought into law enforcement investigations, to do my own work on the same targets they were trying to catch.

The officers knew that in a corrupt system, once their investigation surfaced, they could become the targets of a dishonest prosecutor, or a legislative committee that wanted to keep the status quo.

They brought me in as an outside, objective observer, who would know the truth from the inside when the case finally surfaced. I accepted information in confidence from people who would be killed if certain people knew they had talked to me.

But most leaks are not nearly so cloak-and-daggerish. The most frequent reason to leak to the media is to give them advance notice, so they can gather better information and produce a better story, when the time comes.

Sometimes, in the real world, you will leak to the media to counter your opposition's leaks. A well-timed leak can mean millions of dollars in corporate America.

It can decoy attention away from what you need to do quietly. It can change the course of a political campaign, or a corporate takeover. Without "Deep Throat," the Watergate cover-up might never have been proven.

Plumbers Stop Leaks

In many cases, there is risk for the source who leaks. The Nixon White House during Watergate appointed groups of "plumbers" to stop leaks to fire and/or prosecute those who were leaking. Leaking classified information is a federal crime.

Those kinds of investigations have a chilling effect on others who are thinking about becoming a confidential source. Between 2009 and 2013, the Obama Justice Department prosecuted eight different cases involving leaks to the news media.

According to the *New York Times*, only three leakers had ever been prosecuted before by all previous administrations.

I cannot give you guidelines about when/whether to leak. That's up to your conscience. But if you decide to become a confidential source, I can help you do it successfully, with less risk.

What is Off the Record?

You can no longer be sure what "off-the-record" means. The Washington press corps has created half a dozen gradations for talking to the news media secretly.

They accept information for "background only." Or "deep background." Or quotes for "non- attribution."

Few people outside the Washington bureaucracy know what those terms mean. Even insiders are sometimes confused.

Before you tell anything to a reporter in confidence, be sure you both understand the terms on which you give – and the reporter receives – the information.

A Clear Contract

There should be a clear verbal contract before you stick your neck out. That contract is critical. If it's broken, you could lose your job, your reputation, or your life. The reporter's career could be destroyed.

Talking to a reporter, and then adding, "Now, that's off the record" won't work. The contract must be made *before* the information is given. You can't spill the beans and then ask a reporter not to tell. The agreement cannot be made retroactive.

Most good reporters won't accept information if they have to pledge they'll never use it. Their job is to gather, publish and broadcast information, not store it in their heads. They may already know what you're about to tell them. Promising you they will never write it would prevent them from using it.

"In Confidence"

I recommend that you abandon the term off-the-record, and say instead, "I'd like to tell you something in confidence." The reporter will usually say, "What do you mean by that?" Then you begin to negotiate the terms on which you will give the information, and what the reporter can do with it.

Go over, step-by-step, your joint agreement on exactly what you expect of each other.

Variations of the contract:

- **You may use the information I'm about to give you** in any way you choose, so long as you are very careful not to quote me directly, and give no clue about where it came from. This kind of information is often attributed to a "confidential source" or a "highly reliable source."

- **You can indicate my organization or group.** The story's credibility is increased if the source is less vague. "A confidential source in the police department." Or "a highly-placed executive in a major oil company."

- **You must agree to hold the story until a later time.** "I want you to be aware of this," you say, "Because I know you'll need to do some advance work." Lengthy police investigations are often leaked in advance to the media on this basis. Television, particularly, needs extra time to create visuals.

- **You may use this information if you can confirm** it with an-other source. This involves a lot of trust on your part. It is usu-ally used if you think very few people know, and the story would immediately point the finger at you as the source. The information may be more widespread than you realize.

- **Backgrounding.** "I want you to be aware of some things that are happening. In the next few days or weeks, a story will break, and then you'll understand the importance of what I'm about to tell you. But you cannot disclose that I briefed you."

- **No quotes.** "You may use everything I'm about to tell you, and use my name, so long as you don't quote me directly. You must paraphrase what I say." This is a protection for the source, in case there is bad public reaction to a trial balloon. "That's not exactly what I said. Let me clarify."

- **"You may never attribute anything to me** unless I specifi-cally give you permission." This is a time-saving device if you have a continuing confidential relationship with a reporter. There is an ongoing contract every time you talk.

Caution the Reporter

If the information is leaked for later use, be sure to discuss with the reporter the care that must be taken in gathering background ma-terial.

Stories like the coming retirement of a key executive; the intro-duction of a new model or product; the filing of a lawsuit; a revolu-tionary medical technique. If questions are asked, there is always a risk the competition may find out, and break the story.

Competitive Risks

In some contracts, the reporter agrees to hold your information un-til the agreed time *unless the competition is about to break the story.* If that is imminent, then the reporter may go with the story. This will involve your being able to trust the reporter to be honest with you about any competitive threat.

A good reporter will also insist that you agree, under this kind of contract, to tip the reporter if a competitor approaches you, asking questions about the story.

I once negotiated with a law enforcement agency that was willing to let us put a camera into their sting operation and videotape thieves selling stolen property to undercover police officers posing as fences. I had to agree to hold the story until arrests were made.

So much stolen property had been purchased in the operation, it would take six months or more to process the arrest warrants. It seemed like a simple contract, at first. But we kept running into "What ifs?"

You're Worse Than a Lawyer

Eventually, after two hours of negotiation, we came to an agreement that was satisfactory to both sides.

"Jones," one of the cops said, "You are worse at picking nits than any lawyer I ever dealt with."

"I have to be careful," I told him. "My reputation as a reporter who can be trusted is critical. We have to be very clear on what we've agreed to."

Confidentiality Guidelines

Here are five broad rules that you should review when you make a confidential source agreement with a reporter:

- **You must know and trust the reporter**
- **Does the reporter have authority to make the deal?**
- **How many others will know who was the source?**
- **How far will the reporter go to protect you?**
- **The exact words to be used in referring to the source**

Let's go over each rule.

Know the Reporter

I call this a contract, but it is a contract you probably cannot legally enforce. If you are a secret source, and want to remain invisible, how can you publicly accuse the reporter of violating a section of the contract?

Some reporters can be trusted more than others. All those who call themselves reporters do not live up to the generally recognized ethics of journalism.

As a general rule, reporters for major publications and broadcast outlets will be more reliable to deal with in confidential relationships. The ethical standards at *The New York Times* should be higher than the *Podunk Tattler* or an online blogger. But not always.

Older May Be Better

Older, established reporters are usually more reliable in this kind of agreement. The primary motive for some younger reporters is *getting the story to prove they can*. Older reporters, with an established reputation for getting the story, will let a story die rather than taint their reputation for integrity in dealing with sources.

If you don't know the reporter, call friends in your field and ask what they know. Your call, however, can be a tip to those friends. Once the story breaks, they'll realize you were the leak.

Undercover References

When I left my job as Washington correspondent for *The Miami Herald*, I moved under deep cover for eight months to investigate political and law enforcement corruption for WHAS-TV in Louisville, Kentucky. I knew nobody in law enforcement there.

I risked being killed if my undercover work was discovered. To protect my cover, only the station owner, manager, and news director were aware of my assignment. I was not on the payroll. The news director brought cash to my house every Friday night to pay my salary and expenses.

Jimmy Walker, a young reporter at the station, was detached to help me. They used a phony excuse for his lengthy absence. I never even went to the station until I came out from under cover.

To succeed, I needed confidential sources.

So I called law enforcement officers with whom I had worked closely all over the country. I told them in confidence about my new job, and asked if they knew anyone in the Louisville area that might be helpful.

Several did. They called ahead. You will be approached by a reporter named Clarence Jones, they said. He is a reporter you can trust. With those kinds of recommendations, I immediately began confidential relationships with honest officers who were enthusiastic about helping me.

Complaining if You're Burned

In most cases a reporter's immediate superior will know you are a confidential source. If you feel a reporter has violated a confidential agreement with you, you should complain loudly to that superior. And perhaps to the entire world. Violating a confidence is one of the most serious sins a reporter can commit.

Do You Have Authority?

Does the reporter have authority to promise you confidence? In some news organizations, only an editor or news director can give that pledge. There are atrocity stories of reporters who pledge confidence, then run to tell their editor what they've learned. "Hell of a story," the editor says. "We'll lead the front page with it."

"Wait a minute, boss," the reporter says, in panic. "I told my source we'd hold this until next Friday."

"You did, but I didn't," the editor says, with a smirk. He shafts both the source and his own reporter.

If you have any question about the reporter's ability to pledge confidence, bring the editor into the negotiation before you make your agreement.

Who Else Will Know?

How many others in the news operation will be aware that you are the source?

Secrecy is often broken by accident, not intentionally. The more who know, the greater the chance of a leak.

When Janet Cooke wrote her famous "Jimmy's World" feature story about an eight-year-old heroin addict, she refused to tell her editors at *The Washington Post* how she found the boy, or where he lived. She said she was doing it to protect the confidential agreement that led her to the family of junkies.

The *Post* published the story, graphically illustrated with an artist's drawing of "Jimmy" with his fist extended toward the reader, as if he were shooting up.

She won the Pulitzer Prize before the story was unmasked as fiction. Embarrassed, the newspaper had to admit the hoax and return the prize. Because of that danger, most newsrooms now require a cross-check by editors or attorneys who know the identity of sources for stories that hinge on confidential information.

But in today's jungle of online news and amateur reporters who have no real training, confidential agreements are EXTREMELY DANGEROUS if you're the source.

How Far Will You Go?

You should ask how far the reporter is willing to go to protect your confidence. Would the reporter go to jail rather than disclose you as the source?

Shield Laws

Some states have shield laws that give reporters legal protection for confidential information. The law shields them from subpoenas so they cannot be forced to disclose their confidential sources.

Most states shield ministers, lawyers and accountants from being forced to disclose information given them in confidence. There was an assumption that reporters had that same kind of shield under the First Amendment until the 1972, when the U.S. Supreme Court in *Branzburg v. Hayes* ruled otherwise.

If a state wants to give reporters that protection, it may, the Supreme Court said. But if the state does not, then a judge may decide whether the public good is more important than the reporter's claim of First Amendment rights.

The judge can order the reporter to disclose the source. Refusal can become contempt of court, and that can mean a jail term until the court order is obeyed.

The Exact Words

One risk you might not think about is the way in which the reporter will refer to the source. This part of the contract may be especially important. Confidential sources often ignore it, leaving it to the reporter to disguise the source.

The problem here is that the reporter can unintentionally identify you. "A veteran executive in the power company's research and planning division" may tell everybody in the company you are the source, since nobody else in the division has been there more than two years.

Your leak will be a lot safer if you discuss with the reporter *the exact words* to be used in referring to the source.

Confidentiality and Libel

Confidential sources raise major problems in libel litigation. To win libel suits, the facts published or broadcast by the media must be accurate. In the case of a public person or public official, the media must *believe* the story is true when it is published or broadcast. (See **Libel** and **Privacy**)

If the story is based entirely on confidential sources, reporters cannot prove truth without disclosing the source. In some states, their refusal to answer questions during pre-trial discovery will result in an automatic judgment against them.

Affidavits & Escape Clauses

One way to deal with that issue is to give the reporter a sworn affidavit, with a written agreement that your identity will be kept confidential unless it is needed to defend a lawsuit.

This technique is invaluable if the story is extremely sensitive.

I worked as producer and editor for a series of investigative reports for WPLG-TV in Miami after a group of doctors at a major hospital became concerned about several staff physicians.

They said heart specialists were performing experimental, unnecessary surgery on elderly patients so they could publish their findings in medical journals. The death rate in those procedures was very high.

The Doctor Was Not In

Some anesthesiologists at the same hospital were not even present during major surgery, their colleagues told us. They substituted interns, but the patient was billed as though the more experienced anesthesiologist had been there the entire time.

A number of more ethical doctors on the staff were alarmed about what they knew, but were reluctant to go public with their accusations.

If we broadcast this story, we told the whistle-blowing doctors, we will almost certainly be sued. We can't broadcast the story unless we know we can defend such a lawsuit.

So they leaked internal hospital records to us, and gave us sworn affidavits about what they had seen and heard in the operating room. On the back of each affidavit, we gave the doctors a written agreement never to disclose the doctor's identity unless the statement was needed to defend ourselves in court.

In our script, we said, "We have sworn affidavits from a dozen doctors who say they have seen ..." There was never even a suggestion of a lawsuit from either the doctors or the hospital. They knew we had the evidence that would convince a jury.

Anonymous Calls

An anonymous telephone call to a reporter is sometimes all it takes to get the story started.

When I was working at WHAS-TV in Louisville, a caller one afternoon told me half the traffic tickets written by city police were "fixed." I thought he was a nutcase and tried to brush him off.

So he began giving me specific percentages of cases that were nolle prossed (dismissed by the prosecutor) for different kinds of offenses. My ears picked up.

"Sounds like you have some kind of computer analysis," I said. "You're right," he said, "And if you're a good reporter, you'll find a copy."

Fixing Traffic Tickets

Then he hung up. Within a week, I had found a source who had a copy of the court analysis. I learned that political precinct captains had the power to fix tickets. So many were brought in, the court clerk had to work overtime to mark the cases as dismissed before each court session.

That was the first story.

Based on my experience, I knew the dismissal of drunk driving arrests is a major money-maker in a corrupt system.

So I hired a group of law students to help me collect all the data on several years of drunk driving arrests. We learned that not a single drunk driver had ever spent even one day in jail. That was the second story.

Missing Students

Most drunk drivers who were found guilty were ordered to attend traffic school. So I went to the traffic school records and discovered that half the drivers sentenced to attend class never showed up, and nobody did anything about it. That was the third story.

In the process of investigating all these court cases, I learned that one particular bail bondsman was a key player in arranging for charges to be dismissed. That led to a documentary on corruption within the bail bond system.

As a result, the Kentucky Legislature outlawed bail bondsmen. For a time, Kentucky was the only state in the Union where the state acts as the bondsman.

All that from one anonymous call.

Beware Caller ID

But be careful. With caller ID, your identity can be easily discovered. Use a pay phone, or the code that blocks caller ID.

Another way to get information to reporters is to mail it in a plain envelope. The reporter is protected in that way, too.

If the source ever becomes the focus of a lawsuit, a grand jury or legislative investigation, the reporter can honestly say, "I don't know who sent those papers to me."

Still another technique is to write a detailed memo and circulate it widely inside your organization. A copy will probably wind up in a reporter's hands. It could have been leaked by lots of people.

Partial Shield Laws

Some states have partial shield laws. The reporter cannot be forced to reveal the source, but any physical evidence provided by a confidential source can be obtained through a court process.

This happened to me once in Kentucky, which had a partial shield law. I had broadcast a tape recording of a police official carefully explaining the payoff system to a man who wanted to open an illegal gambling joint.

The tape had been made as the officer drove the ambitious gambler around in his squad car. You could hear the police radio in the background.

How Was the Tape Made?

I was hauled into court and asked how I obtained the tape. I refused to say, and the judge upheld my right to remain silent. But the prosecutor was able to obtain the audio cassette.

It was put through extensive laboratory testing. The police wanted to know how the tape was made, and how I got it. There might have been other microphones in other cars. They wanted to know where the leak was. They never found out.

Fingerprints & Copy Machines

Another caution: wipe fingerprints from anything you mail a reporter anonymously. Use rubber gloves in handling the documents and the envelope you put them in.

If you're sending copies of restricted documents, make the copies at a public copying machine, or one that is used by dozens of people. Pay for the copies with cash. With microscopic analysis, sometimes copies can be traced back to the machine that made them.

Your risk of being identified can be a law enforcement agency or a litigant in a lawsuit that is trying to find out how the reporter got the information.

Lawsuits give litigants powerful resources. Once the lawsuit is filed, the plaintiff has subpoena power to search for evidence, and to question witnesses under oath, just as a police department, legislative committee or grand jury can.

Leave it on Your Desk

Another favorite trick is to simply leave a document on your desk, as the prosecutor did in the movie, *Absence of Malice*. One of the first skills young reporters develop is reading upside down.

When a corruption investigation surfaced in Miami, I tried to obtain the list of people who were being notified that their conversations with a court fixer had been intercepted through a police wiretap. I was told that the list included dozens of public officials.

Disclosure a Federal Crime

But it was a crime to disclose the list. I checked my mailbox each day, looking for the Plain Brown Wrapper. No luck.

One afternoon, I received a call from someone I knew. "Can you come over to the boss's office right away?" he asked. "He needs to talk to you about something. It's important."

I dropped what I was doing and ran over. When I arrived, the man who had called me was sitting in the outer office, alone. The receptionist was gone. The boss' office was empty.

I Must Look Stupid

"The boss is down in the men's room," my contact told me. "Go on into his office. He'll be back in a minute."

I thought it was strange to be ushered into the inner sanctum with the boss absent. Then it became stranger. My contact left me in the office alone, and closed the door.

On a table in plain sight was the list of people intercepted on the wiretap. Beside it was a blank legal pad.

I know I look dumb, but that day I must have looked truly stupid. My contact in the outer office rolled a pencil under the door.

I was able to produce a story listing the public officials who had talked to the fixer.

SKILLS

SPEECHES

How to Wake Up
The Videographers

You are giving a major speech.

You know the media will be there. You *want* them to be there. The audience you need to reach is the entire community, far beyond the civic club or union hall. So you spend a lot of time writing the speech. Polishing phrases. Trying them out on your co-workers.

The big day comes. Sure enough, three television cameras are there, directly in front of the platform. The lights come on as you're introduced, and you begin, with all the cameras rolling.

But most speeches begin with jokes and fluff. By the time you reach the heart of the speech, the lights are dark and the cameras dead. The photographers are back at their seats, eating their pie. Not even paying attention.

Where's the Good Stuff?

Speeches are like white water rafting. Hard to tell where the exciting stuff is. You coast on smooth water, so quiet you can hear birds in overhanging trees. Then, quite suddenly, there is a rush of sound ahead. You come around the bend into rapids and the roar of white water.

When you get to that point in your speech, the reporters will nudge the photographers. Wake up! Get the camera rolling! But by the time the cameras are going, you may be back in calm water. The photographers shrug their shoulders and go back to their pie.

You may interrupt dessert several times. The real message may never reach the television audience.

Don't let it happen next time. Here's how to make sure the photographers will be alert and rolling at the critical moment:

Release Advance Copies

Give copies of the speech in advance to every reporter there. This gives them an opportunity to read through and pick the sections they want to record.

Since TV reporters will only have air time to report your major thrust — perhaps one side issue — they will mark those sections, and tell the photographer to shoot them.

Back at the station, this saves editing time. They know exactly what they have in the camera. It doesn't have to be logged, and they don't have to go back and forth, searching for a usable bite.

Print & Radio Like It

Radio reporters will usually record the entire speech. A transcript helps them, too, find what they want to use.

Print reporters won't have to take notes. They will follow along, marking the spots where you deviated from the prepared text. You'll find the quotes on tomorrow's front page are much more accurate this way.

Leak Part of It

Leak portions of the speech to the morning newspaper the day before. This will work only if what you're saying is truly newsworthy. If it is, the morning paper will have a story:

In a speech prepared for delivery at today's meeting of the Chum and Chowder Society, Power Company President Mike Megawatt says electric bills will rise much higher if his company is not allowed to burn coal in its Smoky Hollow plant.

Environmental groups are expected to oppose any shift from natural gas.

The advance story in the newspaper convinces radio and television assignment editors they should have reporters there to cover it. A local radio newscaster may read the newspaper story on the air, word for word.

The newspaper will be there to see what else happens. You might say something in the question-and-answer session following the speech. Or the audience might lynch you.

IMPORTANT: Don't leak everything to the newspaper in advance. Save the best quotes. That way, your audience won't feel like they're hearing a secondhand speech. There will also be fresh material for radio this afternoon and TV tonight. The newspaper will run a second story about the speech tomorrow.

Signals for the Good Stuff

Many of the best, most newsworthy speeches are not written in advance. They're spontaneous and unrehearsed. So you need to develop signals that tell TV photographers and radio reporters you're approaching something worth recording.

You're moving along, and you know the exciting stuff is just around the corner. You look over. The cameras are idle. To wake up the photographers, give them a warning. Something like:

Listen Up, Now

- **"Now, if you don't hear anything else** I say today, I want you to hear this. This is important." Or –

- **"What I'm about to say is going to make a lot of people angry**. It's going to cause a lot of hard feelings." (They're rushing now to turn on the cameras and tape recorders) Or –

- **"Nobody else has been willing to say this** in public. I think it's time we talked about it."

That kind of tease not only wakes up the photographers, it also whets the appetite of your live audience.

Tell 'em What You Told 'em

Remember to tell them what you just told them, but make it shorter. You'll discover that the summary is the perfect form for the time limitations of broadcasting. After every important section of a speech, either prepared or off-the-cuff, **summarize**. The summary will usually be the sound bite broadcasters use.

You should never again make a speech without drawings, pictures, charts, video – something visual.

Show Me While You Tell Me

You must show me something while you're telling me something. Otherwise, I won't remember. Television has conditioned Americans who listen, learn and remember only if the message is in both sound and pictures.

Often the pictures will be the stronger element in their memory, and the more powerful motivator. You can do it with a wide variety of techniques that range from poster boards and flip charts to projectors and large-screen HD TVs that are being fed from a laptop.

Try Not to Read It

Try not to read your speech. A speech read to a live audience is never as good as one that seems spontaneous. Conversational. Impassioned. Unless you're an accomplished reader and actor, reading a speech puts the audience to sleep. Or makes them pull out their smart phones to check for messages.

You computer can generate and print very large type that's easy to read at a glance. Rather than print the entire speech, have a simple outline. Bullets in 72-point type. Then you can glance at the screen and talk extemporaneously about it.

Speech TelePrompTers

If the speech is especially sensitive and you can't trust yourself to deliver it extemporaneously, you can rent a TelePrompTer® that works just like those the anchors use in TV studios. Barack Obama is so tied to his portable teleprompter, he has a completely different style when it's not there.

You may have noticed little panes of glass on each side of the podium. Many years ago, when I first spotted them on TV, I wondered if they were bulletproof glass to protect the speaker. Awfully small, though.

Those panes are the reflectors for a small computer monitor. The monitor is lower, where you can't see it. On the monitor screen, the speech scrolls by. The glass reflects the words and the speaker reads them. The speed of the scrolling is controlled by an operator who keeps pace with the speaker.

Presidential Speeches

All recent presidents have used TelePrompTers for important speeches. Watch a presidential speech closely on TV. The President will read a sentence or two from the prompter to his left, then switch to the prompter at his right. It looks like he's simply making eye contact with the entire audience.

Occasionally, though, he'll give it away by lapsing into a steady rhythm, swinging back and forth between prompters. One sentence to the left, turn; one sentence to the right, turn; one sentence to the left, turn again.

The Contact Lens Trick

Suppose you wear contact lenses, but need reading glasses. Some people who work hard at their speech technique have a contact lens for one eye with a reading prescription; a lens for the other eye with a distance prescription.

If they're reading from a prepared text, they read with one eye. When they look up and make eye contact with people in the audience, they use the other eye. It takes concentration, practice, and a strong stomach. Looking at the audience with the reading lens can make some people instantly seasick.

Wireless Microphones

One of the neatest gadgets to free you from the podium and let you be more animated is a wireless microphone. They're widely available now in electronics stores for less than $100. A professional-quality system that will do a better job in very large auditoriums or hotel ballrooms will run $350 to $500.

I highly recommend them.

In most cities, stores which cater to musicians and entertainers will stock the widest range of wireless microphone kits. You'll need several adapters to make sure the kit will work with virtually any sound system. The technicians at the music store can help you with that.

Podium Paralysis

A wireless mike cures Podium Paralysis. Behind a podium, many people grab hold and can't let go. The podium inhibits their normal gestures. We can't see the speaker's body English.

Coaching clients for a major speech, I often suggest that they come out to the side of the podium. Perhaps lean on it, to give the impression of a more intimate, off-the-cuff conversation. You'll need a wireless mike to do that. Otherwise, the audience can't hear you.

The tiny wireless microphone is clipped to your tie or lapel. A wire runs to a transmitter clipped to your belt. The transmitter is battery-powered, about the size of a cell phone.

The mike transmits to a small radio receiver, which plugs into the room's loudspeaker system. The wireless lets you wander to a poster board or a projector screen, so you can point at what you're talking about.

Freedom to Wander

When I finish speaking and take questions from the audience, my wireless mike allows me to walk into the crowd and have a close-up conversation with those who ask questions.

The mike picks up their voices, as well as mine, and amplifies the conversation through the speaker system. The people who ask questions feel they get a much more personal response this way.

Remember to Turn It Off

During breaks, remember to turn the mike off. Otherwise, everything you say in the hall – and the splash in the restroom – will be amplified through the speaker system.

When the speech is over, don't leave too soon. Stay long enough to let reporters covering the speech talk to you. In this way, they can make their stories unique. Stories get better play if they're not a carbon copy of the competition's story.

SKILLS

TALK SHOWS

Learning to Be Acceptably Rude

There are two kinds of talk shows.

The first are the syndicated shows that have replaced the old-time, freak show at the carnival. New, miniature replicas of the Inquisition, where exhibitionists confess the most intimate details of their lives and lusts while the voyeuristic crowd, aroused and loving it, plays holier-than-thou, clucking their tongues, pointing their fingers, screaming their condemnation of the vile guests in the pit.

There are people out there who love them. Jerry Springer's show is a great example. His early ratings leaped past the competition when fist-fights between bizarre guests, and sometimes the audience, became a regular event.

About the Other Kind

This chapter is about the other kind of talk show, where guests philosophize, discuss current events and sometimes engage in cerebral, witty exchanges with hosts like Piers Morgan, David Gregory, George Stephanopoulos, Anderson Cooper, or Bill Maher.

If you're a guest for one of those shows, the studio will seem like a huge, dark cavern. The ceiling will be a jungle of black, oddly-shaped stalactites, wires, booms, catwalks and stage lights.

Over in one corner, there may be a cozy little set designed to create an illusion. Perhaps a cardboard bookcase, a fake fireplace, or a mural of the city skyline. Sometimes a potted palm and two chairs, where you and the moderator will chat as though you were at the beach without your sunglasses.

Or it may be a panel show, where you sit at a desk facing a group of reporters who fire questions at you. Other guests may be there to attack your point of view. Some of your adversaries may be in another city thousands of miles away, connected by satellite.

It's Cold in There

The air conditioning is set low in television studios to counteract the heat of the lights. If it weren't that cold, you'd sweat and be uncomfortable. The thermostat is usually set for men who wear coats and ties. Women wearing thin, short-sleeved dresses sometimes have to fight to keep from shivering. Long sleeves will help you cope with the cold.

If the audience remembers what you wore, you wore the wrong thing. Wear clothes and jewelry that won't distract us. Unless you're trying to tell us something about clothes or jewelry.

Arrive Early

It's a good idea to arrive about a half hour before the show is scheduled. Producers have nightmares about guests arriving late, or missing the show entirely. Being on time is just as critical for a recorded show as a live one.

At most stations and networks, the studio and crew are scheduled solidly for months in advance. If you miss today's slot, there may not be another opening. Getting there early gives you time to get acquainted with the place, the moderator and the other guests.

Time for Makeup

You'll need some extra time to apply makeup. For field interviews, women should wear the same makeup they'd wear to work. But in a TV studio, the light will be much brighter and harsher. You'll need heavier makeup. You may look better if your eye shadow and cheek blush are a tone darker than usual.

Outside the studio, men don't normally use makeup. In the studio, to look normal, you need to wipe pancake makeup across your beard area and the shiny places. The floor crew will have makeup and a communal sponge. You may want to bring your own.

It's available in most large drug stores, or online, in different shades to match skin tone. To apply, wet a small sponge, rub it on the hard cake of makeup, and then wipe it on your face. It doesn't smell, and will wash off easily when the show is over. Receding hairlines and noses are particularly shiny in bright studio lights. And even if they shave just before they go to the TV station, some men with very dark beards look like they came in from skid row.

Apply just enough makeup to look normal through a studio camera. If it's done right, you can walk out of the studio and nobody will know you're wearing it.

The Choice Place to Sit

By arriving early, you can get a better idea of the ground the moderator intends to cover. If there are more than two people on the show – and you have a choice – take an end seat, rather than the middle. From the end, you can look at the other guests without moving your head back and forth. In the middle, it's like a tennis match as the conversation bounces back and forth.

Hiding the Mike Cord

Clip your mike so we won't see the cord. This may take some effort, but it's worth it. If the mike is clipped to a tie, run the cord inside a buttoned shirt to the waist band, then inside the waist band to one side. The only cord we'll see will be at the mike.

Clipped to a coat lapel, the cord can run from the lapel under the coat to your waistband at the side.

Women's clothes can make this a lot tougher. With a pullover top, you may have to run the cord inside your blouse, then out at the neck. Another route tapes the wire up the center of your back, then under a collar to the front where it's clipped.

You Can Take More Control

In some ways, in-studio interviews are very different from field interviews. Most of these shows will not be edited. They're broadcast live, or recorded and broadcast later just as they were shot. You will have more control over subject matter.

Through your answers, you may be able to lead the discussion from one area to another. Your answers can be a little longer. But if you begin to ramble, a good moderator will cut you off, try to force you to answer the question, or move on to the next subject before you make your point.

In a recorded field interview, you can make your point repeatedly. They'll edit and use just one. You must be much more clever on a talk show. To repeat the same thought, you have to state it very differently. Otherwise we think you're getting forgetful, and don't realize that you said that before.

Or that you've been programmed by a speech writer and can't hold a conversation without a memorized script.

Quick and Snappy

When the moderator asks a question, the best answer is usually a concise, one-sentence statement of your feeling or opinion, followed by your explanation of why. If you begin to talk too long, and get cut off, you'll still make your point.

Compared to other forms of radio and television, talk shows are boring. They normally feature "talking heads." The host will often insert video clips, just to break the boredom.

Talk shows work best when there is quick, snappy dialogue between guest and moderator, or between guests. The quicker the exchanges, the more interesting the conversation seems to listeners and viewers.

Yell and I'll Believe You

The person who is loudest and most aggressive is usually the most believable. Particularly if the obnoxious person goes unchallenged. That's also why so many talk show hosts are so aggressive and insulting. It keeps the audience awake.

A talk show on radio or TV will often have more than one guest. Sometimes they have very different points of view. There are no rules to give each guest an equal share of that time.

The assertive guest will get more time than the others. So you have to learn how to be what I call "acceptably rude."

Learn to Be Acceptably Rude

For television and radio, you'll find that you're much too polite. Your mama taught you to be nice. You wait until others have finished their thought. You're patient while they ramble, trying to find their point. When they make a mistake, or say something that is obviously untrue, you've been conditioned to sit quietly until it's your turn.

DON'T DO THAT.

As soon as the moderator or another guest says something that's inaccurate, interrupt. "Wait a minute!" you say loudly. "That's not true, and you know it's not true. Why would you say something so obviously phony?"

Not Challenged, It Must Be True

If you don't interrupt, the thought or statistic will be lodged as truth in the minds of viewers and listeners. It is much harder to dislodge it several minutes later. Interrupting also gives you an opportunity to take center stage.

If the guest or moderator you've interrupted comes right back, then the show becomes more interesting.

I remember hosting a talk show on capital punishment. The proponent was the state attorney general. The opponent was an American Civil Liberties Union lawyer. Both had done this before. They knew how to mix it up to make it interesting.

All I had to do as moderator was introduce them and then separate them for commercial breaks. The half-hour went by in a flash. As I passed through the control room on my way back to the newsroom, a technician who'd watched the taping said, "Boy, that was good television. I'd watch that!"

Conflict Makes Us Listen

Sharp conflict is a major element for intellectual debate and spectator sports. We like contests where the two opponents are evenly matched and eager to do battle. Team sports with lopsided scores – boxing matches where the fighters only dance and clinch – make us go to the bedroom, the bathroom, the kitchen, or another channel.

Knowing how far you can go without being obnoxious or rude is very difficult unless you've seen or heard yourself on camera. In my media training for the talk show format, I push people to be more rude and assertive.

I goad them until they feel they're out of bounds. Then they look at the playback. They're not nearly as rude or assertive as they thought they were. Recorded audio and video tend to tone down the conflict. It takes some practice to position yourself with just the right amount of assertiveness.

If you overdo it, you'll seem shrill. You turn us off. Or you can overpower another guest and make us feel like you're a bully. We will side with the underdog.

Take Along Your Visuals

If you have visuals (video or still pictures) that can help tell your story, let the producer of the TV talk show know several days in advance. The producer needs to look at them and decide whether to use them.

Your visuals may have to be converted to fit the station's technical format. You and the producer work out in advance how you'll cue the visuals. You can do it like a sportscaster – "OK, let's go to the video." This accomplishes several things for you:

- **By pre-planning** the use of the visuals, you have much more control over the content of the show

- **Switching the camera** from talking head to the visuals makes it possible for you to continue much longer than the usual 10 or 15 seconds; if the video is good and captures our attention, you can talk as long as the video runs

- **If you're in a debate format**, your pictures will be much more compelling to sell your side of the issue; and they may also enable you to have more time than your opponent

Bring the Book or Product

If you're there to talk about a book or a product, bring it along so the studio cameras can show it while you're discussing it.

If you're dealing with a very technical subject, or one that involves a lot of numbers, the producer may want to sit down with you well in advance.

This way, the station's artists can sketch or diagram what you're talking about to make it more understandable.

Avoid the Monitor

In the TV studio, there will be monitors that show what the audience is seeing. After the show begins, avoid the powerful temptation to watch the monitors. It's very difficult not to sneak a look at yourself on TV, but the camera may catch you. Very amateurish.

Pay attention to what other people are saying. Look at them. Remember, the director will be constantly switching to cutaway shots to make the video more interesting. Don't get caught on camera picking your nose or yawning when someone else is talking.

Bring an Assistant

In the **Interview Guidelines** chapter I suggest having a staff member present for an interview, to help you retrieve information you can't remember.

When you participate in TV or radio talk shows, the assistant is even more vital.

The assistant should bring a briefcase with pertinent documents, a legal pad and a Magic Marker®. The aide sits in the TV studio, where you can see the cues, but the camera can't. If you forget a point or a number, the staffer writes it on the legal pad and holds it up like a cue card.

During radio talk shows, the assistant can sit across the desk, in plain view, and slip you written notes.

Between Rounds

If you're in a debate format, the assistant can run over during commercial breaks to whisper in your ear, or hand you a document to use during the next block.

Just like the assistants who help boxers between rounds, your staffer can patch up your cuts, tell you what seems to be working, and which strategy to abandon. The aide will probably have a better feel for how well you're doing than you will.

Pace Yourself for Time

Once the show begins, you need to pace yourself, and be aware of time. If the conversation is lively, 30 minutes goes very quickly. When it's over, you may realize that you never got to the main point you wanted to make. If it looks like the moderator is not going to reach that area, look for some way to take the conversation there yourself. Something like —

"You know, we've danced around this entire subject without getting to what I believe should be our main concern." Then tell us what it is.

Time Signals

There are some strategies that can be played with time segments of the broadcast, particularly if you're debating with another guest. A 30-minute show usually has two or three commercial breaks. The floor crew holds up signs that tell the moderator when to break for a commercial. A big "2" means two minutes. A "30," thirty seconds before the break.

The signal that tells the moderator to hurry is both hands rolling — the same signal a football referee uses to restart the clock. In television, that means speed it up.

If they need to slow down and fill time, the floor manager may give a signal that looks like stretching taffy — "Stretch it out." Waving at the moderator means, "End the show. Tell everybody good-bye." And a finger drawn across the throat means:

"End it NOW. RIGHT NOW."

If you're aware of those signals, it helps you form an answer that will fit before a break. The moderator won't have to interrupt you in mid-thought.

Time Strategy

If you want to drop your big bomb so the camera can catch your opponent's surprise and fluster, make sure there's enough time before a break. You'll lose the effect if you drop the bomb and the moderator says, "We'll be right back." That will also give your opponent about two minutes to hide the shock and come up with a good alibi.

Surprise!

There are few surprise witnesses or shocking new evidence in criminal trials these days. Unlike the *Perry Mason* show, most rules of court procedure now give each side an opportunity before the trial to take depositions from every witness who will testify. They get to examine every shred of evidence long before the trial begins.

One of the attractions of live television debates is the chance that we'll see the gladiators use a surprise attack. We love to see them speared to the wall, writhing in mortal agony. There's no better place to drop new documentary evidence than in front of a live television camera.

The Zap! Scenario

The scenario can go something like this:

SENATOR BACKWATER: Nobody has a better voting record than I do when it comes to civil rights issues. I have spent my entire life fighting for justice and equality, regardless of race, creed or color.

CHALLENGER UPSTART: (reaching into a briefcase) Funny you would say that, Senator. I just happen to have a picture here of you, at age 21, leading a Ku Klux Klan parade down the main street of the little town where you went to college. I'll hold it up so the cameras can see it.

SENATOR BACKWATER: (flustered) That's a damned lie. Whatever trash you have there is a phony, cheap counterfeit.

CHALLENGER UPSTART: I thought you might say something like that, Senator, so I did some more research and came up with this column which you wrote for the college newspaper. Let me refresh your memory. In it, you say that black people – you actually used the "N" word – are genetically inferior and should never be allowed to enter the campus because they would not be able to understand abstract thought or civilized behavior.

And I have here a sworn affidavit from the editor of that newspaper, certifying that you are the same Phineas Backwater who led Ku Klux Klan rallies and wrote this essay. I'll make all of this material available to the reporters here in the studio just as soon as this debate is over.

ZAP!

Be Sure It's True

No other forum can match the impact of live, juicy exposure on television. But you must be sure the information is absolutely true. If it's not, you'll be accused of dirty tricks. If you hit below the belt, or take cheap shots, you'll look shady and sleazy. In the end, you'll be damaged more than your opponent.

Evasion Is Amplified

If you're on the receiving end of a tough question, radio and television make an evasive answer much more obvious. Pauses and stumbling for the right word are amplified.

It's probably best to answer the question as directly as you can, put your position in its best light, and move on. Use the question that points to your weakness as a springboard to reach your strength. Like:

OTTO MAKER: Yes, we fought the recall of that model because there has not been a single death as the result of a failure of that part. Not one. On the other hand, we voluntarily recalled the 1994 model when we realized we had a problem with a bolt in the rear suspension system.

Nobody had to force us to spend 80 million dollars for that recall. We did it voluntarily, once we were able to confirm there was a problem. And while we're talking about accidents, let's look at the difference in fatal accident frequency for domestic cars versus imports. I just happen to have the latest study here with me, charted so the camera can pick it up.

Take the Tough Ones First

For best overall effect, get the troublesome questions out of the way early. Then you have the rest of the show to counter with a brighter side. TV producers format their news shows that way. Put all the bad news at the beginning of the newscast. Close the show with a light, funny feature story – a "kicker" that leaves the audience smiling or feeling maybe everything's not so bad after all.

Radio Talk Shows

Some radio talk show hosts are so insulting you have to be a masochist to be their guest. You'll feel flattered when the producer calls you. But it may not be in your best interest to accept.

On the show, you'll get some wacko calls. Laughter is sometimes the best defense for stupid or insulting questions. The callers to these shows tend to be from the far ends of the opinion spectrum.

You're not going to change their minds. State your point, and if the host doesn't cut them off, move on with something like a chuckle and "It's very clear to me that I'm not going to change your mind and you're not going to change mine. But I respect your right to that opinion."

INSIDE THE MEDIA

EDITING

Did I Really Say That?

Editing is an art form. Your interview can be edited so skillfully, you can't tell what they took out, or stitched together. You can't see the scar where a good plastic surgeon makes the incision.

Or – when they've finished editing what you said, you may think the editor used a chain saw.

Once you've given an interview, you're at the mercy of the reporter and the editor. A tiny fraction of what you say in the interview will ever be published or broadcast. Maybe none of it. You may wind up on the cutting room floor. Simply a notation in the print reporter's shorthand pad.

Broadcast Interviews

The usual hallway interview, on the run, as you go in or out of a meeting, will last less than five minutes.

A sit-down session for radio or TV may go 10 to 20 minutes. Out of that, a maximum of 20 to 30 seconds will be used – and that much, only if they use several of your sound bites, separated by reporter narration or bites from interviews with other people. For one sound bite, they'll normally use 10 seconds – or less.

Newspaper reporters may spend an hour or two with you for a daily story; a day or two for a lengthy profile. Magazine writers may live with you for a week.

FACE Formula for Print

Print reporters are choosing the same kind of formularized quotes for their stories that radio and TV use. They simply use more of them. The FACE Formula applies for all media. (See **Interviews-Broadcast**) The editing for television is more complicated, because it must deal simultaneously with both audio and video.

Building the Edited Story

Audio phrases can be shuffled and spliced together for a radio story, and you can't hear the edit. Editing video requires some finesse to hide the shuffling and splicing. Here's how they do it:

Jump Cuts

Edits that splice one phrase to another that was spoken later in an interview are clearly visible. You can't miss them. They're called "jump cuts." The interview subject will always jump where the cut and splice was made.

At the beginning of the interview, you may have been leaning forward, elbows on your desk. Then you loosened your tie. At one point, you shifted back in your swivel chair and put your hands behind your head.

In the first phrase they edited, the knot in your tie was tight against your throat. The next phrase, butted against it, shows your tie loose. One arm is on the desk. In the third sound bite, you're leaning back with your hands behind your head.

As you watch the edited video, it looks like you suffer from a strange nerve disorder that makes you suddenly jerk from elbows-on-table to hands-behind-head. You also seem to have a tie with a magic knot that tightens and loosens itself.

Cosmetic Cutaways

In the early days of television news, they decided jump cuts were too distracting. They developed a way to hide them.

A cutaway shot is edited onto the story for only a second or two. It replaces the video of you , but the sound is not changed. It is as though we had looked away while you were speaking. As soon as the jump cut passes, we see you again.

In that brief cutaway second or two, we forget that your tie was tight against your throat before we looked away. Or that you were leaning forward a second ago, and you're now leaning back.

Favorite Cutaways

The three most frequently used cutaways are:

- **Two-Shot** – A wide-angle shot that shows both the reporter and the subject of the interview. The interviewee is talking, but the camera is too far away for viewers to tell whether the movement of the lips matches the words we're hearing.
- **Listener** – The reporter listening, or the reporter making notes.

It is sometimes shot from behind, and over the shoulder, of the person being interviewed. Many reporters have a bad habit of nodding during listener cutaways.

- **Crowd Shot** – Edits of speeches are covered by a cutaway to the crowd, or a closeup of one person in the crowd, fervently listening or applauding.

Print Also Edits

Print journalism interviews are heavily edited, too. Unless the full transcript is printed, a newspaper story takes a phrase here, a phrase there, often out of sequence.

But if the words are direct quotes, the ethics of print require an ellipsis (. . .) to tell readers where the edit points are.

That's the difference. People who work in television understand that a cutaway means an edit point, but many viewers don't know that.

Broadcasting Needs a Signal

To avoid criticism about the editing process, I believe broadcasting needs to create some signal to tell viewers where edits took place. During the cutaway, for instance, an audio beep could be inserted. If the beep were standardized, it could become broadcasting's equivalent of the ellipsis.

In both broadcasting and print, an ethical reporter is very careful to make sure the edited version of an interview does not change the meaning or intent of what was said.

Jump-Cut Commercials

In the 1960s, the "hidden camera" was a favorite technique for television commercials. A woman, supposedly unaware of the camera, was asked to compare her laundry before and after it was washed in Brand X.

Somewhere along the line, somebody said those commercials were misleading if the edit points were hidden with cutaways. So commercials began letting the jump cuts show.

Some news organizations, concerned they will be accused of distortion, now let jump cuts show in sensitive interviews. Or show a quick flash where the cut was made.

Reverse Questions

Another editing device for broadcasting uses the "reverse question" between answers. In most TV interviews, there is only one camera. It shoots the interview subject, but not the reporter asking the questions.

So after the interview, the reporter is shot re-asking the same questions asked during the interview. The camera is reversed, shooting in the opposite direction, over the shoulder of the interview subject. The reverse-shot question can then be used as a bridge to get from one answer to another.

Instead of a cutaway at the edit point, we see and hear the reporter asking a question. Then we jump to the answer. The effect is a continuously flowing conversation.

Listen Carefully

The danger in the reverse question technique is that the question may not be phrased exactly as it was when you answered it the first time. A slightly different question, spliced to the old answer, can be misleading.

When a TV reporter completes your interview, listen carefully as reverse questions are shot. If they're not restated exactly as they were when you were answering the question, politely point that out to the reporter.

If you have some reason to suspect the reporter's integrity, have a staff member make a shorthand transcript of the reporter's questions during the interview. The staffer can then compare the shorthand notes with the reverse questions that are recorded.

If you have any reason to doubt the reporter's competence or integrity, make your own recording of the entire interview. Make sure the reporter knows you're recording the interview, to avoid legal problems. The recording is the only proof you'll have if you complain about the editing of the story

Double-Shooting

On a major TV network documentary – particularly a sensitive, controversial subject – interviews will be "double-shot." The entire interview is recorded by two cameras – one camera shooting the interview subject, the other shooting the reporter.

In that way, reporter's questions and reactions are recorded exactly the way the interview subject saw and heard them. There can be no reverse question distortion. But few local stations or network field crews have the resources to double-shoot interviews.

One of your goals should be learning how to craft a quote so the reporter – whether print or broadcast – will use it exactly as you spoke it, without editing or taking it out of context.

Editing by Headline

A perennial complaint about newspapers is the inaccuracy of headlines. That, too, is a form of editing. When the headline distorts the story, you should complain.

Headline writers are true specialists. They must condense the thrust of the story into five or six words. And the words must fit the column, very much like a crossword puzzle.

On deadline, the headline writers sometimes write the headline after reading only three or four paragraphs of the story. If they had read a little further, they would have a very different perspective, and a more accurate headline.

Editing by Committee

Newspaper and magazine stories go through the hands of a series of editors. At each stage, the story may be changed to suit the whim of the latest editor. That process can gradually distort the story and make it inaccurate or misleading.

The traditional newspaper story formula made it easy to shorten stories with little distortion. It was called the inverted pyramid. The main points of the story were at the top. Then the importance of the information dwindled into pure trivia in the last paragraphs. If the story didn't fit the page, they simply cut it from the bottom.

The inverted pyramid has largely been replaced by the Sony Sandwich story formula. It is harder to shorten during the editing process without affecting its accuracy.

Soft Leads

Soft leads are very popular in today's newspapers. In some of these stories, the real news is delayed until the middle of the story. Their readers have already seen the story on TV or the Internet, but want to know more from the newspaper version.

The newspaper reporter attempts to give us something broadcasters and the Internet did not cover. So the story becomes an artistic production, beginning like a novel, with a "soft" lead, like this one:

David Dentz got out of bed, stretched, yawned, and brushed his teeth. He wondered why he hadn't heard his three-year-old son, who usually got up before his parents.

Dentz checked his son's room. He wasn't there. The TV was dark.

Then Dentz looked out the patio door and stark terror gripped him. There, on the patio, was a huge Bengal tiger, licking his chops.

The tiger had devoured David Jr.

But What Was the Score?

Sports writers, competing against live coverage of the ball game, go all-out to give us a feature slant on yesterday's game. So much so, they sometimes forget to tell us the final score.

Stories with soft leads are much harder to edit. The editing takes extra time and skill. So do the headlines. With deadline pressure, these stories are sometimes chopped from the bottom to make them fit. This can badly distort them. When it does, you need to complain. (See **Fighting Back**)

INSIDE THE MEDIA

FAIR & BALANCED

The Swing Back to News With an Obvious Slant

U.S. Constitution, AMENDMENT # 1 –

Congress shall make no law respecting an establishment of religion, or prohibiting the free exercise thereof; or abridging the freedom of speech or of the press; or the right of the people peaceably to assemble, and to petition the government for a redress of grievances.

Take another look. Nowhere does the First Amendment to the U.S. Constitution say the press in America shall be fair. If your Mama told you the news media would be fair and balanced, your Mama was a liar.

Early History

The early journalists in this country were revolutionaries. They used their printing presses to spread their personal opinions – especially about politics and religion. What they published was neither fair, nor balanced.

The American Revolution was conceived and sustained by writers like Thomas Jefferson and Tom Paine. They believed with religious intensity that ideas – and the freedom to express those ideas, no matter how warped or crazy – were sacred. So they preserved that belief in the Constitution.

It was a novel idea. A noble experiment. The press was the only business given Constitutional protection, even though newspaper stories in those times were grossly distorted to make the editor's friends appear saintly, his enemies grotesque.

During and after his presidency, the newspapers of his time targeted Thomas Jefferson with unfair, unbalanced abuse. Yet he wrote: "If I had to choose between government without newspapers, and newspapers without government, I wouldn't hesitate to choose the latter."

Editorial cartoonists who disagreed with Abraham Lincoln drew the President in caricature as a gorilla.

Until early in the 20th Century, most newspapers announced their political bias on their front pages or mastheads. You didn't need to look at the declaration of their political point of view. You knew, from reading them, the owners and editors were Whigs or Tories, Republicans or Populists.

Many of these early, personalized publications did not care whether they made money. They were evangelists, publishing their prejudices and points of view because they were true believers in their causes. For some, it was also because they loved the notoriety of being ornery.

Advertising's Influence

Early newspapers had little or no advertising. Any money they made came from subscriptions and street sales of the paper. Then advertising began to creep in. If you needed the money, it was important not to alienate advertisers, or the readers those advertisers were paying to reach.

The "press" which had been a conduit for ideas began to be a money-making venture as well. It was economic pressure that forced newspapers to be more fair. As advertising became an accepted part of daily and weekly newspapers, the advocacy was toned down.

Still, the mass circulation dailies in the early 1900s were not exactly fair. Sensational stories fueled the circulation wars. They mangled both truth and the small group of people they wrote about – people unfortunate enough to be caught in the crossfire.

Watergate Era Fairness

The American news media in the Watergate era (early 1970s) were probably more fair than at any time in our history. A new ethic had crept into American journalism. Journalists were supposed to be objective observers relaying information that was not infected with their personal point of view. Or the views of their corporate parent.

The pendulum is now swinging the other way.

Again, it is money and profit that are pushing media outlets to be unfair and unbalanced. As I've written in other chapters, I believe the shift in media ownership to mega corporations has put profit above accuracy, truth, fairness and public service. Political zeal combined with the profit motive can create an enormously powerful voice.

And on the other end of that economic spectrum are bloggers who in many ways replicate the evangelistic zeal of the 18th Century press. They are often individuals with axes to grind who do not publish on the web for money. They do it out of an angry, dedicated mission to sell their view of the world to their readers.

If It Bleeds, It Leads

"If it bleeds, it leads" was the old mostly true axiom for television news. Since ancient Roman times, the audience has been blood thirsty. They love to watch battle. To experience death and destruction vicariously.

Much like sports fans who go to football games, automobile races and air shows with a secret thought that they might witness the modern gladiators being killed or maimed.

In public opinion polls, people say that they detest political attack ads and candidates who savage their opponents. But those tactics almost always succeed in electing candidates who use them.

Rise of the Media Mega-Corporation

The powerful force at work in 21st Century America is media ownership by mega corporations. Their profit is based on the number of people who read or watch their news.

Advertising rates are based on newspaper circulation or "eyeballs" viewing TV commercials.

Sometimes the corporate owner has a well-known political stance and uses the media ownership as a tool to advocate that point of view.

Sometimes the corporate owner doesn't have a political agenda, but makes a calculated bet: That more readers or viewers will be attracted to slanted news that fits their view of the world.

The Creation of Fox News

Case in point: the rise of Fox News. In 1984, Rupert Murdoch bought a controlling interest in 20th Century Fox, the Hollywood movie studio. He was already a major player in British and Australian media.

Then he bought six American television stations, which became the nucleus for the Fox Broadcasting Company.

In 1996, Murdoch created the Fox News Channel - a 24-hour network to compete with Ted Turner's CNN. Murdoch had always maintained that most news media have a liberal point of view. One of

Murdoch's goals as a media mogul was to offer a more conservative point of view to balance the scales.

Roger Ailes' Political History

To create and then run the Fox News Channel in 1996, Murdoch chose Roger Ailes. Ailes had been in television since the early 1960s. When he and Richard Nixon crossed paths during the 1968 Presidential campaign, Ailes convinced Nixon that he could make him a more likeable candidate. He did, and Nixon won.

From that point until 1992, Ailes was a favorite on-camera coach, strategist, and producer of TV campaign commercials for major Republican candidates. During that time, he persuaded Rush Limbaugh to expand his radio show to television.

His work with Republican politicians subsided when Ailes was hired to run the MSNBC cable channel in 1993. Three years later, Murdoch got him to jump ship and create the Fox News Channel.

Ailes persuaded most of his top staff members at MSNBC to go with him to Fox News. And he has been incredibly successful at getting CNN viewers to jump to Fox.

Fox News' Catch Phrase

Interesting that Fox News' catch phrase is "fair and balanced." If they say that often enough, most people will believe them. They appear that way to viewers who are far-right in their political beliefs.

Murdoch has always believed that sex sells news. He owns *The Sun* – Great Britain's largest newspaper. Since 1970, page three of *The Sun* has always featured a photo of a good-looking topless model. Murdoch also owns America's largest newspaper, *The Wall Street Journal*. No topless photos there. Yet.

Murdoch Believes Sex Sells News

Following *The Sun's* marketing tradition, almost all female Fox anchors are gorgeous, well-endowed women in form-fitting dresses. Their makeup and hair emulate movie stars. But they keep their clothes on.

To independents, the slant in Fox stories is immediately obvious. If Barack Obama walked on water, the Fox story tease would be "President Can't Swim."

Most political observers give Fox News major credit for the rise of the Tea Party and the roadblocks they have created in Congress.

The Liberal Side

Meanwhile, MSNBC (which Ailes once headed) has become the liberal voice of cable TV. Their reporters and commentators let you know right away that Republicans are incompetent, evil idiots who are responsible for all of government's ailments.

John Stewart's *The Daily Show* on the Comedy Central cable channel is aggressively anti-Republican. Some polls show young people get more news from this show than any other news outlet, and are better informed about current events than those who watch early morning news shows. But as this book goes to press, conservatives seem to have a much greater voice in news media content than liberals.

The Unbalanced Points of View

It may be that liberals tend to be more tolerant of other points of view, and are less aggressive in attacking their opponents. Talk radio is a bastion of conservatism. To attract and keep its audience, it must be in constant attack mode. Fear, contempt, and attack are staples there.

(Think of the basic techniques used by popular right-wing authors and commentators like Rush Limbaugh, Ann Coulter, Glenn Beck and Sarah Palin.)

If you line up the best-known conservative commentators, you find a cluster of conservatives who are now on Fox, or were once featured there – Beck, Palin, Sean Hannity, Bill O'Reilly.

The same is true of liberals at MSNBC – Think Chris Matthews, Rachel Maddow, Ed Schultz and Keith Olberman. *The New York Times* op-ed page frequently publishes the work of liberal writers like Paul Klugman and Robert Reich. Bill Maher is probably the most vicious liberal voice when he skewers conservatives and Republicans from his weekly show on HBO.

Market Research & Point of View

If market research shows the audience is moving toward a more liberal point of view, watch for other news outlets to show more liberal bias.

This has always been the central dilemma for news reporting: Do we tell them what they need to know, or what they want to hear? If profit is the central, driving force, you give them what they want.

The First Amendment was designed to prevent government from influencing news media content. The Founding Fathers could not have possibly imagined today's ownership of news outlets.

Today's most frightening question: If the "press" is simply a profit-making machine, does it deserve Constitutional protection?

Government Control and Influence

U.S. Supreme Court decisions have made it clear that government cannot interfere in any way with the content of the *printed* press.

For a long time, government *has* regulated broadcast content. That is rapidly fading. Partly because the Federal Communications Commission (FCC) can get in the way of media owners who want to expand and monopolize their markets.

Those owners have a large army of lobbyists working to prevent or remove any government control over them.

There are some laws making it a crime to disclose national defense secrets. The courts have said government can punish the publisher, but cannot prevent the publishing. Court decisions call this "prior restraint."

Civil suits can be filed against the media *after* they damage your reputation or invade your privacy. (See **Libel** and **Privacy**) But you cannot prevent them, in advance, from doing the damage.

Broadcasting Different

Despite the First Amendment guarantee of free speech and free press, for more than half the 20th Century, Congress passed laws, and created agencies, to tell broadcasters what they could — and could not — say on the air.

The FCC can still take away the license of a broadcaster who breaks the rules. But that is rarely done.

The Fairness Doctrine

For many years, the broadest exercise of governmental control was through a regulation called the Fairness Doctrine.

Because radio and TV were a new form of distributing information, Congress, the FCC and the courts ruled early in the 20th century that broadcasting was not "the press" that was given special freedom by the founding fathers.

Broadcasters, the government ruled, had to be fair in covering controversial topics.

How did they evade the Constitution to get to that conclusion?

Early Radio

As AM radio spread across the world in the 1920s, radio signals began to override each other. As the number of stations grew, finding a clear channel became more and more difficult. Even if you found one, there was no guarantee it would stay clear very long.

Broadcasters went to Washington to solve the problem. Their lawyers came up with a theory that would get around the First Amendment and allow Congress to regulate the new medium.

It went something like this: Radio waves cross state lines. Therefore, broadcasting is interstate commerce. The Constitution gives Congress the right to regulate interstate commerce.

Of course, newspapers cross state lines, too.

So a second argument was devised. Broadcasters do not own the medium that carries their signal. Radio waves must go through the sky. The sky belongs to the public. Therefore, government has a right to regulate how the public sky is used.

1927 Federal Radio Commission

Congress created the Federal Radio Commission in 1927 to give order and decency to the airwaves. Anybody using the public sky had to get a license. The commission decided who was morally fit to hold a license and use the public sky.

Shortly after it was created, the Radio Commission began to regulate not only radio signals and equipment, but what broadcasters *said* over the air. And how they allocated air time.

Creation of the FCC

In 1934, Congress rewrote the Radio Act and created today's FCC. There was no question that Congress, through the FCC, restricted freedom of both speech and the press. Most people accepted it as a practical, though unconstitutional solution. Without it to control how broadcasting signals were used, broadcasting simply would not work.

In the early days, radio created an immediate political problem. During a campaign, the owner could use a radio station to help one side, and hurt – or ignore – the other. The Equal Time rule was conceived to prevent radio from influencing politics.

Equal Time is Not Fairness

Many people confuse fairness and Equal Time. If a broadcaster criticizes them or their business, they demand equal time to reply.

Equal Time for Politicians Only

But Equal Time applied only to candidates for political office. Congress and the FCC designed it that way.

To carry out the pretense of press freedom, the FCC's Equal Time rule had a clause exempting news coverage. The same kind of clever maneuvering that enabled Congress to waltz around the First Amendment could also take Equal Time for a spin.

Presidential Debates

In 1960, after Richard Nixon and John F. Kennedy agreed to a series of nationally televised debates, Congress ordered a temporary suspension of Equal Time requirements for that year's presidential campaign. That meant the marginal candidates would not have to be included. The question came up again in 1976, when the networks planned a series of debates between challenger Jimmy Carter and incumbent Gerald Ford. Then-Cong. Shirley Chisolm, also a candidate for the presidency, demanded that she be included.

Carter vs. Ford vs. Chisolm

The Equal Time rule seemed to be on her side. Other, more obscure candidates would also have to be invited to the debate. So a plot was hatched. The networks canceled the debate. Then the League of Women Voters announced it would sponsor a debate between Carter and Ford.

Aha! the networks said. If you sponsor a debate between the two major candidates, it will be a news event, and we will cover it. Equal Time will not apply.

Chisolm and the National Organization for Women (NOW) ran to the FCC. The FCC announced it had been misinterpreting Congress' intent by requiring equal time for all candidates. Equal Time did not apply to the League event.

Chisolm v. FCC
538 F.2d 349 [D.C. Circ.] (1976)

Chisolm and NOW took the FCC decision to court. A panel of U.S. Circuit judges agreed with the FCC's decision. Government can't make news judgments for broadcasters, the court ruled.

The U.S. Supreme Court refused to hear an appeal, in effect endorsing the lower court opinion. The League-sponsored debate was televised, with only Carter and Ford on the platform. Compare broadcasting's Equal Time requirement to an almost exact parallel in the print media.

Equal Newspaper Space

In 1913, the Florida Legislature passed a law protecting the election process from unfair newspaper influence. It was introduced by a lawmaker who was a newspaperman and signed by a governor who was a newspaper publisher.

It said that candidates had the right to reply to newspaper attacks or endorsements during a political campaign. The newspaper had to give equal space to the other side, and print it in the same section of the newspaper. Until 1972, the Florida Equal Space Law had never been seriously challenged. That year, Pat Tornillo, leader of the teachers' union, ran for the Florida Legislature. *Miami Herald* editorials attacked Tornillo. *The Herald* denied him equal space.

Miami Herald Publishing Co. v. Tornillo
418 U.S. 241, 94 S.Ct. 2831, 41 L.Ed.2d. 730 (1974)

Tornillo went to court. After he had lost his political race, the Florida Supreme Court sided with Tornillo. The state justices said the Equal Space Law was not a violation of the First Amendment. In their ruling, they heavily emphasized the similarity to the federal Equal Time rule for broadcasters.

The Herald appealed. This time, Tornillo and Florida's Equal Space Law lost. Writing the opinion for a unanimous court in June, 1974, U.S. Supreme Court Chief Justice Warren Burger said:

The choice of material to go into a newspaper ... whether fair or unfair ... constitutes exercise of editorial control and judgment. It has yet to be demonstrated how governmental regulation of this crucial process can be exercised consistent with First Amendment guarantees of a free press.

In his opinion striking down all equal space laws for print, the Chief Justice did not mention the court's very different attitude about Equal Time and the regulation of broadcast material.

The Rules are Disappearing

But those rules are disappearing. In 2000, the federal appellate court in the District of Columbia ordered the FCC to repeal its Personal Attack and Editorial Reply rules.

They were an outgrowth of the FCC's old Fairness Doctrine, and very similar to the Equal Time requirements for political campaigns.

Both the National Assn. of Broadcasters and the Radio-Television News Directors Assn. had argued in court against the FCC's Equal Time, Personal Attack and Editorial Reply rules.

Rather than enhance broadcast news, they said the rules actually discouraged radio and television from assuming their Constitutional responsibilities as part of the American "press."

Coping with the right-to-reply and Equal Time requirements was so difficult, they said, most stations simply avoided editorial endorsements of candidates, as well as serious political and investigative reporting.

On October 26, 2000, the FCC complied with the court order and repealed both the personal attack and editorial reply rules that had required broadcasters to give those attacked on the air a chance to reply. The court process had taken 20 years.

The Old Fairness Doctrine

The old Fairness Doctrine was a much broader concept which evolved over a period of years as the FCC heard complaints about broadcasters abusing their licenses to use the public airwaves.

The Fairness Doctrine said broadcasters must be fair in covering "controversial issues of public importance." Because broadcast outlets were limited, the FCC said stations had an *obligation* to inform the public by carrying all points of view on those issues.

Supreme Court Endorsement

The Fairness Doctrine was not approved by the U.S. Supreme Court until 1969. The justices ruled in *Red Lion Broadcasting Co. v. FCC* that the scarcity of broadcast channels required a different kind of Constitutional treatment for broadcasters.

The court said TV and radio – because of their special license and privilege to use the public sky – had to be fair.

Note that cable TV was gradually taking over the delivery of television signals. The public sky argument could not apply to broadcasting by cable.

But cable companies were required to include major local TV stations in their lineups. So government still had some control over those cable channels that were also broadcast.

Government Deregulation

As part of its philosophical belief in deregulation, the FCC conducted a series of hearings on the Fairness Doctrine and issued a report in 1985.

It concluded that the explosion of new technology had made the old argument about scarcity of channels obsolete:

The public has access to a multitude of viewpoints without the

need or danger of regulatory intervention. ... In stark contraven-
tion of its purpose, [the doctrine] operates as a pervasive and sig-
nificant impediment to the broadcasting of controversial issues of
public importance.

In that 1985 report, the FCC said the Fairness Doctrine had actually reduced public discussion, not broadened it. In practice, stations
had avoided controversial issues, rather than go through the hassle of
airing opposing points of view.

The 1985 report said the FCC believed its own Fairness Doctrine
was unconstitutional. But the Commission refused to repeal it, saying
it would leave that decision up to Congress or the courts.

Congress disagreed with the FCC, and in early 1987 wrote the
Fairness Doctrine into law. President Ronald Reagan vetoed it. Con-
gress could not muster enough votes to override. In August, 1987, the
FCC finally repealed the Fairness Doctrine.

Public Affairs Programs

The FCC once required a certain amount of news, public affairs
programming, and public service announcements at all stations. No
longer.

Public affairs programming at local stations was often a weekly
talk show, where guests discussed a current issue. They were usually
very boring. They're almost extinct.

The Future for the FCC

Some in Congress have proposed doing away with the FCC alto-
gether. Let the free marketplace and competition decide how broadcasting will be conducted, this point of view says.

If it is not eliminated, the FCC may evolve into an agency which
simply regulates the technology of broadcasting, with no control
whatever over its content.

Other forces at work that could end restrictions on station ownership, as well as broadcast content:

- **Powerful lobbying efforts** by huge corporations which want
  no restrictions on the number of media properties they own –
  including the number of competing outlets in the same market
  area.

- **Present attitudes** in both major political parties that private
  industry should have as little government regulation as possible.

- **The decline of print** as the predominant news medium. Future courts are more likely to look at broadcasting, cable TV and the Internet as modern versions of the "press" the framers of the First Amendment would have protected from government interference.

INSIDE THE MEDIA

LIBEL

Can They Do That and Get Away With It?

It depends on who you are, as well as what they show and tell. No matter how powerful the media seem to be, there are ways to get even if a story damages you unjustly.

Sue. For libel, or invasion of privacy.

The lawsuit might make you a millionaire. But before you rush to the courthouse, you should know what you're getting into. Collecting damages may take years. You'll need a very good, very expensive lawyer, because libel law is extremely complicated. It's constantly evolving.

A Long, Painful Process

Your lawsuit will be a very long, painful process. The defendants will have on their side some of the best legal counsel available. Because they carry insurance to protect them against this kind of attack, they can spend an enormous amount of money defending themselves in court.

Appearing on a panel at an American Bar Association conference in 1998, lawyer George Vradenberg told how much money was spent defending two major libel suits. This was a very rare disclosure. Vradenberg was on the legal team representing CBS in the lawsuit filed by Vietnam War General William Westmoreland.

CBS spent $8 million before the Westmoreland suit was finally settled in 1985, Vradenberg said. He estimated *Time* spent twice that much defending another libel suit the same year.

If your suit has no merit, the judge might issue a summary judgment and make you pay attorneys' fees for the other side. A large percentage of libel suits never get to a jury. They are found to be without merit by the judge, and dismissed.

If your case has merit, don't expect a quick settlement. Settlements tend to encourage other suits. In the long run, it's sometimes cheaper for the media to fight to the bitter end – and lose – than to put up with the hassle of a new lawsuit every week.

Your Life An Open Book

Once you file suit, you bare your entire life. If there is anything in your past that could be embarrassing or painful, it will almost surely be found, placed in the public record, and reported. One of the best defenses the news media launch in a civil suit is a good offense.

Your suit will give the defendant subpoena power to get records, and drag in witnesses who must testify under oath. They will explore everything about your finances, your family, your medical history, your professional career, your education and your sex life.

Still want to sue? OK. You should also look at the **Privacy** chapter. Invasion of privacy by the media can also be attacked in a civil suit. Some of the rules and tactics for the two kinds of litigation are similar. But some aspects are also very different.

In matters of governmental regulation, in the past there were different standards for print and broadcasting. No longer. In libel and privacy, the courts make few distinctions between the two media.

Applying established legal standards to material published on the Internet has been enormously complicated. That area of the law is still in an early stage of development.

Defamation Becomes Libel

You have been defamed if someone spreads information that damages your reputation. It becomes libel if there is no legal immunity or justification for the defamation.

If your friends, your family, the people at work or the club think less of you after they see or hear the story, you have evidence of your being damaged. The people who see the report don't have to know you for the story to damage your reputation.

Disclosure of the information can hurt you financially, by decreasing your future income, or your ability to borrow money. It can damage you emotionally, by causing embarrassment, anguish and ridicule.

News stories defame thousands of people every day in America, yet relatively few suits are filed. The law provides protection for the media, based on the Constitution's First Amendment guarantee for freedom of press and speech. To win a libel suit, you must prove more than the fact that you were defamed.

Issue #1 - Truth

The law says they can defame you and get away with it if the story is true. Truth is an almost perfect defense in a libel suit.

How do you prove something is true? How many witnesses does it take, what kind of evidence? There are no rigid rules.

Truth is what a jury will believe.

A half-dozen burglars and robbers testify they met you at your jewelry store every Sunday morning at 11 o'clock to fence what they'd stolen. Your priest says you never missed 11 o'clock Mass on Sunday morning.

After the thieves have been torn apart on cross examination, the jury will probably believe the priest, even though the witness score is 6-1.

Relaying the Defamation

A journalist does not have to initiate the libel. If the media pass on something someone else says about you, the media outlet generally must take responsibility for the truth of that statement.

Suppose you fire one of your employees. The angry employee then holds a news conference and says you are a drug user who regularly encourages teenage employees to use cocaine, which you supply. A reporter covers the news conference and reports what the disgruntled employee says about you.

It's True You're Accused

It is true that the accusation was made. But that alone will not protect the media outlet which publishes or broadcasts what the employee says.

If the media act as a relay for the employee's accusations, they must be prepared to prove to a jury that you are, indeed, a drug dealer who encourages teenage employees to use cocaine and supplies them with the drug. If the media convince a jury that you do those things, you cannot win a libel suit, no matter how much damage has been done to you.

Issue #2 - Privilege

If the damaging information comes from part of a governmental process, the news media have very limited responsibility for the truth of that information. This is called privilege.

The legal theory says government officials should be able to do their jobs freely, without worrying about libel suits. A Supreme Court justice once said freedom of speech does not give you the right to yell "Fire!" in a crowded theater when there is no fire.

But a senator can run up and down the aisles of the Senate Chamber yelling "Fire!" – or anything else – without fear of reprisal.

And the media can report with impunity what the senator said. The courts have said the public needs to know – through the news media – what public officials are doing and saying.

Suppose that during a debate in the Senate Chamber, a U.S. Senator announces that you are a war criminal who murdered hundreds of innocent civilians in Iraq. The story is widely reported. As a result, you lose your job. An angry crowd sets fire to your house. Your children are beaten on their way to school.

What the senator said was absolutely false. But you cannot win a slander suit against the senator, or a libel suit against the media. What the senator said is privileged, unless he said it in a private conversation, completely outside the governmental process.

Judicial Process Privileged

If you are charged with a crime, or sued, almost everything in the judicial proceeding (part of the governmental process) is privileged. The civil or criminal complaint, records or testimony, the contents of a governmental audit, what a policeman says during the investigation of a crime – all will almost always be privileged.

Notice as we go through this chapter how often I hedge with qualifiers like probably – almost always – generally – usually – virtually. The law is constantly changing. The rules can be bent – and often are – by judges and juries who feel they should cure an injustice.

The rules are different in state and federal courts. Most courts would probably extend privilege to what is said in political advertising and debates, or presidential press conferences, even though they technically are not part of the governmental process.

Issue #3 - Absence of Malice

In the early 1960s Martin Luther King, Jr. was waging war against racial segregation in Alabama. He moved from city to city, encouraging black followers to break the law. Use segregated rest rooms, he told them. Sit in segregated sections of the bus. Demand service in restaurants and hotels that – by law – bar African-Americans.

King had embraced Mahatma Gandhi's non-violent technique that successfully forced the British to abandon India, one of its largest colonies.

King knew that if the law is bad, the quickest way to change it was to get media coverage of public officials enforcing bad law. The civil rights movement became a major national story. The police who enforced the law became the villains in that story as they used clubs, fire hoses, attack dogs and tear gas to rout and arrest the demonstrators.

Martin Luther King v. Alabama

King became a master at using the media in his campaign. On the front pages of the world's newspapers, and night after night on television, the confrontation between the police and King's followers was the top story.

A committee went to *The New York Times* and paid $4,800 for a full-page ad pleading for public support to continue the campaign in Alabama. *The Times* published the ad without checking its accuracy. In the advertisement, the police and other unnamed public officials were portrayed as the evil force trying to stop King and racial justice. The demonstrators, the ad said:

> ... are being met by an unprecedented reign of terror.

> ... In Montgomery, Alabama, after students sang "My Country, 'Tis of Thee" on the State Capitol steps, their leaders were expelled from school, and truckloads of police armed with shotguns and tear-gas ringed the Alabama State College Campus. When the entire student body protested to state authorities by refusing to re-register, their dining hall was padlocked in an attempt to starve them into submission.

> ... Again and again, the Southern violators have answered Dr. King's peaceful protests with intimidation and violence. They have bombed his home, almost killing his wife and child. They have assaulted his person. They have arrested him seven times — for "speeding," "loitering" and similar "offenses." And now they have charged him with "perjury" — a felony under which they could imprison him for ten years.

Montgomery Police Commissioner L. B. Sullivan and a group of fellow public officials sued *The Times* for libel.

Although they were not named in the ad, they said they were defamed because the ad blamed law enforcement, state and local gov-

Winning with the News Media

ernment for the "reign of terror." They said it suggested the police were somehow involved in bombing King's home.

Times Ad Not Entirely True

The New York Times could not use the truth privilege, because some of the statements in the ad were false:

- The students on the State Capitol steps did not sing "My Country, 'Tis of Thee." They sang the National Anthem

- Nine students were expelled for demanding service at a segregated lunch counter, not for the Capitol steps demonstration

- Students protested the expulsion by boycotting a single day of classes, not by refusing to reregister

- The dining hall was never padlocked

- King had been arrested four times, not seven

In Montgomery, a state court jury found *The Times* had, indeed, libeled those local public officials and should pay them the maximum in damages allowed by Alabama law – $500,000. The Alabama Supreme Court upheld the verdict. By the time the U.S. Supreme Court got the case, a second half-million dollar verdict had been returned. More cases were pending.

New York Times Co. v. Sullivan
376 U.S. 254, 84 S.Ct. 710, 11 L.Ed.2d 686 (1964)

In 1964, *New York Times Co. v. Sullivan* made new libel law for the nation, and changed the rules for publishing truthfully. The decision became one of the largest landmarks in libel litigation history.

Before the U.S. Supreme Court's *Times* decision, the media had to prove their stories were true in a libel case.

With this ruling, the burden of proof shifted to the victim of the libel, who must prove the story is false.

The press cannot be held responsible for an untrue story about a public official, the Supreme Court said, unless the libel is published with **malice**. The plaintiff must prove the journalist or news outlet had a grudge against the libel victim; knew the information was false, or had reason to doubt the truth of what was published.

The Supreme Court decision in the *Times* case coined a new phrase to define malice. The media must be found guilty of **reckless disregard for truth** before a public official can collect for libel.

If You Can't Take the Heat

In their decision, the justices acknowledged that many public officials would be damaged by untrue stories as the new ruling was applied. But the court said the democratic process demands full and free debate – a continuous open season on public officials.

The public must be able to hear every accusation thrown at those in public office, and decide whether they deserve a position of public trust. If you can't take the political heat, the court warned, stay out of the kitchen.

Justice William Brennan, writing the *Times* decision for the court, said:

> *... The general proposition that freedom of expression upon public questions is secured by the First Amendment has long been settled by our decisions. ... The maintenance of the opportunity for free political discussion to the end that government may be responsive to the will of the people and that changes may be obtained by lawful means, an opportunity essential to the security of the Republic, is a fundamental principle of our constitutional system.*

What Is Reckless Disregard?

How far must the news media go to check out damaging information about a public official to meet the absence of malice test? That's up to a judge or jury.

In the *Times* case, the Supreme Court felt the newspaper had no warning that it needed to check the accuracy of the ad. The committee which submitted the ad included some very prominent people.

A hypothetical: Suppose the mayor has been waging war against local chemical companies that have polluted the river and neighborhoods near the firms. The mayor has a reputation as Mr. Environment. His campaign has persuaded city departments and many local companies to stop buying from the polluters. They have switched to suppliers in other cities.

Anonymous Calls

An anonymous caller tells a reporter the real motive for the mayor's crusade: Mr. Environment has a hidden interest in a Chicago company whose business is booming as a result of the mayor's crusade. The company in which the mayor is involved is a horrible environmental villain in its Chicago neighborhood.

To be fair, the reporter asks the mayor if the charge is true. The reporter gets an angry denial, and then writes a story that says: "Our sources tell us the real reason for the mayor's crusade. He holds a financial interest in a Chicago chemical firm that signed a contract with the city after the mayor's environmental campaign put three local firms out of business. The mayor denies it."

Anonymous = Reckless

Reckless disregard for truth? Almost certainly. If the only evidence is an anonymous tip, most juries will say the reporter and the outlet that spread his story were reckless with the truth. If the mayor proves they were wrong, the jury will punish them by ordering them to pay damages to the mayor.

But suppose the reporter pursues the tip, drives to Chicago, and finds two employees at the chemical company who say the mayor is often in the main office of the plant. They say the mayor has also been talking to employees at the plant, asking them for suggestions to improve the company.

Even if the mayor proves to the jury he has no ownership interest, the jury will probably decide the reporter was not reckless with the truth. That the media outlet, with strong evidence, published the accusation *believing it was true*.

Who is a Public Official?

The court in the *Times* case did not clearly define who is a public official.

All of the plaintiffs in that case were elected or appointed government officials. Other cases since then have drawn some guidelines.

You can probably assume you are a public official, and that reckless disregard for truth is the level of proof you will need to win a libel suit if you are:

- **An elected or appointed** public official

- **A candidate** for public office

- **A law enforcement officer**

- **A public school teacher** or administrator

- **A public health nurse**, social worker or administrator of a government-funded medical facility

- **A private citizen or company hired to do work** for the government

- **A private auditor hired to monitor** government spending

Case Law Guidelines

The cases seem to say public officials are those government employees who have the most contact with the public; those who have
major roles in developing and carrying out governmental policy, and
those who contract to do work for the government.

Where a school teacher or administrator would be seen as a public
official, a maintenance worker at a public school or police department
would probably not be. Court decisions have said public officials are
especially those employees whose responsibilities are government
spending, public health or public safety.

Issue #3A - Public Figures

Back to the 1960s. As integration spread across the South under
court edicts and the muzzles of army rifles, a federal court ordered the
University of Mississippi to admit James Meredith, its first black student. To insure his safety, he was escorted to the campus by a squad
of U.S. marshals in September, 1962.

That night, the marshals and a small army of reporters were driven
into the university administration building by an angry mob. As the
night wore on, a full-fledged riot developed. The mob began to shoot
at the marshals and the building.

Small groups charged, carrying Confederate flags, trying to break
in. A reporter was killed. The federal government was once again in a
shooting war with the rebellious South.

Who's Leading the Charge

In the heat of the battle, an Associated Press reporter called the
AP's Atlanta bureau to report a famous man – retired U. S. Army
General Edwin Walker – was giving technical advice to the rebels.
The general, he said, was leading and encouraging the charges at the
Old Miss administration building. A bulletin was quickly teletyped.
The story was published all over the world.

Gen. Walker had been in command of the federal troops dispatched to keep peace during the school segregation confrontation in
Little Rock, Arkansas, in 1957. A career soldier, he believed strongly
the Communist Party was a huge threat to America.

As commander of U.S. forces in Europe, he had recommended
that his troops read the John Birch Society's *Blue Book*, which accused former President Dwight D. Eisenhower and other national
leaders of being communist dupes.

Walker was relieved of his European command. He retired and went on the lecture circuit. The wire services transmitted a picture of the general, flying an American flag upside down outside his home as a distress signal that the country was in trouble. He ran unsuccessfully for governor of Texas.

So the AP reported the famous general was leading the charge against the U.S. marshals. Walker denied it. The AP story had run all over the country. Walker chose to file his libel suit in Texas.

He testified he *was* on the Old Miss campus that night, but had counseled the mob to use restraint. Walker categorically denied leading any charge against the marshals. The state court jury awarded Walker $800,000. The trial judge reduced it to $500,000.

Associated Press v. Walker
388 U.S. 130, 87 S.Ct. 1975, 18 L.Ed.2d 1094 (1967)

The AP appealed, and again the U.S. Supreme Court reversed. In 1967, the court extended the *New York Times Co. v. Sullivan* guidelines to "public figures." Public figures, like public officials, cannot win a libel judgment, the court ruled, unless the media show *reckless disregard for truth.*

In the chaos of the riot – under deadline pressure – the court decided the AP was not guilty of "reckless disregard" and should not be penalized.

The Man Oswald Missed

An aside – seven months after the Old Miss riot, a sniper took a shot at Walker while he was sitting at the dining table in his home. The bullet came through a window, but missed Walker. Evidence before the Warren Commission indicated the unsuccessful assassin was Lee Harvey Oswald. Oswald then went on to Dallas.

The Associated Press vs. Walker decision was sandwiched into another "public figure" case, in which the justices used the same legal standards, with a different result.

Curtis Publishing Co. v. Butts
388 U.S. 130, 1 Media L. Rep. 1568 (1967)

The Saturday Evening Post published a story that said University of Georgia Athletic Director Wally Butts had called University of Alabama Coach "Bear" Bryant on the telephone to "fix" a game between their football teams in late 1962.

The sole evidence came from Atlanta insurance salesman George Burnett, who claimed one of his telephone calls was accidentally patched into a call between the two coaches.

Burnett said he listened as Butts gave Bryant the Georgia team's offensive plays and how they planned to defend against Alabama. Burnett said he made notes as he eavesdropped on the conversation.

Investigative Reporting Standards

Butts filed a libel suit in federal court contending the story was untrue, and that the magazine failed to follow accepted standards of investigative reporting.

Editors at the magazine had not looked at Burnett's notes of the call; had not talked to another man supposedly with Burnett at the time of the phone call; and had not reviewed films of the game to see if Alabama changed its tactics.

The magazine was not under deadline pressure and had time to do a better job of checking out the story.

A jury awarded Butts $60,000 in general damages and $3 million in punitive damages. The trial judge reduced the punitive damages to $400,000.

The U.S. Supreme Court approved the outcome in the lower court. Butts was a public figure, the justices decided; the *Sullivan* case guidelines should be extended to public figures; but the magazine had been guilty of reckless disregard for truth.

Rosenbloom v. Metromedia, Inc.
403 U.S. 29, Media L. Rep. 1597 (1971)

In 1971, the Supreme Court loosened the truth standard even more. George Rosenbloom was a distributor of nudist magazines in Philadelphia. The police arrested him in 1963 and seized his entire inventory.

Newscasts on radio station WIP said the magazines were obscene and referred to Rosenbloom as a "girliebook peddler" in the "smut racket."

Rosenbloom was tried and found not guilty of distributing criminal obscenity. He then went to federal court and sued the radio station owner for libel. Rosenbloom was not a celebrity. None of the jurors at the start of the trial had even known who he was. A jury awarded Rosenbloom $750,000. The trial judge reduced the judgment to $275,000.

When the case reached the U.S. Supreme Court, the justices overturned the verdict and extended the *Sullivan* standard even further. People caught up in "issues of public concern" could not win a libel suit, the court said, unless they proved reckless disregard for truth.

The Court Pulls Back

The Rosenbloom decision shows how confused the issue had become. The court was badly split. There are five separate opinions, using different legal reasoning. The bundle of opinions runs 32 pages, single-spaced.

In 1974, through *Gertz v. Robert Welch, Inc.* a more conservative Supreme Court pulled back. Chicago police officer Richard Nuccio had been convicted of second-degree murder in the shooting of a teenager. Attorney Elmer Gertz was hired by the shooting victim's family to file a civil suit against the officer.

Communists vs. Police

American Opinion was a monthly magazine published by Robert Welch, Inc. – parent corporation for the ultra-conservative John Birch Society.

The magazine had been running a series of stories about a communist plot to discredit local police agencies. There was a secret conspiracy, the magazine said, to create a national police force that would help the communists overthrow the government.

An article in *American Opinion* said Gertz was the architect of a conspiracy to frame Officer Nuccio. It inferred Gertz had a criminal record; and said he had been a leader in several communist organizations. One of them, the magazine said, was responsible for the attack on police officers during the riots outside the 1968 Democratic Party Convention in Chicago. None of this was true.

Gertz v. Robert Welch, Inc.
418 U.S. 323, 1 Media Law Rep. 1633 (1974)

Gertz sued for libel in federal court. A jury awarded him $50,000. The trial judge overturned the jury's verdict, applying the *Rosenbloom* case standards. Gertz had become a public figure by being caught up in an issue of great public concern.

The Court of Appeals agreed, based on the U.S. Supreme Court's previous libel rulings. But this time, the higher court reversed both the trial and appellate courts and set new standards.

Private persons like Gertz who are drawn into major public issues must prove falsity in the libel, the Supreme Court said, but are not required to prove reckless disregard for truth.

For private people who are libeled, most states require proof of media negligence or lack of reasonable care. This is much easier to prove than reckless disregard for truth.

Who is a Public Figure?

Justice Lewis Powell in the *Gertz* decision did not define "matters of public interest." He made an effort to better define who is a public figure, but – in some ways – he made it more difficult.

The Powell decision talks about "all-purpose" public figures – celebrities – people whose names are household words. Elmer Gertz was clearly not a celebrity.

Powell also writes about "limited" public figures – those who make the choice of thrusting themselves onto the public stage; those who try to influence the outcome of a public controversy, then fade away when the controversy ends. Elmer Gertz did not fit that definition, either. He had avoided reporters while the Nuccio civil suit was in progress.

Celebrities Risk Attack

Public officials and celebrities, the *Gertz* decision said, have chosen to step into the limelight and subject themselves to public scrutiny. They need less protection because they have more opportunities to counter false information published about them. The Powell opinion said:

Private individuals are not only more vulnerable to injury than public officials and public figures; they are also more deserving of recovery.

Gertz went back, had another trial, and won $482,000 in damages, interest, and court costs.

Media Coverage of Public People

Now you can understand why the news media concentrate on stories about politicians, actors, athletes and rock stars. The libel rules are much more lenient for celebrities. The media don't have to be absolutely sure the story is true, so long as they don't suspect it may be false.

Stories about celebrities also sell. The public seems to have an insatiable appetite for them. Mobs of photographers (paparazzi) follow and surround celebrities everywhere they go, hoping to get a shot that will sell for thousands of dollars.

The Carol Burnett Case

If you're a public official or public figure and you hear a journalist is about to damage your reputation with a false story, run – do not walk – to the media outlet and warn them. Take a lawyer with you.

That's what Carol Burnett did when she heard the *National Enquirer* was about to print a false story about her being drunk in a restaurant and arguing with Secretary of State Henry Kissinger.

She put the *Enquirer* on notice, but they published it anyway. Clear evidence, the jury decided, of malice and reckless disregard for truth.

The jury awarded Burnett $1.6 million.

Issue #4 - Fair Comment

British Common Law developed another area where the press could defame people and get away with it – theater critics.

If a critic says an actor's performance is shoddy, and the script miserable, the review does great damage to everyone involved with the play. Not just their reputations. Their livelihood.

Today's standards say that if you go on stage to display yourself or your talent, journalists have the right to throw figurative tomatoes if they don't like what they see. That same kind of license has been extended to journalists who test cars, rate restaurants, or review other kinds of consumer services and products.

A damaging story can kill a new business. A favorable story, in the right place, can make millions for a new product. There are *some* restrictions. Most courts would probably rule that the journalist who decides to judge artistic or engineering merit can be successfully sued for libel if the review misstates the facts.

Libel on the Internet

The Internet has unleashed a huge torrent of new, unresolved libel questions.

Are the Internet service provider and/or the owner of a website legally responsible for libelous material posted by a customer?

Do they have any obligation to investigate the accuracy of damaging posts?

What jurisdiction do U.S. laws and courts have over the publication of material on the web which originates in another country?

Does the critical review of a product or service posted by a customer have the same protection from libel as a similar review published by an expert in the field?

Do blogs have the same First Amendment protection as stories and opinion columns in newspapers?

All that is still evolving. Whatever I write here will soon be obsolete.

Libel on the Internet is what the next court decision says it should be. And the libel lawsuit after that will probably alter that. Appeals take many years. Until the U.S. Supreme Court agrees to accept a case, Constitutional issues can vary from one Circuit to another until the Supreme Court nationalizes them.

A Summary of Libel Law

Let's recap:

- If someone says something that damages your reputation, you have been defamed, and can sue for slander

- If the defamation is published or broadcast, the slander becomes libel

- You cannot win a libel suit if the damaging information is true

- Since *New York Times Co. v. Sullivan* (U.S. Supreme Court, 1964) the damaged person must prove the story is false; before the *Times* case, the media had to prove the story was true

- To win, public officials and celebrities must prove the story is false PLUS that it was published or broadcast with malice, defined as ***reckless disregard for truth***

- If the media *relay* defamatory information, they are responsible for its truth EXCEPT for certain privileges

- The media have immunity for accurately reporting what happens in government or courts, even if the information is false and defamatory

- The media have libel immunity for most reviews criticizing those who choose to perform in public (actors, athletes, entertainers); or stories about the performance of products and services offered for sale on the open market – especially their safety

INSIDE THE MEDIA

NETWORKS

Television's Scattered Audience
Batters Network Money Machines

Once upon a time (the 1950s) in a media land far, far away (The United States) there were three very large broadcast television networks. They were incredibly profitable. Gold mines. Each night in homes across the land, 75 per cent of the natives huddled before the tube, warmed by the glow of prime time network shows.

All three carried nightly newscasts. A full 15 minutes. They did not expand their daily news to 30 minutes until September, 1963.

Ted Turner launched cable channel CNN in 1980, providing the first round-the-clock television news. Rupert Murdoch launched the 24-hour Fox News Network in 1996, also delivered by cable.

Hundreds of Networks

The TV audience has scattered now, drawn to other sources of news and entertainment. As this book goes to press, there are more than 50 broadcast networks, and many hundreds of cable and satellite networks. Some of these are national, some regional.

The prime time (eight to 11 p.m.) television audience is now split a thousand different ways. Some pessimists in broadcast television worry that broadcast TV will be devastated by new technology and changes in the economic model, following the destructive path that has driven newspapers nearly extinct.

To understand this section, you need to be clear on the industry terminology. A **broadcast network** delivers its programs by *broadcasting* through the air, using a network of local stations to transmit those shows.

Satellite systems also transmit programs through the air, from space to earth. But the industry doesn't call them broadcasters.

Most programming provided by a broadcast network can also be delivered by cable, satellite, telephone lines, or the Internet. But only the broadcast signal can be picked up by a TV set with an antenna.

Cable Must-Carry

The quality of broadcast signals is almost always inferior to the video delivered by other means. So to keep broadcasters competitive, Congress and the FCC dictated that their signals must also be transmitted by cable systems in their local communities. It is called "must-carry."

The smallest cable companies must set aside at least three channels for commercial stations and one channel for public broadcasting. As the number of channels provided by a cable company increases, the number of required must-carry channels also grows.

And the FCC says the channel number on cable must be the same as the broadcast channel, to make it easier for customers to find.

Original Model Destroyed

With so many choices, there will never again be the huge, nationwide audience on which the original broadcast network financial model was based. It is truly difficult to measure the broadcast network audience now.

How many people in the audience record programs and watch them later? How many people watch those programs on cell phone screens, or in bars? How many get their television over the Internet? How is the audience watching a broadcast network show delivered by cable calculated?

With so many choices, it is clear that the number of people watching a specific broadcast network show has dwindled. But accurate totals are hard to come by.

Measuring TV Viewing

The best way I could find to measure the diminishing broadcast network audience was Nielsen ratings for the most-watched broadcast network shows in prime time.

Nielsen is the company that calculates TV audience numbers and demographics. But this is just a way to show trends, because over the years the measuring methods have changed. (See **RATINGS**) And the accuracy of all those methods has been challenged.

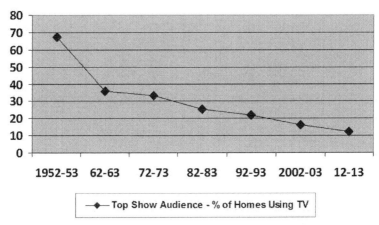

------ Top Show Audience - % of Homes Using TV

Diminishing Prime Time Audience

This Nielsen chart shows the percentage of homes that watched the top-rated broadcast network show that season. "I Love Lucy" was the most-watched network show for four years in the 1950s.

In 1952-53, Nielsen said 67 per cent of all the homes in America loved Lucy more than any other show.

"All in the Family" was top-rated for five of the years in the 1970s; "60 Minutes" in 1982-83 and again in 1992-93; "CSI" in 2002-2003 and "NCIS" in 2012-13.

So where did the audience go? Mostly to shows on cable. To video games and movies on DVDs and Blu-ray. To the Internet.

Network TV Affiliates

In the beginning (late 1940s, early 1950s) virtually all local TV stations were affiliated with either ABC, CBS or NBC. Without their network feeds, these stations would have had very little to broadcast.

In those pioneer days, local stations produced very few shows of their own. Few stations were on the air 24 hours a day. It was fairly standard to close the broadcast day about midnight, after a quick late newscast, with the national anthem playing while an American flag fluttered in the breeze onscreen.

The entire news staff at many stations was one anchorman (at first, there were no anchorwomen) who was also news director, reporter and photographer. These were primitive times. News programming was really radio, but you could *see* the announcer.

Some early stations didn't even own a movie camera. Polaroid photographs were shot by the anchor, who also served as news director/reporter/photographer. At six o'clock, he sat at a desk, read the news, and held the Polaroids before a studio camera. The network affiliates were almost all VHF (Very High Frequency) stations on Channels 2-13.

Low-Rent Independents

Once a community had three TV stations, a new station had no network to affiliate with. New stations were called "independents." They were low-rent, low-prestige operations, with very few employees, and no news.

Mostly, they ran old movies. And they were usually UHF (Ultra High Frequency) stations on channels above 13. UHF signals were inferior, both in signal quality and in reach. Cable in those early days could deliver a high-quality picture for a UHF station, but very few homes had cable. There was little incentive to produce original programming for cable. Too few viewers were connected.

Growth of Cable Systems

Cable finally conquered its major obstacle in the late 1980s when – for the first time – a majority of American homes were connected to a cable system.

Once most homes were subscribers, commercials for cable programming also grew, raising the money to stimulate more channels and new cable programs. By 2012, according to Nielsen, 90.4 per cent of all American households paid for TV delivery by a cable, satellite or telephone company.

But an interesting shift is developing. If you're a geek who wants to show off your technical know-how, or a skinflint, or both – you can now cut the cable/satellite cord and watch hundreds of TV programs that are streamed on the Internet.

In 2012, Nielsen said, there were 22 million homes receiving their TV signals that way. If you're already paying for Internet service, some people figure there's no need to pay double for TV service.

Original News Monopoly

The networks originally had a monopoly on the delivery of national and international news. They built their own coaxial cable system, connecting their affiliate stations, in virtually every part of the country. They had bureaus in a number of foreign countries.

Satellites changed all that. More and more communications satellites were launched. By the late 1980s, most local television news operations had their own satellite capability.

They could send reporters anywhere in the world and beam stories back, live, with a local angle. Once they could do that, network coverage seemed second-rate to the local audience.

The Affiliate Relationship

The relationship between the networks and their local affiliates is often misunderstood. It became even more so in 1997, when the networks asked their affiliates to start identifying themselves as "Channel 8 - NBC" or "Channel 10 - ABC."

They wanted to build more loyalty to network programs on those stations after the news. It also helps the confusion among viewers after ownership changes in which stations switch networks. The tie between a network and its affiliates does not usually involve ownership. They supply services to each other.

Network-Local Station Contract

When advertisers buy network time, they want to reach the largest possible audience. So the network contracts with local stations to broadcast network programming.

In return for that service, the network has traditionally paid the local station a fee, based on market size. It was historically only about what it cost to operate the local station for the time allotted to network shows. As network profits dwindled, the old network-local station relationship changed.

Local Station's Percentage

The real money for the affiliate comes from local advertising slots that are built into network programs. Each hour of a network show carries about 10 minutes of commercials. About three minutes of that 10 minutes is set aside for local commercials.

Watch a network show. Most of the advertising will be national — cars, detergents, aspirin, beer or office machines. But some of the commercial breaks will advertise Aunt Millie's Delicatessen or a local car wash. That's the local station's cut.

New Network Deals

One of the ways that the Fox network grew so quickly was by offering affiliates of the Big Three better deals to join the new network.

And because the Fox network at the beginning was not producing shows around the clock, local stations who joined the network had more time to run local shows and take all the advertising profits for those time slots.

Cable systems have traditionally paid cable content providers like A&E, CNN or The Discovery Channel who provided them programming. In order to get an immediate audience, Rupert Murdoch in 1997 paid cable operators $10 per home to include his startup Fox News Channel in their systems. A truly radical idea.

Conflicts and Hybrids

The networks and their affiliates need each other. But the changing technology and increasing competition from other delivery systems are creating enormous conflicts, and new hybrids.

When a television station has a website, the video shot for broadcast or cable can also be streamed there, where it is available on demand. Links to other, related sites and additional, full-text resource material can be included in the Internet version.

The quality of streamed video has increased tremendously. Especially if the viewer's connection has a very fast download speed. Movies over Netflix, for instance, can look as good as DVDs played on a large HDTV screen. Some experts predict that the Internet could deliver more TV programming in the future than cable or satellite.

Network News Cooperation

There is usually a cooperative working relationship between network news organizations and the local affiliates. Suppose a tornado touches down in your area. There's no network correspondent available to cover the story. The network will call the local station and ask for a copy of its tornado video.

Sometimes, the network will ask for a complete "package" from a reporter at the local affiliate. When the reporter "sigs out" at the end of the story, you can tell whether he's network or local.

If he's local, he says, "In Topeka, I'm William Windy, *for* ABC News." The story was done *for* the network. The reporter is telling you he's not a network correspondent.

A network correspondent would close his piece, "In Topeka, I'm William Windy, ABC News." When a network uses video shot by an affiliate, it usually pays the reporter and camera crew a fee. They're moonlighting for the network.

Signing out by the reporter has fallen out of fashion lately. Partly because networks have fired so many reporters and photographers, they often have to depend on affiliates to do their reporting for them. It's harder for viewers to tell whether the reporter is a network correspondent.

If an affiliate reporter has provided the story package, the network anchor introduces the piece by saying something like:

"William Windy in Topeka has the story." Sometimes the anchor will say, "William Windy of ABC affiliate WNDY has the story." Sometimes not.

If the network sends a crew to a town to cover a story, the crew will usually use the local affiliate's newsroom, satellite system, and editing facilities.

News Appetite Increases

Until the middle 1970s, news was rarely a moneymaker for local stations or networks. It was considered a prestige item. Local news on stations affiliated with the three networks distinguished them from the independents, which did not have news.

Watergate whetted America's appetite for news. CBS' *60 Minutes* grew to be one of the most-watched shows on the air in the early 1980s, and still ranks regularly in the top ten.

Ted Turner & CNN

When Ted Turner started CNN in 1980, few people believed the country could absorb that kind of news saturation. Many thought Turner was on an ego binge that would drive him to bankruptcy. In 1997, Turner donated a billion dollars to charity and thumbed his nose at those who had doubted his success.

CNN was so popular, a number of round-the-clock news channels were created. Regional, 24-hour news channels are proliferating – some operated by local newspapers. Everybody is scrambling to have constant, ready-when-you-are news.

If you haven't connected an antenna to your TV set lately, you're probably not aware that many local stations are now broadcasting four or five different shows at the same time. Some are full-time local weather, sports, or entertainment guides.

New Digital Channels

The FCC ruled that all broadcast TV stations had to switch from analog to digital signals in 2009. Digital provides much higher quality. Paradoxically, digital TV needs less bandwidth than analog. So the stations had bandwidth to spare when they made the switch.

You'll find now that Channel 3 in your area may be the station's primary programming. If you use the remote to go up one channel, it may be Channel 3.1, not Channel 4. Channel 3.1 may be local weather, full-time; Channel 3.2 can be a documentary that repeats every hour. Channel 3.3 can be non-stop public service programs.

Network-owned TV Stations

A growing number of local TV stations are owned and operated by one of the national TV networks. They're called "O and O's."

Until 1985, the FCC limited the number of TV outlets owned by any one company to five VHF and two UHF stations. The rule was enacted to prevent monopolies that could narrow the control of TV content and limit the different points of view available to the public. As a result of that rule, each major network had five O and O's.

Station Ownership Expanded

In 1985, the rules were rewritten, allowing one company to own as many as 12 stations, so long as that owner's stations reached no more than 25 per cent of the national audience. The only limit now: one owner's stations cannot reach more than 39 per cent of the population.

Notice the similarity to the evolution of local newspaper ownership. In the early days of the Republic, newspapers were all locally owned. Today, a huge majority of newspapers are owned by mega media corporations a thousand miles away. TV station ownership is following the same path.

Rupert Murdoch has been a major lobbying influence in this growth, so he could make Fox an equal competitor with ABC, CBS and NBC. In 2013, ABC owned eight local stations; CBS owned 16; Fox owned 18, and NBC owned 10. Ownership is constantly shuffling. In some recent years, the networks made more profit from their O&Os than they did from their network programming.

Radio Consolidation

The 1996 law also eliminated national ownership limits for radio stations and allowed companies to own (based on a ratings formula) up to about 20 per cent of the radio stations in the same city.

As a result, there was a rapid consolidation of radio station ownership – more than in any other medium.

By 2013, Clear Channel Communications, Inc. owned 850 radio stations that reached 110 million listeners. It was the largest radio conglomerate. In many cities, it owns more than one station.

As a result of large corporate owners whose primary goal is profit, local radio reporters who gather, write and read the news are virtually extinct.

Stations that carry news (many don't) either read it off the wire, or simply relay stories written and voiced by a national news service.

Lights On, But Nobody's Home

With today's technology, it is possible to own and operate a radio station with no local staff. The lights are on, and the station is broadcasting, but nobody's home.

All programming can be sent to the station by satellite. Halfway across the country, someone monitors and adjusts the control room dials. If the telemetry indicates something needs fixing, they call a local technician to do the work.

Most of the early network anchors, correspondents and top news executives had begun their careers in newspapers. They understood the responsibility that Constitutional protection implied.

New Owners, New Goals

By the late 1990s, with the major network audience split and profits down, the networks were gobbled up by corporations with a different kind of heritage. For the most part, the people who run these companies have no journalistic background. Their primary goal in life has always been to make money for the corporation and its stockholders.

They found new ways to make their broadcast and cable properties money machines. The news segment of their operation is a tiny niche. News is only a fraction of the programming for a major national TV network.

Gatekeepers and Corporate Greed

Journalists in this culture have always been described as gatekeepers, choosing which stories they will allow the public to read, hear or view. The crucial issue now is how the new media owners handle news that could help or harm the mother corporation.

The movie *The Insider* is a classic example, based on real events. A tobacco insider leaked documents to *60 Minutes* that showed tobacco executives had known for years their product was addictive and deadly. It was a great news story. All the top tobacco company CEOs had sworn before a Congressional Committee that they did not believe tobacco was addictive. A huge national lawsuit against the tobacco industry was pending.

But because the sale of CBS was being negotiated at the time, corporate lawyers prevented *60 Minutes* from broadcasting the story. They felt the story would result in a major lawsuit, and they were afraid Viacom might back out of the deal. So the insider took his information to *The Wall Street Journal*. The *Journal* ran with it.

Disney's Hiring

In January, 1999, *Brills Content* reported that ABC's *20/20* – afraid of offending its parent corporation – suppressed a story that would have exposed hiring practices at Disney World. According to the magazine, background checks were so loose, convicted child molesters were able to obtain jobs there. The allegation surfaced again in the *New Yorker*. Disney denied it.

Comcast, the cable giant, now owns NBC. If a major Congressional investigation should look into problems in the cable TV business, would NBC cover that story with no holds barred?

Since 1776, there was a philosophy that believed democracy is best served by a wide range of news outlets to give the public as many points of view as possible. That was a guiding principal when the FCC was created to regulate broadcasting.

Growing Corporate Greed

Growing corporate greed and the belief that government should regulate as little as possible has led to today's argument: Since the Internet provides an unlimited number of outlets, mega-media ownership is fine.

But the number of outlets does not really measure the effectiveness for wide-ranging points of view. Thousands of Internet bloggers will never reach as many people as one mega-corporation with multiple outlets that reach a third of the population.

In my 30 years of reporting for both newspapers and television, I worked for companies that were owned by one family, and those that became large, public corporations.

In my experience, truly aggressive, watchdog reporting died when corporate executives took control. I write about that experience in my memoirs: *They're Gonna Murder You – War Stories From My Life At The News Front*.

One of the book's chapters is titled "Bosses with Balls."

INSIDE THE MEDIA

NEWSCAST

For the End of the World, You Get Two Minutes

Time dictates almost everything in radio and television news. Broadcast deadlines are absolute. The news begins at exactly six o'clock, or ten, or eleven. The lead story in broadcast news must be ready when the anchor says, "Good evening."

Sure, you could place that story later in the newscast. But if the audience is expecting today's big story and it's not ready at the top of the newscast, they'll switch to the competition.

A Precise Fit

Time restricts broadcast stories in another way. The producer who assembles the newscast must build a collection of recorded stories, live material and commercials that will fit the time slot exactly. The time tolerance is so precise, listeners and viewers will notice if there is an awkward split-second of dead air. Producers live with stop-watches hanging around their necks.

A television newscast, in its entirety, will be 30 or 60 minutes long. The time slot is rigid, just as the "news hole" in a newspaper (the space set aside for news stories) can't be stretched.

The newspaper news hole varies from day to day, depending on how much advertising has been sold. The newscast length remains the same.

Radio Even Shorter

Locally produced radio news is now extremely rare. Most local stations buy their news from a national provider. A radio newscast producer will have only five or 10 minutes. Most radio news stories are 10 to 15 seconds long. In radio, 30 seconds is a *very* long story. Unless it's National Public Radio.

The 17-Minute Newscast

Time is absolute, and it is precious. After you subtract commercials, weather, sports, good evening and good-bye, a 30-minute local TV newscast is only about 17 minutes of news.

Most stories will run 30 seconds, or less. A few will have the luxury of a full minute. For a major story – 90 seconds.

Network half-hour newscasts contain about 22 minutes of news. They don't have weather and sports segments.

There is an old, inside joke about a young reporter asking for more time for a story. "What do you think you're covering?" the producer yells. "This story isn't worth two minutes. For the end of the world, you get two minutes. (pause) But only if you have good video."

TV Alters the Mind

Television has radically altered the way most Americans receive, retain, and react to information. Fifty years ago, first graders had an average attention span of 20 to 30 seconds. Today, that is beyond the limit for most adults.

Television's ability to flick from one picture to another – sometimes several times per second – has conditioned us to *expect* frequent changes of scenery on the tube. When it doesn't happen, our attention drifts.

A new form of TV commercials evolved in the mid-1990s. Dubbed "MTV-style," they got their name from music videos. It had become trendy to edit videos with extremely rapid cuts. Some shots were so brief they were virtually subliminal.

Young People See the Cuts

Marketing researchers ran some tests to see how much of the information in these commercials could be retained by the audience. Commercial time is precious. No reason to increase production time and cost if the product doesn't work.

They found that young people who had grown up with television and video games could see all the cuts. Older people whose learning process as youngsters developed without television could not see some of the very quick cuts.

The theory from that research is that heavy doses of television at an early age sharpen the natural ability to see and retain visual information that flicks by in milliseconds.

For TV, the 90-Second Rule

The TV industry spends billions of dollars on market research. Consulting firms are constantly studying viewers to learn what turns them on, and what makes them switch to another channel.

It was those consulting firms that issued the Ninety Second Rule. Sure, the rule is broken. But unless it is exceptionally well done, any story longer than 90 seconds tends to make viewers go to the kitchen, to the bathroom, to the bedroom, to sleep in their chair, or – horrors – to another channel.

Those same studies led to another time guideline: Never let anybody talk on camera for more than about 10 seconds. Many network sound bites are three and four seconds long.

The voice can continue, but you must constantly give viewers new video. If you want to retain or improve your audience ratings, change the picture as often as possible.

Channel Surfing

The short attention span was cut even shorter with the invention of the TV remote control.

If the program is not constantly stimulating, we surf to another channel. As a result, one theory says the public also has a very short attention span for government and politics. If elected officials do not make us happy within a few months, we get irritated and impatient. We are ready to zap them and sample someone else.

The Internet can shorten the attention span of Americans even more. Most people surfing the Net do not really read. They scan, looking for links to something they *might* want to read. They jump from one page to another every few seconds.

Under 10 Seconds

When you watch network news tonight, time the interviews. Virtually all of them will run less than ten seconds. The exception is Public Broadcasting, which believes its audience is more mature, better educated, and able to concentrate longer.

The same time limit is used for live shows which feature experts talking and arguing about current events.

The larger the television market (and the more vicious the competition), the more research will be done to attract and retain the audience. As a general rule, the bigger the market, the shorter the sound bites.

Surveys year after year show America's greatest fear is stage fright. I believe the real fear is looking stupid or incompetent in front of a lot of people. How can you possibly say anything intelligent about a complicated, controversial subject in ten seconds or less?

That's what makes talking to broadcast reporters seem so terribly difficult and scary.

Transferring Skills

But once you learn how, you'll discover it works in many other places where you need to communicate – to sell ideas. The people in those audiences have also had their minds altered by TV.

You'll be much more effective if you use some of television's techniques for your next civic club speech – when you testify at a legislative hearing – when you're trying to convince your staff or board of directors.

You need to be brief. You need to communicate with visuals as much as with words.

The most common formula for a TV news story that involves a reporter is the Sony Sandwich. Some stations call it a "wrap" or a "package." Most television stories will follow this simple formula, or some variation. And now newspapers have adopted it, too.

TV Creates Tribal Unity

Walter Cronkite once said television provides a headline service. He started as a newspaper reporter. Newspaper people love that quote. For much of television coverage, Cronkite was right.

But there are other times when neither the written nor the spoken word can come close to the awesome impact of the television sound camera.

Television has unified us more than any other force in history. The storytellers in ancient tribes gave people their sense of time and place and identity. But each person crouched around the campfire came away with a very different mental picture of what the chief or medicine man was reciting.

Then books served that purpose for civilization. But still, no matter how well written, every reader had a different mental image.

Identical Memories

We now have identical memories of the major events in our lives and recent history. Those moments, captured on film and video, bind us together as a people. They are more powerful, more intimate, more emotional than books.

Computerized encyclopedias now include news clips with full sound and video. The same images and sounds will pass to future generations.

We sometimes have to think a minute – did I see it on television, or was I really there? Major news events like:

- **Martin Luther King, Jr.** speaking at the Lincoln Memorial in 1963

- **Law enforcement officers** using clubs, fire hoses and attack dogs on Civil Rights demonstrators

- **Combat** during the Vietnam, Iraq and Afghanistan wars

- **The first astronaut** stepping onto the lunar surface

- **The shootings** of John F. Kennedy, Lee Harvey Oswald, Robert Kennedy, and Ronald Reagan

- **The explosion** of the Challenger spacecraft

- **The destruction** of the World Trade Center towers on 9/11

- **The long string** of mass shootings in the years that followed

- **The 2011 tsunami** in Japan

- **Catastrophic storms**, forest fires, floods and earthquakes

For those stories, television forgets about time. When it does – and when luck and skill put a camera and microphone in just the right place – no other medium can match its impact.

Newscast Mechanics

As a first step for coping with broadcast news, you need to understand some of the mechanics of producing a newscast. TV news stories are short, but broadcasting them is very complicated.

Some of the things they do are very puzzling if you don't know about the gadgets, the formats, how they dictate the production of stories, and the newscast itself.

Many of the story forms for television news are dictated by the audience's attention span. That's why the double or triple anchor format was invented.

If viewers begin to nod, the new face and voice bring them back to attention. Many local stations believe male-female anchor teams offer maximum appeal and attention-span advantages.

Anchor Balancing Act

The anchors are usually attractive people, easy to look at and listen to. The shift back and forth between male and female voices offers constant attention fresheners.

If they're not listening closely, men in the audience enjoy looking at a beautiful woman. Female viewers like to watch a good-looking anchorman. And the chemistry between a man and a woman on camera makes ad-libs more interesting.

Television stations balance their anchor teams in the same way a political party tries to balance its ticket. A city with a large black population needs African-American anchors.

Stations with significant ethnic communities search for anchors who may have lost their accents, but have identifiable ethnic names and *look* Spanish, or Italian, or Polish.

Voice Monotony

Television and radio amplify monotony. Five seconds of a blank screen, or dead silence on the radio, seems like forever. Listen carefully to good disk jockeys – the way they talk to keep your attention.

Broadcasters train themselves to read so their voices go up and down, now slower, then faster without a breath, then a long pause. Paul Harvey – one of radio's most successful commentators – was almost a caricature of this technique, but you can better understand it by listening closely to how he did it.

Bup, bup, bup bup, rising intensity. Stretched word. Quick phrase. Pause. Slow phrase. Pause. Rising volume. Diminishing volume. Pause And that's (pause) the rest of the story.

In putting together a newscast, the producer tries to pace the show the same way.

Pacing the Newscast

A long TV story will be followed by several short ones. The plane crash report may be played just before a break. When they come back from the commercial, there will be a fluffy, breezy story to make us feel better.

The simplest and briefest television story is called a "copy story" or "reader." The anchor reads the entire story, on camera. There may be some kind of still picture or graphic electronically inserted in one corner, over the anchor's shoulder.

TelePrompTers

While we're talking about copy stories, you may wonder how anchors read the news without looking at the script in their hands – and why they bother to even have a script.

TelePrompTer® devices enable anchors to read stories while looking directly into the camera lens. The pages in the anchor's hand are a printout of the script, which was typed into a computer.

How it Works

In front of the camera lens in the studio is a plate of clear glass, mounted at an angle. The computerized script is reflected or projected on the glass.

The angle of the glass is fixed so the anchor can see the reflection of the pages. But the camera shoots right through the glass. At home, we can't tell the glass is even there. And because of the reflection in the glass, the anchor can't really see the camera lens.

TelePrompTer at Bay News 9
Tampa/St. Petersburg

The script is printed in large type and very short lines – usually two or three words per line – so it can be read without noticeable eye movement. In front of the camera lens, a computerized script scrolls by. The anchor can see it, but the audience can't.

The anchors can see what's on the air in the studio monitors. Large monitors are mounted off-camera, and smaller monitors are usually built into the desk, where the audience can't see them.

The speed at which the script rolls can be controlled by a technician, or by the anchors themselves. Each time a page goes by on the monitor, the anchor turns a page on the desk, in case something goes wrong with the TelePrompTer.

Should that happen, the paper script is a backup. The anchor can continue by reading from the script on the desk — glancing down and looking up, one sentence at a time.

Stumbling is a Clue

When experienced anchors stumble, and suddenly start reading from the script in their hands, it's usually a clue that something has gone wrong. The pages in the TelePrompTer may be out of sequence, or frozen. When the prompter's problem is fixed, the anchor goes back to reading the script there.

Most anchors glance down at the script on the desk each time they turn a page. They give the illusion that they've read the entire page at a glance, memorized it, and then recite it to you.

If they don't look down occasionally, the viewers begin to wonder why the anchors never look at the pages they're holding. Maybe they're in Braille?

Graphics That Aren't There

The graphic over the anchor's shoulder is inserted electronically, in the control room. You know, of course, the drawing, or picture, is not actually there in the TV studio. If it's a story about a postal rate hike, there may be a postage stamp, or a mailbox in the key. A copy story about a murder may key a gun, or a knife.

This is part of television's constant effort to show you something while they talk. It helps you understand and pay attention. It doubles your retention.

You should do the same thing when you talk to the Kiwanis Club or the County Commission.

Invisible Weather Maps

The same electronics that put a graphic over the anchor's shoulder can make a blank wall look like a weather map. This is one of TV's most interesting and time-honored electronic illusions.

The meteorologist works in front of a wall that is painted bright green. At home, you see a map of the area, the state, or the nation on the wall. It's not really there.

How Weather Maps Work

An electronic device merges two sources of video. The camera shooting the weathercaster is tuned to be blind to the color on the wall. The picture it takes is a cutout of the forecaster. The picture is blank everywhere else.

Another video source is fed into the device. It can be a computer-generated map, video, slides, or a live radar scope. The device inserts into the map the camera cutout picture of the weathercaster.

Electronic Cookie Cutters

Imagine two sheets of cookie dough. A cookie cutter (the studio camera) stamps out the image of the forecaster. That becomes the cookie.

The rest of that sheet of dough is thrown away.

The same cookie cutter then stamps out the same image on the second sheet of cookie dough.

This time, you throw away the cookie and keep the remaining dough. There is a hole in the sheet of dough that will exactly match the silhouette of the cookie.

Then the cutout from the first sheet (the weathercaster) is inserted into the second sheet of cookie dough (the weather map). It is done so seamlessly we think the weathercaster cutout and the map are all part of the same sheet of video.

Smoke and Mirrors

When the forecaster is pointing to a storm system over the Great Lakes, the Great Lakes are not there. On each side of the set, where viewers can't see them, are TV monitors showing what we're seeing at home.

The forecaster appears to be looking at the map on the wall. Instead, the forecaster is watching a monitor. If the forecaster's finger pointing to the Great Lakes is actually over Arkansas, the forecaster can see it on the monitor and make a correction.

Originally, the background color was blue, chosen because it was the color most absent in human skin tones. Later equipment worked better with a shade of green. Occasionally, anchors will have something in their clothing that is too close to that color.

A Window in Your Chest

An anchor's tie or scarf with the same green will make that part of the anchor invisible. We will see the weather map where the tie or scarf is. Just as though the anchor had a window in that part of the body. This same equipment is often used in commercials. A pair of hands holding the product seem to be unattached, floating in air. They're actually at the end of a sleeve that is the blue or green color. The arms disappear. We only see the hands and the product.

Voice-Over Story Formula

In a voice-over (V/O) story, the anchor begins to read the story on camera. About 10 seconds into the copy, the director in the control room (below) switches the picture from the anchor to video of what the anchor is talking about.

The anchor continues to read, live, while we see video. The video may have sound with it, played very low. This is called *natural sound.* The anchor voice is *over* the picture and background sound.

As the anchor talks about last night's Academy Award winner, you see the actor accepting the statuette. If the video is used with natural sound, you will hear the applause in the background.

V/O to SOV

In the voice-over-to-sound-on-video formula (V/O to SOV), the anchor begins the story on-camera, just as before. The story becomes voice-over as we watch the actor accept the Oscar.

Then the anchor stops reading. The sound on the video source is turned up, full volume. We see and hear the actor thanking his parents, his wife, his mistress, his childhood friends, his director, and his dog. Then the video switches back to the studio and the anchor reads the introduction to the next story.

For a V/O to SOV story, everything must be timed precisely. After the copy is written, a producer with a stopwatch takes it to the anchor, who reads at a normal pace.

They time from the point where the live V/O begins, to where the actor in last night's ceremony will speak on video. The V/O video is edited to run exactly as long as it takes for the anchor to read the copy.

The Countdown

When the anchor reads the copy during the newscast, the director in the control room punches a stopwatch as the voice-over source begins. The anchor must read for exactly 16 seconds.

The director works with a microphone in the control room. The anchors wear hidden earphones. The floor crew all have headsets. In some highly automated studios, there is no floor crew. By flipping a selector switch, the director can talk to anyone in the studio, or to all of them. As the anchor reads the V/O section of the story, the director watches a stopwatch and begins a verbal countdown.

When the countdown reaches five seconds, the anchor will hurry a little, or slow down, to finish the voice-over just as the sound-on-video (SOV) begins.

Scripting the Story

There is a form for television news stories, just as there is a form for movie scripts. They're different.

The notations at the left side of the television script are instructions for the editor who will put the story together. It is a blueprint that shows how the story is built. The editor can build the story that will be broadcast while the reporter does something else.

The control room needs the script if the story is read live. It indicates when to roll video, when to bring up supers, etc.

Winning with the News Media

V/O - SOV - V/O

The voice-over to sound-on-video to voice-over (V/O-SOV-V/O) is a variation of the same formula. The anchor begins with a copy story, on camera.

Below is a typical script:

ANCHOR LIVE	THE CITY'S GARBAGE COLLECTORS SAY THEY'LL STRIKE AT MIDNIGHT UNLESS THE CITY COUNCIL GOES ALONG WITH THEIR DEMAND FOR A 15 PERCENT PAY INCREASE.
V/O (meeting video)	THE GARBAGE COLLECTORS' UNION MET AT TWO A.M. THIS MORNING, AND WOUND UP WITH A UNANIMOUS VOTE, SETTING THE WALKOUT DEADLINE.
SOV (Union Pres)	"The Council says we don't care about our city. Well, I say they don't care about us. We're human beings. We have to eat, too."
V/O (Mayor at CH)	THE MAYOR HAS CALLED AN EMERGENCY MEETING OF THE CITY COUNCIL TONIGHT IN A LAST-DITCH EFFORT TO STOP THE STRIKE.

If the story is more complicated – getting the mayor's point of view, for instance – it will usually be handled by a reporter, who will "package" the story in Sony Sandwich form.

The Lead-In

On the air, the Sony Sandwich is introduced by the anchor. The anchor copy is called the lead-in. It is a headline, designed to tell you generally what the story is about, grab your attention, and make you want to listen to what the reporter is about to say.

The reporter's entire story is recorded, both sound and video. That's why it is very difficult to change the length after the newscast starts.

INSIDE THE MEDIA

PRIVACY

Get Out of Here ...
And Leave Me Alone

Many lawsuits against the media now claim invasion of privacy, not libel. Jurors have strong feelings in this area. Privacy cases often focus on personal, emotional beliefs in conflict with each other.

Appellate courts take widely different views of similar cases, depending on the judges' personal experience and attitudes about the news media. Jurors are swayed more by an attorney's appeal to their outrage than by the law and legal precedent.

Today's technology gives the media powerful new tools for intrusion into private lives. Cameras are tiny and easy to hide. Conversations are easily recorded surreptitiously. Computers and the Internet provide the ability to rummage through the closets of your life in ways that have never before been possible.

An Evolving Legal Concept

Personal privacy is a relatively new legal concept in this country. It is still evolving.

The Bill of Rights protects citizens against unreasonable search and seizure. But that is a protection from government intrusion – not media corporations, or individual journalists.

We inherited criminal trespass from British Common Law. But that protects your real estate from intrusion. The idea of a right to privacy in your personal life was not even conceived until the 1890s, when newspapers became more sensational with stories of gossip and sexual scandal. They even published pictures.

Law Lags Behind Technology

The law has generally lagged well behind the technology. In the 1950s, the old statutes forbidding wiretaps became ineffective. Better ways had been invented. It was no longer necessary to physically tap into telephone lines. Electronic "bugs" and inductance devices were widely used to pick up conversations and were technically not an illegal "tap."

A comprehensive federal statute to protect the privacy of conversation was not adopted until 1968. There still is no national standard to protect personal privacy from the telephoto lenses of the media.

Physical Trespass

Trespass is physical intrusion onto your property. It can be a criminal act. Shooting a picture, and publishing or broadcasting it, can be two different kinds of intrusion. If the picture taken by a trespasser is never shown to anybody else, then a simple trespass took place.

Shooting Without Entering

But a picture can be shot and shown to others without trespassing. A news story and photographs can bring thousands – perhaps millions – of people into the most intimate parts of your life.

In September, 2012, a photographer with a very long lens photographed Britain's Prince William and his wife, Kate Middleton, sunbathing at a remote chateau in France. They were on a vacation. Middleton was topless.

The future king threatened to sue for invasion of privacy. But the case would have been complicated. The photos were shot in France, first published in Great Britain, then circulated worldwide on the Internet.

In the United States, if the photographer was not trespassing, their privacy was probably not legally invaded. But a jury might feel differently. Notice (just as I did in the **LIBEL** chapter), how often I write probably – maybe – almost certainly– in this chapter.

These laws are constantly evolving. Privacy is what the next jury believes it should be. Until/unless an appellate court disagrees.

Privacy lawsuits provide a way to punish the media who make your private life a peep show. Courts have said paparazzi stalking you in public places – as well as shooting and publishing your picture – can also invade your privacy.

Where Cameras Can Go

Let's go back now to trespass – physical intrusion – and work forward to the latest electronic eavesdropping.

A photographer has the same freedom of movement as anyone else. If you can walk down the sidewalk, so can a news photographer with a camera.

We have public places in this society where anyone can legally go, unless a state of emergency is declared. Places like streets, parks, subways, beaches, public buildings.

Privacy decisions in court often hinge on what is reasonable and customary. Customs, and what seems reasonable, change.

No Privacy in Public

Generally speaking, you have little or no right of privacy from the media if you are in a public place. So long as everybody in that public place can see you, the media can photograph you, write about what you did there, and publish the pictures.

You have little legal recourse. If you don't want to be seen and photographed, don't go out in public.

Off-Limit Public Places

There are some public places which by custom are not truly open to the public. A public school classroom, for instance, is in a building built with tax dollars. The teacher is a public employee.

But custom says you can't just barge in and interrupt the class. Even if your child is a student there, you're expected to check in at the principal's office and get permission to enter.

Reporters and photographers are expected to do the same thing, and would probably lose a lawsuit if they suddenly entered, cameras rolling, disturbing the teacher and the students.

It All Depends

There I go again. Fudging with the *probably* word. Because every case is different, and the law so new. The outcome will depend on how judges and juries react to the facts and conflicting values.

We sometimes give the news media special access so they can represent the public and report what happens. At a major trial, for instance, seats are reserved for the media and many spectators are shut out. There's just not enough room for everybody.

Special Media Access

Reporters and photographers are customarily allowed beyond police lines at disasters so they can see, record and photograph the victims and the rescue effort.

Later in this chapter I'll cover cases where journalists accompanied government authorities with special power into people's homes. Can reporters and photographers go with them? For years, the courts said yes. Then the U.S. Supreme Court said no.

Cameras in Congress

There are some public places where citizens are welcome but cameras and microphones are barred. Television cameras were not allowed to cover proceedings in the U.S. House of Representatives until the 1970s.

The U.S. Senate allowed television camera coverage of its committee hearings as early as the 1950s (McCarthy & Kefauver committees) but did not allow daily, continuous coverage of proceedings in the Senate chamber until 1986.

Cameras in Courtrooms

Almost all American trials are open to spectators. Because the Constitution guarantees a right to trial by a jury of your peers, case law has almost always said the public has a right to be represented by the media to make sure the justice system is working properly.

But news cameras are not welcome in many courts. Almost all federal trial courts forbid cameras.

News cameras were barred from the trial of Oklahoma City Federal Building bomber Timothy McVeigh. But the trial was televised, through a closed-circuit system, to a room where survivors of the bombing and families of the victims could watch.

That was made possible by a special law Congress passed after survivors and family members pleaded for access. Security was extremely tight, to make sure the news media did not acquire any of the video or pictures.

The O. J. Simpson Trial

U.S. District Court Judge William Hoeveler of Miami, who chaired the American Bar Association's Resource Team for High Profile Trials told a media-law conference in early 1998:

> *You will not see cameras in the federal courts for quite some time because of the O. J. Simpson criminal trial. It set cameras in the federal courts back at least 10 years.*

In that case, the saturation coverage showed the mistakes and frailties of the judge, police officers, witnesses, attorneys and journalists.

Inside the judicial system, there was a protective reaction – Maybe we shouldn't let the public watch. The pressure of national coverage affects people. It can sometimes be embarrassing.

The Simpson case also made the media look bad, in their mob scene chases of witnesses; the feeding frenzy for any scrap of information, the payoffs for exclusive interviews. The backlash from the Simpson case had a chilling effect nationwide.

Moves to Ban Cameras

When a law or court order allows cameras in courtrooms, judges usually have broad discretion to ban cameras if they think the cameras will interfere with a fair trial. After the Simpson trial, more judges and more states moved in that direction.

About the same time, U.S. Supreme Court Justice Antonin Scalia, who once favored courtroom cameras, said he had changed his mind.

Federal Court Status

Fellow Supreme Court Justice David Souter said publicly, "The day you see a camera coming into our courtroom, it's going to roll over my dead body." He retired in 2009.

Reportedly, there is an agreement among Supreme Court justices that no cameras will be allowed there unless the nine justices unanimously approve. That may take a while.

Bills have been introduced in every Congressional session since 1997 that would require the U.S Supreme Court to allow video coverage of its open sessions. The bills have never gone to a vote.

The court DID begin audio recordings of its sessions in 1955. The audio tapes, however, were kept at the National Archives, and were not available to the public until 1993. Even then, the recorded arguments for the court's current term were not available until the beginning of the next term – as long as a year later.

That changed in 2010. The session recordings for each week can now be downloaded every Friday from the Court's website. In a few, rare cases, the Court has allowed immediate release of the recording because there was such intense public interest in their proceedings.

The audio of a case argument released immediately was Bush vs. Gore, which decided the 2000 Presidential election. There were immediate releases of Court sessions in 2013 on gay marriage and the National Affordable Health Care Act.

As this book goes to press, 37 states routinely allow TV coverage of trials, but in most, the judge or participants can object and prevent broadcast coverage if they argue successfully that cameras would prevent a fair trial. All states allow broadcast coverage of appellate proceedings.

In July, 2011, a three-year experiment began, to test cameras in 14 volunteer U.S. District courts. They allow video recording of civil cases in those pilot courts if all parties agree. The Judicial Conference of the U.S. created the experiment, and will study the results to recommend whether video recording should be allowed in federal courts.

Opponents of cameras in court have always argued that they intimidate witnesses and jurors, and prevent a fair trial. But in appellate courts, there are no witnesses or jurors.

Courtroom Construction

In the 1970s, my television station in Miami (WPLG-TV) was the plaintiff in a suit that eventually made news cameras standard in Florida courts. For many years, oral arguments before the Florida Supreme Court have been videotaped and archived.

During that process, I became convinced that all objections to cameras' disruptive influence can be overcome with the construction of soundproof booths in courtrooms. Photographers could work there, shooting through a glass panel, and nobody in the courtroom could even tell whether the cameras were there.

Semi-Public Places

Back to personal privacy. The next areas in which the media can intrude on personal privacy are semi-public places. Privately owned, but open to the public. Stores, restaurants, bars, offices. Anybody can walk in. There is an understood, open invitation.

In a truly public place, a reporter or photographer cannot invade your privacy unless they physically harass and intimidate you. When they walk into a semi-public place, the rules shift.

Most cases that have gone to trial seem to indicate still photographers or TV camera crews can come in shooting, but must leave if the owner/manager of the semi-public place orders them out.

If they don't leave, they become trespassers. This increases the likelihood a court will decide they also invaded personal privacy. This would apply to almost any place of business. A pioneer case in point:

Le Mistral, Inc. v. CBS
61 A.D. 2d 491, 402 N.Y.S. 2d 815, 3 Med L. Rptr. 1913 (1978)

The owner of Le Mistral restaurant in New York City won a privacy suit against CBS, claiming that a television crew barged in, refused to leave, created a scene, and frightened the restaurant's customers. Witnesses disagreed on how long the camera crew tarried, but the jury felt they overstayed their welcome.

The CBS crew had entered the restaurant with a health inspector, hoping to videotape unsanitary conditions in the kitchen.

The restaurant manager couldn't stop the health inspector, but argued that the inspector's right of entry did not include the right for a television crew to tag along. The jury agreed.

If You Go, the Camera Can

Again – the camera crew has the same right of entry as the general public. The photographer has the legal right to walk into the reception area of a doctor's office, but can't barge past the receptionist into the examining rooms, where patients have their clothes off.

In semi-public places, the outcome of a privacy suit often hinges on the behavior of the two litigants. Juries tend to rule against people who are loud or obnoxious, and act like bullies.

Moral of this story: If a television crew enters your place of business and you ask them to leave, be nice.

The nicer you are – and the pushier they are – the better your chances of winning a privacy lawsuit.

The Most Private Place

The most private place is the home. Here, criminal law says in most states that you commit a felony – not just trespass – if you enter without an invitation, even if the door is unlocked.

Because of that long tradition that holds privacy of the home so sacred, many successful privacy suits against the news media involve intrusion there.

Do reporters and photographers have the right to come to your front door and try to talk to you?

The U.S. Supreme Court decided long ago (1943 – *Martin v. Struthers*) that unless there is a "Do Not Enter" sign at your front gate, no trespass is committed if someone enters your property and knocks on your front door. The court followed custom in America.

Once they're asked to leave, they become trespassers if they refuse. A rented home – or a hotel room – carries with it the same sort of privacy rights as a home you own.

Dietemann v. Time, Inc.
449 F.2d 245 [9th Cir.] (1971)

Another early, trail-blazing case: In California, a *Life* Magazine reporter went into the home of a naturopathic doctor and feigned symptoms of cancer. The doctor wired her to a gadget with flashing lights, and told her she was feeling bad because she ate rancid butter on a certain date.

While she was receiving the diagnosis, her "husband," a *Life* photographer, was shooting pictures with a hidden camera. He was also wearing a "bug" that transmitted the entire procedure to a prosecutor parked up the street in a van.

When the prosecutor arrested the doctor, *Life* was there to photograph the bust. The pictures taken inside the house were featured in an article on quack doctors.

The naturopath sued for invasion of privacy, and won. In upholding the verdict, the appellate court made it clear that it simply did not like the idea of reporters coming into people's homes with hidden cameras and microphones, acting as agents for law enforcement.

Cantrell v. Forest City Publishing Co.
419 U.S. 245, 95 S.Ct. 465, 42 L.Ed.2d 419 (1974)

In Ohio, a newspaper reporter and photographer returned to an area that had been devastated by a flood. Their story focused on one family, where the father had been killed when a bridge collapsed. The children, at home alone, let the newsmen into the house. The kids told how the flood had changed their lives.

The reporter never saw the mother. But in his story, the reporter cheated. He included a sentence about how tired she looked: "She wears the same mask of non-expression she wore at the funeral."

The story gave the clear impression that she was present during the interview.

In deciding that the family's privacy was invaded by the story, the court made a special note of the reporter's deception. This is another case where the specific behavior of those involved had a powerful influence on the outcome.

Fla. Publishing Co. v. Fletcher
340 So.2d 914, 2 Med. L. Rptr. 1088 [Fla. S. Ct.] (1976),
cert. denied 431 U.S. 930 (1977)

In Jacksonville, Florida, a fire killed a 17-year-old girl, at home alone. When firefighters removed the body, her silhouette remained, unburned, in the charred floor of her bedroom. A fire marshal who had run out of film asked a newspaper photographer to take a picture of the unburned spot where the girl died.

It was a dramatic shot. The newspaper published it with a caption, "Silhouette of Death."

The mother sued for invasion of privacy, saying the fire marshal had no right to bring the photographer into her home; that the newspaper had no right to invade her life by publishing a picture that caused her so much pain.

At the trial, a jury found the newspaper guilty of privacy invasion. On appeal, the verdict was overturned by the Florida Supreme Court.

The higher court said it was the custom for journalists to accompany fire and police officials at disaster scenes, and the photographer served a semi-official function when he shot the picture at the fire marshal's request.

Police Raids and the Media

Over the years, courts disagreed for many different reasons about cops bringing reporters and photographers along on raids. In my years as a reporter, I went into many homes and businesses with cops who had a search warrant to enter.

I was not there – but a crew from my station was – one night in the late 1970s when the Hialeah Police Department invited my station along on a huge raid. They said they were going to break up a major, illegal gambling operation.

Our reporter and photographer sat in on the briefing, then went to a private home with the cops. The police search team was ready for World War III with their riot guns and flak jackets. At a pre-arranged signal, they burst into the living room of the house. Our photographer was right behind them.

Penny-Ante Poker

Inside were a group of senior citizens playing penny-ante poker. No arrests. No story. The owner of the home sued my station for invasion of privacy. Our attorney – media specialist Sandy D'Alemberte – persuaded a judge to dismiss the suit. He argued it was standard procedure for the media to accompany the police when they served search warrants. It was.

Later, D'Alemberte warned our news staff that sometime in the future, courts would decide that reporters and photographers have no right to enter a home with the police.

The U.S. Supreme Court ruled on this specific issue for the first time in 1999.

Operation Gunsmoke

In early 1992, the U.S. Justice Department launched "Operation Gunsmoke." U.S. marshals and local police were to concentrate on fugitives with outstanding arrest warrants for drug arrests and violent felonies.

A special public relations brochure was printed, telling marshals how to include reporters and photographers on arrests they planned.

Dominic Wilson was one of the targets of Operation Gunsmoke. Wilson was a fugitive who had violated his probation on charges of robbery, theft and attempt to rob. The wanted bulletin listed him as armed and dangerous.

The Raiding Party

A reporter and photographer from *The Washington Post* were invited to accompany a squad of officers when they raided a home in Rockville, Maryland. They believed Wilson was there.

It was the home of Wilson's parents. At dawn, marshals, county police officers, and the newspaper team entered the house. Wilson's parents were still in bed. When the father heard a noise, he ran into the living room wearing only his briefs, to find a group of men in plain clothes, some of them with guns drawn.

The father yelled at the group, asked what they were doing, cursed them, and was quickly thrown to the floor. His wife ran in, wearing her nightgown. She was kept in place while officers searched the house. They didn't find Dominic Wilson.

All through the search, the newspaper photographer was taking pictures. The pictures were never published. The Wilsons sued the officers and the *Post*, claiming their Fourth Amendment rights against unreasonable search and seizure were violated when the officers brought the news media into their house. The search warrant clearly gave the officers the right to enter, they said, but did not give that right to the media.

The Trial and Appeal

The U.S. District Court ruled the law enforcement officers were protected from the Wilsons' suit because they were following standard practice at the time. The decision was appealed. The federal appellate court reheard the case twice.

A majority of the appellate judges finally agreed with the trial court, but were badly split on the decision and the reasons for it. So were other federal appellate courts in similar cases.

The Supreme Court decided to hear the case and make a decision that would apply nationwide.

Wilson v. Layne
526 U.S. 603 (1999)

The Supreme Court ruled unanimously that the Wilsons' Fourth Amendment rights had been violated when the media were brought into the house by the police.

All but Justice Stephens agreed that the police should not pay damages, however, because they were following widely accepted standards at the time.

Writing for the court, Chief Justice William Rehnquist said:

Although media ride-alongs of one sort or another had apparently become a common police practice, in 1992 there were no judicial opinions holding that this practice became unlawful when it entered a home. We hold that it is a violation of the Fourth Amendment for police to bring members of the media or other third parties into a home during the execution of a warrant when the presence of the third parties in the home was not in aid of the execution of the warrant. ... the possibility of good public relations for the police is simply not enough ... to justify the ride-along intrusion into a private home.

Rulings from the Gut

This case, like many others, shows how judges and juries see similar facts in very different ways. After reading as many court decisions as I have, I conclude that they frequently decide from their gut, then look for legal reasoning to support that decision.

Racially segregated schools had the blessing of the U.S. Supreme Court for generations. The first child labor laws were upheld by judges who said children had a legal right to earn money in a capitalistic society.

In time, attitudes change. Court decisions often reflect the common sense in that community, at that particular time. With new technology that makes invasion of privacy easier and more abusive, the law must race to keep up.

Wiretaps and Telephone Privacy

Most states passed laws against wiretapping in the 1920s and '30s. But they were often more concerned with the bootlegging of telephone service than with personal privacy.

Two and four-party telephone service was common in most American homes through the 1940s. Most people just assumed someone might be listening to their conversations. Privacy is not a big concern if you don't expect it.

A wiretap is a physical connection to a communications line – connecting to the wire that carries information. You can tap into a telephone line or television cable and create an extension of that conversation or TV signal.

If the tap is done skillfully, the people who use or own the line cannot tell the wire has been tapped. This is how bootleggers get cable TV without paying for it.

One of the most vulnerable spots for industrial espionage is a telephone line carrying computerized data or e-mail from one office to another. A wiretap can put you inside the company.

Wiretapping by individuals is always illegal.

The early laws let state and local police agencies wiretap with little control or supervision as part of a their investigations. Federal law enforcement agencies were required to get approval from the U.S. Attorney General before they could wiretap. The FBI reported each year how many wiretaps had been used in its investigations.

Electronic Bugs

In the early 1950s, the first small "bugs" were created. Federal law enforcement began using them on a massive scale, without approval from the Attorney General. Since they were not wiretaps, there was no requirement that they be reported.

A "bug" is a small microphone with a radio transmitter. It is easy to hide, and much more intrusive than a wiretap. In a car or a room, it intercepts conversation and transmits it to a receiver.

A "bug" can be designed to pick up not only conversation in a room, but also both ends of a telephone conversation from that room. Some of them use house current, or the voltage in the telephone line, so they never need new batteries.

The invention of miniaturized electronics opened up new worlds of possibilities for privacy invasion.

Their widespread use by law enforcement, as well as private investigators doing industrial espionage, became a major issue in the early 1960s. Congress passed in 1968 – as part of its Omnibus Crime Bill – national standards for electronic eavesdropping.

Federal Standards

Simply stated, federal law says if you participate in a conversation, you may record it. But if you plant a microphone, recorder, or bug to *intercept* a conversation you cannot hear, then you have committed a serious federal crime.

It is the *interception* – the listening in – that constitutes a crime in most laws against eavesdropping – not the recording. Under this law, police agencies must get court approval to intercept conversations if they – or their informants – are not participants.

Electronic Search Warrants

The court approval is an electronic search warrant. If a police officer gives a judge sworn information that you have contraband hidden in your home, the judge can issue a search warrant. It gives the police the right to search your home for evidence of a crime.

In the same way, if a police officer has sworn information that you are about to have a conversation that would become evidence of a crime, the judge can give the officer a warrant to search for that conversational evidence electronically.

The officer must certify that conventional investigative techniques will not work; that the eavesdropping is a technique of last resort.

State Eavesdropping Laws

Federal law gives states power to pass more stringent eavesdropping regulations, if they choose. About half the states have laws that make it a crime to secretly record conversation, *even if you participate* in that conversation.

In those states, it is a felony to record your telephone calls – to record any conversation whatsoever – unless everyone whose voice is intercepted knows a microphone or "bug" is picking up what is being said.

In states that have not adopted more stringent laws and use the federal standard, you may record your telephone calls without telling the other person, if you use a suction cup or other inductance pickup that does not physically tap into the telephone wires. You can wear a small recorder to tape conversation.

In those states, reporters can secretly record what you say and use it later in their stories. In the more stringent states, reporters cannot record your voice without telling you.

Skirting the Law

Florida was one of the first states to pass a more stringent law. It even forbade hearing aids that would give users better than normal hearing that would allow them to intercept conversations.

One of the series I did for WPLG-TV in Miami disclosed a widespread scam. A number of companies had registered phony high schools with the state, and then sold high school diplomas to people who needed them to apply for a job.

I registered a high school — Conman High — with my daughter's parakeet as the principal, and another reporter's cat as the dean of students. Then we invited a diploma mill salesman to come to a reporter's house.

We hid a small microphone in a toaster on the kitchen table. Under the table was a switch that could turn the microphone on and off. A photographer and I were in a tool shed on the patio outside, shooting the entire session through a sliding glass door.

The staffer posing as a prospective diploma customer would turn on the microphone when he asked questions. Like, "Now let me get this straight — my wife can help me when I take the final exam for my diploma?"

The he would turn off the microphone. But it was easy to read the salesman's lips as he nodded and said, "That's right."

Expectation of Privacy

Many of the court cases involving privacy hinge on whether the person whose conversation was intercepted had a *reasonable expectation* of privacy.

If passers-by can hear, the cases seem to say, the media can record.

Juries and judges often decide against the news media if the reporter broke the law to obtain the secret recording, or gained access under false pretenses to bring in the hidden camera or microphone. In their gut, they don't like that.

Computer Hackers

Computer hackers can now get past electronic security barriers and access sensitive data like medical, insurance and bank records to invade your privacy. Laws are still evolving to deal with hacking. A larger problem is finding computer technicians in law enforcement who can outsmart the hackers.

Visual Eavesdropping

So far, there are few laws similar to those for audio and telephone privacy that establish visual privacy from the news media. If a telephoto lens can see you inside your home or business, it has not invaded your privacy. This concept says: You can't call them peeping toms if you leave the blinds open.

Some court decisions have restricted law enforcement from using telephoto lenses, but those rulings do not affect private citizens. Cameras mounted in drone airplanes to capture criminal evidence are the latest battlefront in that skirmish.

If a camera were hidden inside your home or business to photograph things the reporter couldn't see with the doors and blinds closed, most judges and juries would probably feel your privacy had been invaded. You had an expectation of privacy.

Personal Privacy

Intrusion into the secret details of your personal life is another matter. It may involve some kind of physical trespass to obtain those details, but not necessarily.

The concept was first proposed in December, 1890, in an article written by two young lawyers who had roomed together at Harvard – Samuel Warren and Louis Brandeis.

Brandeis would later become one of the legendary justices of the U.S. Supreme Court. Warren's family was prominent in Boston society. They threw lavish parties. Press gossips constantly pestered the family and tried to spy on their parties.

The Right To Be Left Alone

Warren and Brandeis published their novel idea in a *Harvard Law Review* essay. "Instantaneous photographs and newspaper enterprise," they wrote, "Have invaded the sacred precincts of private and domestic life."

It is time, they said, to create a new area of law in America that would guarantee the right of personal privacy. Their definition is still used today: Personal privacy is **the right to be left alone**.

Galella v. Onassis
(487 F 2d 986, 1 Media L. Rep. 2425 (1973)

Even in public places, courts have ruled that paparazzi openly hounding their targets can invade personal privacy. An early case involved Jacqueline Kennedy Onassis.

Ron Galella was a free-lance photographer who stalked Onassis and her family. She sued in federal court and obtained an injunction preventing Galella from taking photos closer than 150 feet.

The judge said Galella had violated her *right to be left alone*. An appeals court decreased the separation to 25 feet. Galella violated the court order and was ordered to pay Onassis $10,000.

Celebrities today pursue that same kind of verdict when they can no longer stand the constant mob of paparazzi. Or they go berserk, sock a photographer, and trash his camera.

Human Decency

This is a hypothetical I use when I conduct media relations seminars for law enforcement:

Suppose a young child has been hit by a truck. The mother is sitting in the street, holding the body, sobbing hysterically. The truck driver, sitting at the curb, is going into shock. He may be having a heart attack. A police officer is trying to help him.

A news photographer arrives and begins shooting close-ups of the mother and child and the truck driver. Does the photographer invade their privacy? At this point in our history, no.

Police, the Media and Privacy

This kind of incident often leads to major confrontations between the police and the news media. Officers, with feelings of human compassion, step in to stop the photographer.

Sometimes, they seize the camera and arrest the photographer for interfering with an officer. These charges are almost always dropped. The officer has no legal right to stop the photographer or responsibility to protect the privacy of the accident or crime victim. It is a public place. No criminal trespass is occurring.

The officer acts out of sense of human decency.

The Naked Mental Patient

In another hypothetical I use in seminars, an attractive female patient has escaped from a state mental institution. She goes to a busy shopping mall, takes off all her clothes, and strolls along, window shopping.

A news photographer happens to be in the mall shooting another story. He follows and photographs the woman until a police officer stops her, wraps her in a blanket, and takes her away.

Does photographing her invade her privacy? Will publishing the photos serve any public good? I asked my students.

The only answer I ever got to justify publishing said it might depend on whether the mental institution was having a major problem with patients escaping. The news story (with her face and private parts covered) might inspire changes to improve security at the hospital.

On the other hand, law enforcement often helps the media invade the privacy of people they have arrested. Because prisoners in a jail cell have some rights to privacy, police officers often arrange a "perp walk." They walk the perpetrator – in handcuffs – in a public place just so the media can photograph him.

Trauma and Grief

The public seems to be increasingly angry about the media's invading the privacy of people who are in deep trauma or grief. They feel these people have *the right to be left alone*. Photographers chasing relatives of crash victims through airports after major airline accidents are almost universally condemned.

For three days, a reporter infiltrated the group of family members in New York after the TWA Flight 800 crash in July, 1996. When she was discovered, what she had done was so sharply criticized she never wrote anything. Her newspaper apologized.

In the aftermath of tragedies like the Watertown school massacre, and a string of other mass shooting incidents in 2012 and 2013, the families of victims asked the media for privacy. For the most part, they were left alone.

Libel & Privacy Differences

Let's look at the differences between libel and privacy. Suppose you are about to be promoted to the presidency of a department store. A reporter discovers that 40 years ago, when you were 15, you were caught shoplifting in that same store.

If the story is published or broadcast, there is no question it will damage your reputation. The embarrassment could even stop your promotion. But you can't win a libel suit, because it's true.

Public Good vs. Privacy

However, you might be able to win a privacy suit. In deciding whether damages should be paid, the judicial scale tries to balance the public good that is accomplished by publishing or broadcasting information, against the damage that is done to the individual whose privacy is invaded.

An early lawsuit set the precedent:

Briscoe v. Readers Digest Assn.
4 Cal. 3d 529, 93 Cal. Rptr. 866, 483 P. 2d 34 (1971)

The *Reader's Digest*, in a long-running series on organized crime, included a brief reference to a man who had been convicted of a crime as a young adult. The story did not focus on him. His case was simply used to illustrate a point. His wife and children, his employer, his friends knew nothing of his criminal past before the article was published.

He sued for invasion of privacy, and won. He argued he had paid his debt to society, become a productive citizen, and lived an exemplary life after he left prison.

Any public good that was served by publicizing that part of his early life, he maintained, was far outweighed by the damage it did to his personal privacy.

The court agreed.

Final Exam Questions

A question from my final exam, when I was an adjunct professor at the University of Miami:

A woman calls you with a story tip. Every Saturday night, she says, the people next door throw a very wild party. They leave all the doors and windows open. From my back bedroom, you can look into their house. By 10 p.m., they're rowdy and obviously high on something. Some of them are snorting a white powder.

I've called the police with no results, your caller says. How would you like to come sit in the dark, in my house, and take pictures of what goes on next door?

Question A: If you accept the invitation and shoot into the house next door, have you invaded the privacy of the people at the party?

Question B: If you publish or broadcast those pictures, have you invaded their privacy?

Final Exam Answers

Answer A: Shooting the pictures will not invade their privacy. You were not trespassing when you shot the pictures. If someone chooses to undress in front of an open window, and you watch, you can't be blamed for staring.

Answer B: The best test answer I ever had from a student was one which said, "If it's just a bunch of party people, you may invade their privacy. A jury might find no public benefit from publishing the pictures. You don't know what the white powder is.

"But if one of the people in your pictures is the police chief – or the governor – that's something else." The outcome of a privacy suit in this example will probably hinge on the jury's weighing personal privacy vs. public good.

Senator Eagleton's Past

U.S. Senator Thomas Eagleton of Missouri in 1972 became the Democratic vice-presidential candidate, running with George McGovern. A newspaper reporter discovered that Eagleton, years earlier, had been a patient in a mental institution.

The story caused Eagleton's withdrawal from the race. But there was never even a suggestion that he sue for invasion of privacy. Why? Because he was a public official. Like libel, privacy law offers little protection to public officials.

Gary Hart and Donna Rice

U.S. Senator Gary Hart of Colorado was the front-runner for the Democratic nomination in 1988. There were recurring rumors that Hart had an active sex life outside his marriage.

The rumors became so strong, Hart challenged the media to follow him and prove whether the rumors were true or false. Acting on a tip, *The Miami Herald* followed model and actress Donna Rice when she flew from Miami to Washington, D. C.

While *The Herald* didn't have photographs of Hart and Rice together, their story said the two had spent the night together in Hart's Washington townhouse. Hart attacked the newspaper for scurrilous, slanted reporting; said he had done nothing immoral, and planned to continue as a presidential candidate. But when the *National Enquirer's* front page later showed Rice on Hart's lap during a weekend boat trip to Bimini, Hart's campaign collapsed. He withdrew from the race.

The stories sparked a national debate on whether politicians have the *right to be left alone* in their private lives. That debate continues. Former U.S. Senator John Edwards' affair with a television producer who gave birth to his child was a long-running tabloid tale.

Is nothing private in the life of a political candidates and government officials?

FDR's Handicap

As a result of polio that had made him a paraplegic, President Franklin D. Roosevelt could not stand without leg braces, holding onto something. He spent his days in a wheelchair.

When he left the White House, he had to be carried in the arms of a servant, then placed in the presidential limousine. But the process was never photographed.

There was a story of a new photographer at the White House who raised his camera to shoot. A veteran newsman knocked the camera down, with a stern warning: "We don't do that here."

Throughout his presidency, news photographers avoided pictures that showed how handicapped he was. It was an era when the media felt an obligation to censor itself for the public good.

Campaign Films

Look at old film of Roosevelt campaigning from the back of a railroad car. One of his sons was usually standing beside him, discreetly holding his arm, to keep him from falling.

There are 35,000 pictures of Roosevelt in his Presidential Library, but only two show him in a wheelchair. Neither was published while he was alive, according to the Freedom Forum in Arlington, Virginia.

Presidential Body Parts

President Lyndon Johnson insisted on pulling up his shirt to show the media his scar after his gall bladder operation. During Ronald Reagan's term in office, network newscasts gave the nation nightly diagrams of his colon and prostate during separate operations.

Before John F. Kennedy was assassinated in 1963, Washington reporters wondered if they should write about his relationships with other women. They were even more troubled by then-Vice-President Johnson's private life. Bored, alienated from Kennedy, Johnson drank a lot. He was always on the prowl.

Suppose something happened to the President, the reporters asked themselves. If there was a national emergency, would anybody be able to find Johnson? Would he be able to function?

Johnson became President, got back into working trim, and the stories were never written. The reporters were relieved. Most reporters and public officials were men, and men had a gentlemen's agreement not to talk about certain things.

The Stripper's Swim

The watershed event for stories on politicians' sex lives occurred in 1974, when U.S. Rep. Wilbur Mills, 65 and married, got into a spat with his stripper girl friend, Fanne Foxe. Mills was chairman of the House Ways and Means Committee.

He and Foxe, riding in a car one night, got into a fight. She jumped out of the car, into the Tidal Basin, and onto the front page of nearly every newspaper in the country.

From that point on, it seemed that nothing in a politician's private life was sacred. There was an avalanche of stories about the sex lives of former presidents. Mills retired in 1976.

Clinton and Lewinsky

When the Monica Lewinsky story broke in early 1998, many people were puzzled by the public's reaction. Polls showed most people believed the President had been unfaithful to his wife. But Clinton's popularity was not affected. Many of those surveyed seemed more unhappy with the media than with Clinton.

As President, Clinton complained about the media's fixation on his affair while they ignored his administration's accomplishments. But when his autobiography was published in 2004, Clinton spent more space on his private than his public life. Invasion of privacy sells newspapers, and broadcast stories, and books.

Public People & Privacy

The rule of thumb seems to be: the higher in government you are, and the more contact you have with the public, the less privacy you have from the news media.

Judges, police officers and school teachers probably have less privacy than government auditors or secretaries, on the theory that their character can affect the quality of their public work.

Outside government, the more visible and newsworthy you are, the less privacy you have. The lines are difficult to draw. Verdicts in one state disagree with those in another.

Recap Libel & Privacy

Let's recap –

- If the story is true, you can't win a libel suit
- If the story is false, public officials and public persons can win a libel suit only if they *prove* the story is false; and was published with malice and/or *reckless disregard for the truth*
- Libel cases have determined that one sure indication of malice is to know a story is false – or to have serious doubts about the facts – and run the story anyway
- True or false, a story can invade your privacy
- You have almost no privacy from a camera in a public place

- If you are in a private place, and a news photographer outside shoots you, that probably does not invade your privacy

- Broadcasting or publishing what is shot with a telephoto lens *can* invade your privacy if a court decides your privacy outweighs any public good that was served

- Photographers can come into a privately owned place where the public is invited, but may invade privacy and become trespassers if the owner asks them to leave and they refuse

- Federal law does not prohibit secret recording of telephone conversations by people who participate in those conversations, but some states have more stringent laws that prevent *all* secret interception and/or recording by private citizens

- Spreading facts about your past – and intimate portions of your present – may do more personal damage than public good, and therefore become an invasion of your privacy

- Invasion of privacy verdicts are often returned when a jury feels: *They shouldn't do that. I wouldn't like it if they did that to me. That person had a right to be left alone*

- In the near future, court cases could decide that people have a right to privacy, even in public places, during moments of deep grief or pain

INSIDE THE MEDIA

RATINGS

Will They Know I Switched From Opera to Wrestling?

Television is one of America's most fiercely competitive industries. Very slight changes in the audience can shift profits by tens of millions of dollars.

It is an industry constantly in metamorphosis, looking for some new game or gimmick that will entice a few more people away from the competition. If the audience wants a little more sex, a little more violence, that's what it gets.

Every producer of TV programming is constantly trying to guess next season's fad or fashion, hoping to invent a show or character or situation that will play to the appetite of that fleeting, fickle audience.

Spin-offs

Once a show becomes a success, there is a stampede to copy and clone it, hoping to squeeze every penny of profit out of the idea before it gets stale and the audience moves on to whatever turns them on.

All in the Family begat *Archie Bunker's Place*, until the audience eventually became weary of the characters and dwindled away. *Happy Days* bred *Laverne and Shirley*. *Cheers* led to *Frasier*.

Much about the CBS hit *Survivor,* born in 2000 on CBS, was copied by the same network the next year to create *The Amazing Race*. *American Idol*, launched by Fox in 2002, led to *Dancing with the Stars* on ABC in 2004.

Sometimes the spin-offs work. Sometimes they don't.

At the very top, television news is controlled by the same people who program entertainment. They're always looking for the magic formula that will seduce people away from the competition. If the ratings research shows the audience wants more flash and trash, stories become flashier and trashier.

From city to city, television news is as varied as radio station formats. There are newscasts anchored by gray-haired veterans as bland and dated as elevator music.

Hard Rock News

In other markets, young, hyper anchors shout stories with the intensity of hard-rock radio. It doesn't matter so much what the words say, so long as you keep the rhythm and beat. Keep it breathless and intense.

"The City Manager's Secret Agony! Tape at Eleven!"

"A Psychic Says UFOs Will Disrupt The Governor's Inauguration! I'll Talk With Her Live, at Five!"

How do they know we'd rather learn about a new diet than the defense budget? How do they know who – and how many – are watching?

Ratings.

Ratings & Demos Set the Price

As a general rule, the cost of commercial time on television is based on how many people will see the advertising. But *who* is in the audience also has a powerful influence on price. TV advertisers will pay more to reach fewer people, if that smaller audience has the right "demos" – demographics.

An audience with a lot of 18 to 49-year-olds is more desirable to advertisers because they spend more.

Gillette, paying to advertise a new razor, wants to know how many men of shaving age are watching. Revlon wants a show with a lot of women. Lexus and Lincoln will place their commercials in shows that appeal to a mature, affluent, status-conscious audience.

What the Market Will Bear

There are no hard and fast rules. The price is based on what the market will bear. It has to be competitive with other forms of advertising. The price keeps going up.

In early 1983, the last installment of $M*A*S*H$ set a new record – $450,000 for each half-minute of commercial time.

The next all-time high was the final *Seinfeld* episode in May, 1998, where commercials cost $2 million per 30-second spot.

Super Bowl Commercials

Unless there is an unusual show like the *M*A*S*H** and *Seinfeld* finales, telecasts of Super Bowl games usually contain the most expensive commercial time on the tube because they have the largest audience of the year.

Thirty-second spots during the 2014 Super Bowl reportedly went for as much as $4 million.

Some portions of the game are more expensive than others. And there is bargaining on price before the game if sales are sluggish. Spots toward the end of the game are usually cheaper, because the audience is expected to gradually tune out.

Ratings Are Estimates

The entire economic foundation of television and radio in this country is built on audience estimates. Broadcast rating services use several techniques to calculate how many people are listening or watching at any given time.

The process has always been mysterious to outsiders. Polling techniques are very complicated, and few people who don't have Ph.D.s in statistics understand how a small sample, properly drawn, can accurately tell you what millions of people are doing.

The entire system is constantly under attack. Periodically, powerful network executives say they're unhappy with the system and would support a new company if it could make ratings more accurate. They only complain if their numbers go down.

Nielsen and Arbitron

Two firms – Nielsen Media Research and Arbitron – were historically the major ratings services for broadcast programming. In 1993, Arbitron abandoned national TV ratings, but continued to be the dominant ratings service for radio.

In September, 2013, Nielsen Holdings N.V. bought Arbitron, which was then rebranded as Nielsen Audio. This gave Nielsen a complete monopoly for measuring TV and radio audiences in America. Nielsen operates in 100 countries, and also measures other marketing and consumer data.

Internet Ratings

In late 1995, Nielsen launched a new service to measure how many people were logged onto the Internet; their demographics, and which sites they visit. There is still a lot of competition for that ratings service. In February, 2013, Nielsen adjusted its TV rating service to count people who watched TV shows on the Internet, as well as through the normal channels of cable, broadcast and satellite.

Rating Techniques

Nielsen has used four basic techniques over the years:

- **Telephone surveys** (rarely used now)

- **Viewer/listener diaries** (used now during "sweeps")

- **Electronic meters** that show when a TV set is turned on, when a show is recorded and watched later

- **People Meters** that show WHO is watching what, and when

Household Diaries

Before electronic metering, families in the measurement sample agreed to keep a diary of the TV shows they watched. They were supposed to make an entry every 15 minutes when the TV set was turned on, showing which station was on, and who was watching. Once a family agreed to keep a diary, their viewing habits were monitored for long periods of time.

Their identity has always been a secret, to avoid any outside influence on their choice of shows. But diary-keeping is a real chore, and there has always been a concern that some families aren't very precise.

They're only used now in remote, small markets and during "sweeps" to gather more insight. When diaries were the only method of measurement, Nielsen would invest major efforts to measure TV audiences during the "sweeps" months of November, February and May.

With electronic measurement, those concentrated efforts were no longer necessary, but advertising agencies are still habit-bound and focus on audiences in those months.

Viewing Meters

In 1959, Nielsen began using viewing meters in New York City to supplement telephone surveys and viewer diaries. The company selected metered households in much the same way it chose families to keep a diary.

The family gives its permission for the rating service to connect a meter to its TV set. Any time the set is turned on, the meter automatically keeps a record of the time and which station it is tuned to. The next step was People Meters.

People Meters

For advertisers, WHO is watching is just as important as HOW MANY are watching. You don't advertise beer in a children's show, or toys on *20/20*. So Nielsen began using People Meters in 1986 to find out WHO is watching in carefully selected samples.

The People Meter is very much like a remote-control TV device. A miniature computer about the size of a paperback book is attached to the TV.

How They Work

The People Meter has lights that blink red and green. There is a light for each family member, and additional lights for guests. When the set is turned on, the red lights start blinking. The people watching push a button on the remote device to log in. The light for that person changes from red to green.

If someone new comes into the room to watch TV, or if someone leaves, they're supposed to use the remote control to tell the meter.

Time to Push the Button

After a certain time, or if the station is changed, the red lights start flashing again. Each person watching must log in to be counted.

Using a remote control to quickly surf other stations doesn't require a new tally if the set is returned to the original station within a certain number of seconds. Stay away from that channel too long, and the meter asks again who's watching.

If the set stays on without a change of stations, and nobody responds when the red lights blink, Nielsen drops that family from the viewer count that day.

People Meters are subject to cheating, too. One member of the household can log in absent family members. But you can't go back and "vote" a show that was on two hours earlier.

There are other measurement problems that Nielsen is trying to solve. Like picture-in-picture sets that allow you to see two stations on the same screen at the same time. Or recorded shows, viewed later, where the viewer zaps commercials. Or shows watched in a bar, or on the Internet, or on a smart phone.

Nielsen has said much more sophisticated People Meters are in the works, that are scheduled to go into service beginning in 2014.

Exactly how many families are measured is a closely-guarded trade secret. The Los Angeles Times in late 2012 estimated there were People Meters in 20,000 American homes.

Winning with the News Media

In each market area, meters in homes are connected by telephone lines to a national computer center. At 3 a.m. each morning, each meter sends its data for the last 24 hours to Nielsen. Instant, overnight ratings are then tabulated for those who subscribe to the service.

"Voting" a Show

Meters are considered much more accurate than diary reports. People in viewing samples have a tendency to cheat. If they have a favorite series, they "vote" for it, reporting that they watched it, even if they didn't.

Viewers also tend to tell the rating service they watched shows they think they *should* watch. They may say they saw a *National Geographic Special* or a symphony concert when they were really watching wrestling.

The same thing happens when people are surveyed about their newspaper reading habits. People want to appear educated and well-read.

In the 1998 Pew Research Center survey, for instance, 10 per cent of those polled said they read *The New York Times* regularly. But *The Times* only sells enough copies to reach one per cent of the homes in America.

In that same survey, 28 per cent said they read *USA Today* regularly. The publisher only printed enough copies of *USA Today* to reach 1.6 per cent of the population.

Meters Increase Viewing

When a family gives permission for a meter to be installed, they watch a lot more television for a while. There's a subtle psychological effect. Their inclusion in the sample makes them feel like their choice of shows is suddenly more important. That tendency to increase viewing time slacks off after several months.

The families aren't told this, but the rating service doesn't start tabulating their viewing during that early surge.

Independent stations seemed to be the big winners when meters were first added to diaries and telephone surveys. One study showed daytime ratings for independents doubled in homes where meters were installed. The analysts could only guess why.

Meter Mysteries

One explanation – people at home alone during the day didn't want other members of their households to know how much time they spend watching daytime television. In those homes without meters, viewers were not reporting accurately in their diaries.

Translating the Numbers

Radio and TV programs are measured in two ways:

- **Rating** – The *percentage of homes watching or listening* to a specific show. This figure is technically the percentage of *homes watching a show who own radio or TV* sets.

  In most communities, more than 99 per cent of the homes have at least one radio and TV set. So the rating number is really the percentage of total households. Ratings are tabulated for local market areas as well as nationwide.

- **Share** – The *percentage of all households with their sets on* who were watching a particular program. It is that program's *share of the entire audience* who were watching or listening while that program was being shown.

HUT Levels

The TV industry has another shorthand term in its jargon – HUT. Households Using Television. A HUT-level of 10 means your show was being watched by 10 percent of the households who own a TV set.

If a town has 100 households and five are watching television – but all are watching the same show – then that show will have a 5 Rating/100 Share. Only five per cent of the homes are watching television. But 100 per cent of the people watching TV at the time are all watching the same show.

A program with a 12 Rating/26 Share was seen by 12 percent of the households who own TV sets and by 26 percent of the households who were using TV during its time slot.

Prime and Drive Time

Rating numbers go up during evening prime time evening hours when more people watch television. Share numbers for all the programs being broadcast at any given time total 100, no matter how many people are watching.

Radio audiences are generally highest during "drive time" –when people listen in their cars as they commute between home and work.

In addition to the rating and share figures, the services can report to their subscribers detailed demographic information on the people watching by age, sex, ethnicity, education, whether employed, and by income level.

Some of this detailed data is routinely included in markets with People Meters.

Market Size

The Nielsen numbers establish audiences in 210 television markets and rank them by size.

Reporters and anchors are always looking for opportunities in higher-ranked markets because the size of the potential audience means stations there can charge more for their advertising, and the salaries of TV news people are higher.

The 2014 rankings for the top 20 markets, and the number of TV households in each market were:

1. *New York – 7,461,030*

2. *Los Angeles – 5,665,780*

3. *Chicago – 3,534,080*

4. *Philadelphia – 2,963,500*

5. *Dallas/Ft. Worth – 2,655,200*

6. *San Francisco – 2,518,900*

7. *Boston – 2,433,040*

8. *Washington, DC – 2,412,250*

9. *Atlanta – 2,375,050*

10. *Houston – 2,289,360*

11. *Detroit – 1,856,400*

12. *Phoenix – 1,855,310*

13. *Seattle/Tacoma – 1,847,780*

14. *Tampa/St. Petersburg – 1,827,510*

15. *Minneapolis/St. Paul – 1,748,070*

16. *Miami/Ft. Lauderdale – 1,663,290*

17. *Denver – 1,574,610*

18. *Orlando/Daytona/Melbourne – 1,490,380*

19. Cleveland/Akron – 1,484,530

20. Sacramento/Stockton/Modesto – 1,387,950

High-Priced Anchors

Slight shifts in audiences can mean millions of dollars. If a network show increases its ratings just one point, that means the audience for the program and its commercial messages increases by about 2.6 million people. That's why on-air "talent" – anchors, sportscasters and meteorologists – are paid so much.

A popular anchor or sportscaster who moves to a competing station can sometimes bring the fans to the new station and cause dramatic shifts in ratings.

Popular local anchors have job benefits like a chauffeured limousine; an extravagant expense account and clothes allowance; a reporting assignment outside the country at least once a year, where the entire family can tag along.

"Hi, Brian"

Network anchors are even more pampered.

Television is an unusual medium. Its anchors have more celebrity status than anyone except the President of the United States. Walk a movie star and Brian Williams down the same sidewalk, and many more people will recognize Williams.

More than just recognize him. They'll speak, wave, call him Brian. They think they know him personally. He's in their living room just about every night. The ability to create that kind of connection with viewers is extremely valuable.

Shooting Craps

Because the ratings are so critical, TV news constantly changes. If the ratings get stuck or go down, they change the format or the pacing or the people.

It's like shooting craps. Keep changing until you hit a winning combination. And, like magic, some new gimmick works. For a while. The process never stops.

TV has altered the American brain and the way it receives, remembers, and reacts to information.

There are those who say TV is ephemeral and shallow; that its performers are pretentious and plastic; that its motives are crass and demeaning.

To some extent, all those criticisms are valid. But when TV is good, it is *very, very good*. No other technique has yet been invented to reach so many people so quickly with so much power.

INSIDE THE MEDIA

RESOURCES

Internet Websites to Help You Find Current News Media Info

One reason for my earlier decision to not publish a 9th Edition of this book is that much of the data in printed books becomes obsolete as soon as they come off the press. So I updated and published it as an e-book.

But I changed my mind about a new, printed version when a number of people said they'd like to have this book in printed form.

The Internet has a lot more stuff, and it is current. At least, most of the time. This chapter will steer you to great resources for media stats, studies, and the full text of court decisions that are cited in some of the chapters of this book.

www.journalism.org

This is the starting page for the Pew Research Journalism Project, a subsidiary of the Pew Research Center. I consider it the best unbiased, independent source available for information about the current state of American news media. This is how the Research Center and Journalism Project describe their mission:

> Pew Research Center is a nonpartisan fact tank that informs the public about the issues, attitudes and trends shaping America and the world. It conducts public opinion polling, demographic research, media content analysis and other empirical social science research. Pew Research does not take policy positions. It is a subsidiary of The Pew Charitable Trusts. ...

The (journalism) project employs a variety of empirical research methods to analyze whether people are getting the information they need for a functioning society. It publishes research on who is reporting the news and what new players are emerging; what is being reported on and what gaps in coverage exist; how news is consumed and how the economic models for news are changing. In addition to reports on these topics, each year the project produces the State of the News Media report, which examines key questions facing the industry.

In their 2013 State of the News Media report, 60 per cent of those questioned said they knew little or nothing about the media's current financial problems. Yet 31 per cent of those questioned said they had recently stopped reading or watching a news outlet because it was no longer giving them the news they were accustomed to.

You'll find fascinating data on this voluminous website that covers just about any question you could ask about the news media. And a lot of stuff you never even thought of. Their 2012 State of the News Media report is a voluminous compilation of which media corporations own what.

This is the best place I've found to keep a close eye on what's happening to news, to the people and corporations who provide it, and those who consume it.

www.freepress.net/

This website also does a great job of summarizing and listing which corporations own what. Can you trust a network review of a new book or movie, for instance, if the same corporation owns the network, the book publisher AND the movie studio?

www.poynter.org/

This is another independently financed think tank that is a major training ground for journalists. It offer classes year-round to help reporters, editors and photographers improve their skills.

Nelson Poynter was the owner of the *St. Petersburg Times* (now the *Tampa Bay Times*). When he died in 1978, his estate created the Modern Media Institute, which owns both the Poynter Institute and the newspaper. The website says:

> *Not only did the unique ownership model protect his publications from the insatiable demands of the Wall Street-owned chains, it also fulfilled Nelson Poynter's dream of a school that would help working journalists improve their skills to the benefit of their communities.*

This is a good place to stay in touch with journalistic ethics, and what news reporters, editors and photographers are doing to uphold them.

www.cjr.org

The *Columbia Journalism Review* is widely considered the conscience of American journalism. It has extensive archives online. This is its mission statement:

> *Columbia Journalism Review's mission is to encourage excellence in journalism in the service of a free society. Founded in 1961 under the auspices of Columbia University's Graduate School of Journalism, CJR monitors and supports the press as it works across all platforms, and also tracks the ongoing evolution of the media business. The magazine, offering a mix of reporting, analysis, and commentary, is published six times a year; CJR.org weighs in daily, hosting a conversation that is open to all who share a commitment to high journalistic standards in the US and around the world.*

www.ajr.org

The American Journalism Review, managed by the University of Maryland's Merrill Journalism College, had been CJR's primary competitor. In the fall of 2013, it printed its last edition and became an online-only publication.

It is too soon to know, as this book goes to press, whether AJR will continue the quality of its printed magazine online. Ram Reider, its longtime editor, left the magazine to become an editor at *USA Today* when the shift to all-digital was announced. AJR also has extensive online archives.

> *"The model for publishing has clearly shifted to digital formats as online readership has grown," Merrill College Dean Lucy A. Dalglish said, in announcing the change. "It no longer made financial sense for the award-winning AJR to continue producing a print magazine because most AJR readers accessed content on the Web. In addition, philanthropy has long been an important source of funding for print magazines devoted to media criticism. That support has steadily declined over the past 10 years."*

www.auditedmedia.com/

The Alliance for Audited Media is the new name for the old Audit Bureau of Circulations. It is the primary method for measuring print media audiences.

You can find extensive total circulation figures for newspapers and magazines there, plus lots of analysis – down to circulation for zip code areas.

www.nielsen.com/

    Nielsen Holdings, N.V. now has a monopoly on measuring both TV and radio audiences in the U.S. Virtually all broadcast advertising is based on Nielsen's estimate of the audience for broadcast areas and times. This website is extensive, and can give you audience numbers and TV market ranks, plus explanations of how they gather the data.

www.findlaw.com/

    This website has the full text of every U.S. Supreme Court decision since 1893. Go to Cases and Codes to search by topic. Includes extensive federal appellate and state court decisions as well.

www.iab.net/

    The Interactive Advertising Bureau provides comparisons for advertising effectiveness in various media. Its data is helpful in measuring trends, advertising spending, audiences and reach for the Internet and mobile devices.

www.nab.org/

    This website for the National Assn. of Broadcasters will give you the point of view for management/ownership of radio and TV stations and networks.

www.naa.org/

    This is the Newspaper Assn. of America website, which looks at the media from the newspaper industry's perspective. It is a good place to get national summaries, but it is short on data for specific newspapers.

About the Author

Clarence Jones Was a Reporter for 30 Years - Half in Newspapers, Half in TV

He was one of America's most honored journalists. The only reporter for a local station to ever win TV's equivalent of the Pulitzer Prize (the duPont-Columbia Award) three times.

Starting at the Florida Times-Union

He started working full-time for the *Florida Times-Union* while he was earning his journalism degree at the University of Florida.

A Nieman Fellow at Harvard

As one of the country's most promising young journalists, he was awarded a Nieman Fellowship at Harvard University.

Miami Herald Reporter

Then he went to the *Miami Herald*, where he was part of a year-long investigation that showed how the Dade County Sheriff's Department had been totally corrupted.

Their stories prompted a referendum that abolished the Sheriff's Department. Miami-Dade is the only county in Florida with an appointed public safety director instead of an elected sheriff.

Jones' last newspaper post was Washington Correspondent for the *Herald*.

Under Cover TV Assignment

Then he accepted one of TV's most unusual assignments for WHAS-TV in Louisville, KY. Using another name and a shell corporation to hide his real identity, he worked deeply undercover for eight months to show how illegal gambling had corrupted government and law enforcement there.

His first documentaries, using film shot inside bookie joints with a lunch box camera, gained immediate national attention.

Return to Miami

After two years in Louisville, he returned to Miami as investigative reporter for WPLG-TV.

For 12 years at WPLG-TV, he specialized in organized crime and government corruption.

Awards at WPLG-TV

His reporting there won four Emmys, three duPont-Columbias, and the Robert F. Kennedy Award. More about his reporting career and those awards is at www.winning-newsmedia.com.

Author & On-Camera Coach

Then he wrote the First Edition of this book (1983) and left reporting to be a news media consultant and on-camera coach. This print version of *Winning with the News Media* is the 9th Edition.

Jones has four other books available now, in both print and e-book formats. The latest before this one, is (*They're Gonna Murder You – War Stories From My Life At The News Front*).Those stories about his career read like a murder mystery or a spy novel. His other books are listed on the copyright page at the front of this book.

He is also a tinkerer, sailor and photographer. He frequently publishes magazine articles showing how to make modifications and gadgets he creates for his 28-foot Catalina sailboat.

·

Made in the USA
Charleston, SC
07 August 2016